"Moral injury always occurs in a relational context. As such, it cannot be healed in a vacuum; rather, the presence of safe, supportive, and—importantly—benevolent relationships where acceptance, forgiveness, and repair can occur are essential. Marrying their vast knowledge of moral injury and the use of metaphors in psychotherapy, the authors have created a unique text to illuminate the sometimes long and windy road to recovery from potentially morally injurious events. Pernicano and Haynes offer mental health clinicians, Veterans, family members, and individuals touched by MI a roadmap for understanding the multi-layered impact of potentially morally injurious events. They do so by utilizing the amazing power of metaphor—a tool with a long history in psychotherapy and increasingly recognized as invaluable in working with trauma. In helping individuals re-story their experiences, metaphors serve as a conduit of human connection and a vehicle of change. This book is as enlightening as it is practical, and a must-read for anyone whose life has been impacted by moral injury."

Valentina Stoycheva, PhD, co-author of *The Unconscious: Theory, Research, and Clinical Implications*, and co-chair, Moral Injury Special Interest Group, International Society for Traumatic Stress Studies

"Years ago, I volunteered as a hospital chaplain near Atlanta, Georgia. One day I visited a World War II veteran facing a dire physical diagnosis. He was near death, but the elderly man asked a profoundly moral question. He pleaded "Will God forgive me for what I did during the war?" He revealed a secret that had tormented him for decades. The pain on his face was evident as his stoic features softened. He said he had killed a surrendering German sailor. He had obeyed orders but now carried a moral injury from what he had done as a frightened young soldier. I was an untrained, recent seminary graduate and new pastor. I was unequipped to help him other than recite my confessional and Scriptural beliefs. I had no tools to offer him comfort. I needed this book then; it is what I wish I could have provided to that unnamed man decades ago. I am so thankful for this new but ancient way of bringing healing to moral injury."

Ray Woolridge, brigadier general, US Army (retired) and co-author of *Escaping Enemy Mode: How Our Brains Unite or Divide Us*

"As a combat veteran, woman, Latina, and sexual-assault survivor, I saw myself throughout the pages and walked away awe-struck by the realness of it all. In many ways, this book parallels my journey to wellness from trauma and moral injury. The authors authentically describe real veteran experiences, acknowledge, and affirm our struggle and resilience; most importantly, they provide a pathway towards healing. I saw my healing journey play out countless times in each veteran story. The metaphor, stories, art, and writing brought me back from a dark saturated type of emotional and physical pain into a fuller life in the light."

Lisa Carrington Firmin, colonel, US Air Force (retired),
and award-winning author of *Stories from the Front:
Pain, Betrayal, and Resilience on the MST Battlefield* and *Latina Warrior*

"The authors, drawing on vivid personal stories from veterans and their extensive professional experience, offer readers a wealth of useful strategies such as storytelling, imagination, and collective engagement to support recovery from moral injury."

Rita Nakashima Brock, PhD, senior vice president for moral
injury recovery programs, Volunteers of America

"This book is an up-to-date overview of the field and a guide for treating moral injury through group therapy, writing, and art-making. The authors' compassion and clinical rigor shine through from page one as they draw on decades of moral injury research and treatment. In addition to providing a thorough understanding of moral injury, the innovative treatment techniques developed by the authors comprise a proven step-by-step process for helping veterans heal. Dozens of gripping veteran testimonials offer a rare insight into the realities of combat and military service and describe many of the ways that those who serve can suffer life-long trauma. This is a valuable and thought-provoking resource for seasoned practitioners, lay persons, and students alike."

Scott Sinkler, director of the documentary *Absolutions:
War and Moral Injury*

"*Healing Veteran Moral Injury* delivers an innovative and impactful recipe for healing that supports, educates, instills hope and dignity, and offers a path to forgiveness for those struggling with moral injury. Pernicano and Haynes use captivating examples that connect the reader to the introduced concepts while honoring veteran stories. This book provides a voice that academic texts and treatment manuals often lack."

Ashley Casto, PsyD, HSP, licensed clinical psychologist

"Building on their combined decades of clinical experience in mental health care and chaplaincy, Pernicano and Haynes offer an approach that integrates forgiveness and acceptance with storytelling in various forms to address the suffering of moral injury, pointing the way to what is possible when mental health and spiritual care professionals collaborate."

Keith G. Meador, MD, ThM, MPH, Ann Geddes Stahlman Professor
of Medical Ethics and Professor of Psychiatry and Behavioral
Sciences at Vanderbilt University and Professor of Ethics
and Society at Vanderbilt Divinity School

Healing Veteran Moral Injury

Healing Veteran Moral Injury highlights the importance of story and metaphor in the change process and in trauma-related work.

Grounded in evidence-based practice and replete with clear, down-to-earth examples that foster empathy and understanding, *Healing Veteran Moral Injury* illustrates the ways in which building a sense of community can help restore trust and meaning-making. Chapters illustrate the power of stories and metaphors and help Veterans identify strategies for healing moral injury and posttraumatic growth. Clinicians and Veterans will come away from this book with tools for building connections, accepting what they cannot change, and developing a more accurate perception of responsibility.

Healing Veteran Moral Injury is intended both for mental health professionals and Veterans themselves as a tool for breaking the silence, pointing other Veterans toward hope and healing, and telling stories of moral pain with fortitude and courage.

Pat Pernicano, PsyD, holds a doctorate in clinical psychology from Baylor University. Her writing, teaching, and clinical work reflect her passion for trauma-informed healing with children, families, and Veterans.

Kerry Haynes, DMin, is retired, having worked as a mental health chaplain at the United States Department of Veterans Affairs, an Army Reserves chaplain, and a pastor. His doctor of ministry work focused on group services for Veteran moral injury.

Healing Veteran Moral Injury

Using Metaphor and Story to Foster Hope and Connection

Pat Pernicano and Kerry Haynes

Routledge
Taylor & Francis Group

NEW YORK AND LONDON

Designed cover image: Getty Images

First published 2025
by Routledge
605 Third Avenue, New York, NY 10158

and by Routledge
4 Park Square, Milton Park, Abingdon, Oxon, OX14 4RN

Routledge is an imprint of the Taylor & Francis Group, an informa business

ISBN: 978-1-032-78970-5 (hbk)
ISBN: 978-1-032-78969-9 (pbk)
ISBN: 978-1-003-49426-3 (ebk)

DOI: 10.4324/9781003494263

Typeset in Palatino
by KnowledgeWorks Global Ltd.

Access the Support Material: www.routledge.com/9781032789699

This book is dedicated to the Veterans who have shared their stories of moral injury so that others might find hope and healing. From Vietnam to the Gulf War, from Iraq to Afghanistan, through all ranks and roles, we are grateful for their service and contributions to this book.

■ Table of Contents

Acknowledgments

This book would not exist were it not for the Veterans who shared their stories of moral injury pain and healing, then permitted us to include their drawings and poignant descriptions. Veterans gave written informed consent and phone confirmation, and each, when contacted, expressed gratitude and hope that what they shared might help others. One Veteran said, "This book may change a life in the same way that the group changed mine. Science with spirituality works!" Another described the program as "a catalyst" that launched him in a new direction. The stories are theirs, but details and demographics have been changed to protect identity; we are ever grateful to them, and they will not be forgotten.

A special shout out to Dr. Brian S. Powers, whose experiences as an Air Force Special Operations officer from the UK in Iraq and Afghanistan and nearly two decades of moral injury study offer a unique lens. As the Executive Director of the International Centre for Moral Injury (ICMI), he has written a powerful and thought-provoking foreword.

Special thanks to Psychologist Ashley Casto for her proposal review and input for the manuscript. She has expertise in PTSD and moral injury and is generous with her time and feedback. She is much appreciated as a colleague and friend.

Dr. Valentina Stoycheva has been generous with her time in doing a proposal review and offering a wonderful, insightful book commentary, with insight into the interpersonal nature of moral injury and awareness of the power of story and metaphor in the healing process. We are grateful to her for her contributions.

Special thanks to Retired U.S. Air Force Colonel Lisa Carrington Firmin for her proposal review and for allowing us to quote her poetry from *Stories from the Front: Pain, Betrayal, and Resilience on the MST Battlefield* (2022) and *Latina Warrior* (2023). Carrington Firmin's writing has created a pathway of hope and healing for other Veterans.

We appreciate Dr. Everett Worthington, Jr.'s written permission to include and cite his REACH model of forgiveness. As a guru in the forgiveness literature, we are grateful for his comments.

Gratitude to Duke University Professor Omid Safi for his touching poem on wabi-sabi from the blog, "Being, Illuminating the Beauty in our Broken Places." This speaks so well to the interpersonal healing needed in moral injury.

Thank you to Hannah Braime for permission to quote parts of her blog on kintsugi from "Becoming Who You Are."

Thank you to Cindy Manginelli of the National Health Care for the Homeless Council (NHCHC) who permitted the authors to cite a PowerPoint presentation (Trauma-Informed Storytelling) from August 11, 2019.

Retired Brigadier General, US Army, Ray Woolridge offers a poignant story of moral pain in his endorsement. We thank him for his meaningful words and insight.

We are grateful for documentarian Scott Sinkler's landmark contributions to this field (*Absolutions: War and Moral Injury*).

We thank Dr. Rita Brock, Senior Vice President for Moral Injury Recovery Programs at Volunteers of America, for her comments.

We thank Dr. Melissa Smigelsky of VA Integrative Mental Health for leadership in the Dynamic Diffusion Network (DDN, 2019–2020) and DDN Quality Enhancement Research Initiative (QUERI, 2020–2025) to enhance moral injury services, measure outcomes, increase visibility, offer training, and broaden dissemination.

Jason Aronson (Rowman & Littlefield) provided Marketplace Copyright Clearinghouse license to reprint, with minor editing, three stories authored by Dr. Pernicano in previous publications: "The Cracked Glass Bowl" in *Outsmarting the Riptide of Domestic Violence* (2012), "The Burden Bag" in *Family-Focused Trauma Intervention* (2010), and "The Unraveled Tapestry" (also titled "The Self-Weaving Tapestry") in *Metaphorical Stories for Child Therapy* (2010). Each is cited in the chapters where they are used.

Routledge/Taylor & Francis granted Marketplace Copyright Clearinghouse license to reprint, with minor editing, portions of previous publications authored by Dr. Pernicano: *Using trauma-focused therapy stories: Interventions for therapists, children, and their caregivers* (2014) and *Using stories, art and play in trauma-informed treatment: Case examples and applications across the lifespan* (2019). Portions of both are reproduced with permission of Taylor and Francis Group, LLC.

Special appreciation to Dr. Kevin Pernicano for formatting the photographs included in this book. This was a time-consuming and significant contribution.

We are grateful for Routledge Editor Anna Moore's professional input from proposal to production. She understood our vision to raise awareness of Veteran moral injury so that Veteran stories could be told and those suffering might find hope and healing. Her patience and kind support have been invaluable.

On a more personal note, this has been a labor of love, and we would be remiss if we did not thank our spouses – Becky (Chaplain Kerry) and Kevin (Dr. Pat) – for their unwavering encouragement and support throughout the process. Kerry and Pat are deeply grateful for the time and space to work together as friends and colleagues while our families patiently waited.

Foreword

Researchers suggest that as early as two years old, we experience moral emotions such as guilt – the purpose of which may be to indicate that we have broken a communal value and need to make amends to stay within the good graces of our social group. However, we can also feel positive moral emotions of pride, satisfaction, and gratitude when we live up to those societal values, negative moral emotions of contempt and anger arise when others have transgressed us and where justice and repair are necessary.

In modern society, these relatively straightforward emotions become increasingly complex. With our identities in the world today defined by nationality, ethnicity, political leaning, and spirituality, and when there are increasing divisions around the idea of "what's right," moral emotions can become more difficult to understand, process, and draw out amongst questions of agency, responsibility, and blame.

Military members, ostensibly embarking on doing good in the world, often find themselves in situations where personal and societal values are violated, betrayed, or suppressed, and as a result, those individuals with front-line moral responsibility reap an enduring sense of negative moral emotions. We note that those who experience this have been morally injured.

Moral injury (MI) is not a mental health disorder – though it can certainly lead or contribute to many: depression, anxiety, addiction, and self-harm just to name a few. In fact, the more we understand the ways in which enduring negative moral emotions affect our relationships, our capacity for social trust, and our ability to see our own agency as important in the world and perceive it as a place in which justice may be done, the more we find that MI – particularly if left unaddressed – is existentially dangerous. Studies have indicated that among those diagnosed with PTSD, it is a strong predictor of suicide and suicidal ideation.

In this book, Pat Pernicano and Kerry Haynes have created powerful ways to navigate MI in a manner that is clinically sound and pastorally effective. MI is multifaceted and is experienced in vastly different ways depending on the circumstances. Haynes' and Pernicano's development of self-forgiveness and spiritual concepts like lament present valuable pathways to help Veterans who have experienced MI find the compassion to work through their own experiences and gain a sense of solace – returning, as Jonathan Shay says, to the possibility of a flourishing life. It is no exaggeration to say that this proposed intervention will be life-saving.

Treatment of MI is vital to alleviate the suffering of individuals (which is obviously crucial); it also points to society's need to hear their testimonies. This is only possible if those who have experienced MI have explored their own woundedness carefully and come to a point when they can bear witness to the truths many of us have the luxury of ignoring.

Those who have experienced MI, particularly in a military context, experience the basest aspects of human nature, cultural violence, xenophobia, racism, sexism, and injustice. As they reveal uncomfortable realities about war and violence, we may understand the phenomenon of MI as something akin to a moral canary in the coal mine: indicating that we need to do societal work to repair unjust policies, have conversations about why our military cultures seem so rife with violent and sexually abusive situations, and show how critical it is that the United States use power in the global community in accord with "what's right" while seeking to make meaningful amends when we haven't.

This book and the work of Pernicano and Haynes are a critical step toward helping us be aware of and recover from MI as individuals and move toward those broader conversations necessary for us to live, individually and communally, with moral integrity.

Rev. Brian S. Powers, PhD
Bernard William Vann Fellow in Christianity and the Armed Forces
Executive Director, International Centre for Moral Injury (ICMI)
Durham University

Introduction

Beth was at the top of her Navy class. She was a quick learner and first in most training exercises, a shining star... until the night onboard ship when the Chief Mate left a door to her quarters unlocked and a group of seamen, who resented her excellence, raped her. She tried to report it, and command looked the other way, her word against theirs. She felt undeserved shame and guilt. She thought, "They said they had my back, like a family – I trusted them. I wonder what I did for them to treat me like that. I wanted to make the Navy my career, and my dream is ruined." Those men, and the Navy, left Beth feeling broken, damaged, and changed.

Joe developed an alcohol problem after he returned from Vietnam. He was haunted in his nightmares by the faces of women and children he had unintentionally killed when, on orders, he flung a grenade up over a rise. His grenade hit the wrong target, and seeing the aftermath sickened him. He was there to serve his country but questioned the morality of the war and believed that Army leadership, all the way to the top, had deceived them. His guilt, and Vietnam, left him feeling broken, damaged, and changed.

Ben carried his "ghosts" with him daily, waking and sleeping. He had been on a humanitarian mission when he found himself in a processing area and overheard laughter as a group of men sexually groped fearful, crying Cuban women who had reached the U.S. in hopes of a better life. He called over to them to "cut it out," turned away in shame, and did not report it, fearing retaliation for himself or the refugees. He carried pain and guilt for many years, wondering if he should have done more. This experience left him feeling broken, damaged and changed.

DOI: 10.4324/9781003494263-1

Susan was a competent non-commissioned officer (NCO) and a trusted, compassionate trainer and leader. One night in Iraq, two soldiers walked in as she was finishing work. Two against one, they began their vicious sexual assault. She was shocked that soldiers would brazenly attack an NCO and she fought them off until a superior heard her cries and interrupted the attack. The assault left her feeling broken, damaged, and changed.

Jim, raised in the inner city, faced daily poverty and gang shootings in his neighborhood. He was drafted and sent to Vietnam at age 17. He did not fully support the war, but he was proud to serve his country; he was badly wounded and sent home 10 months later. His welcome home at the airport included loud, angry protesters who called him a baby killer as they cursed at him. Jim's combat experience and the aftermath left him feeling broken, damaged, and changed.

While Jenny was stationed in Afghanistan, she watched in horror as a man beat a woman just outside the wire. The man stared at Jenny defiantly, daring her to do something. Military orders prohibited interference with the culture, so she had to stay inside the wire. She felt deep pain, shame, and guilt, and the experience left her feeling broken, damaged, and changed.

Henry had been on three combat deployments and was exhausted and demoralized by recent rank casualties. One day, he got a letter from his wife stating she was leaving him, for his best friend and had ended the life of their unborn child. He "lost it" and grabbed his weapon in rage, intending to blow away everyone in sight and take his own life. A battle buddy talked him down and escorted him to Behavioral Health. Later, he judged himself as weak and unforgivable. This event left him feeling broken, damaged, and changed.

These individuals each carried a deep, invisible wound from an experience that violated their core values: military, personal, spiritual, or moral. Their military experiences brought moral pain and left them feeling broken, damaged, or changed. They found themselves at the Veterans Affairs (VA) seeking help for alcohol abuse, sleep difficulties, depression, anger, suicidal ideation, and post-traumatic stress. None knew they were also struggling with moral injury (MI).

This book is about the power of story (fictional, author-initiated, film, writer-based, Veteran-shared), meaningful interactions, and forgiveness to foster connections "up," "between," and "within" Veterans with MI. The connection "up" is spiritual and might be called meaning-making through confession, forgiveness, return to values, and purposeful living. The "between" connection is relational, established through trust, sharing, attachment, compassion, and acceptance. The "within" connection is one of self-acceptance and worth.

Throughout the book, we will share Veterans' stories of pain, grief, and guilt; stories of accepting what cannot be changed; and stories of hope through acceptance, forgiveness, meaning-making, and restoration. Storytelling has been used for meaning-making across cultures and time, and we have incorporated story and metaphor into the meaning making process for healing MI Pernicano (2014, 2019) reflects on how stories and metaphors enhance trauma-informed care through new awareness. We explore the value of storytelling and metaphor early in the book and later introduce stories that anchor each phase of acceptance and forgiveness therapy (AFT; Pernicano & Haynes, 2023). Stories and therapeutic activities prepare Veterans to share their stories of moral pain and provide new ways of looking at themselves and others. Examining one's story through a new lens guides one toward revisioning, restoration, and wholeness rather than re-experiencing old wounds in a way that keeps one feeling broken and stuck in the quicksand of pain.

Over the years, especially in recent years, there have been numerous scholarly publications about the definition, underpinnings, causes, types, and implications of MI. There is still debate about how to define it and best treat the issues that arise from it. This book is not intended as an academic, scholarly publication but as an evidence-guided source for educators, therapists, clergy, family members, community partners, and the general public to help them better understand Veteran MI and one means of recovery. This book is also intended for Veterans to help break the silence, tell their stories, and point them toward hope and healing.

Many civilians are unaware of the scope of moral injuries that burden those who have served our country, and many Veterans do not realize the ways MI keeps them stuck in self-imposed judgment and blame. This book illustrates situations that cause moral pain and offers hope for healing and restoration through story, compassion, and connection. Veterans face barriers in seeking services: within themselves, their families, communities, and the VA system; they need opportunities to access healing and safely share their stories. Breaking the silence may encourage other Veterans to examine grief, self-assigned responsibility, judgment, blame, and guilt in restorative ways.

In 2018, psychologist Pat Pernicano and chaplain Kerry Haynes began to develop AFT, a group intervention for MI. We examined the individual intervention model of adaptive disclosure (Litz et al., 2015), piloted with active-duty Marines; and familiarized ourselves with a spiritually focused group intervention, building spiritual strength (Usset et al., 2021). AFT was designed to rebuild trust and attachment through group process and Veteran relationships, with broad spiritual and psychological components, and to incorporate confession, compassion, and forgiveness. Haynes (2015) had previously developed a spiritually oriented group for MI as part of his doctoral work, using stories and concepts of forgiveness. Pernicano (2010a, 2010b, 2012, 2014, 2015, 2019, 2021) had previously used trauma-focused stories and interventions with children, families, and civilian adults and believed metaphors and stories could be incorporated into work with Veterans. We wove these together into a more inclusive and comprehensive curriculum. A description of AFT is published in *The Journal of Health Care Chaplaincy* (Pernicano et al., 2022). Pernicano and Haynes (2024) also authored a 4-week introductory MI curriculum available in the public domain through the VA's educational resources (https://www.mirecc.va.gov/visn16/moral-injury-psychoeducation-group.asp).

MI is a human condition, a state of being (as opposed to a diagnosis listed in the DSM-V of the 2022 American Psychiatric Association) that develops following exposure to a potentially morally injurious event (PMIE), followed by a hindsight-driven evaluative process. The narrative that develops during that hindsight-evaluative process often includes blame, regret, moral judgment, a skewed sense of responsibility, hopelessness, if-only thinking, and attribution related to the violation of deeply held values.

In a way, MI is a Veteran-written story of unacceptability, guilt, and blame that explains his/her moral pain and assigns responsibility. Metaphorically, Veterans sentence themselves or others to punishment, *life in emotional prison*, and become stuck in seemingly inescapable pain and judgment. In AFT, storytelling, compassion, and connection bring a revised, more hopeful narrative of forgiveness, new meaning, and renewed purpose. This lightens the load of MI, accepting what cannot be changed from the past and intentionally living out the new meaning going forward.

Since MI often occurs in a group or interpersonal context, we consider the group as the "gold standard" for healing and share its benefits – along with examples of group interactions – later in the book (see Chapter 6). However, groups are not always a viable option. The stories, concepts, and elements in this book may be used by those who are not yet ready to meet with other Veterans, who are pursuing self-help, who might find group disruptive or become distracted, who might wish to approach MI individually with a pastor or therapist, or who have no access to MI services at their VA. Whether in a group or with a trusted other, Veterans must have access to compassionate others for confession and validation (Litz, 2023).

This book is not intended to be a comprehensive treatment or program handbook, nor solely about AFT; however, we share some processes and concepts that contribute to healing from MI and illustrate the benefits of metaphor and story. In examining other approaches to MI treatment, we see similarities and differences in theme and approach. Healing from MI is more than symptom reduction, as Veterans often report what might be referred to as post-traumatic growth in their self-depictions of hope and healing (Logan, 2023; Tedeschi et al., 1998, 2004, 2018). Struggles related to trauma, crisis, or life-changing events – both in the aftermath and while pursuing healing – can bring negative and positive changes. These changes reflect new ways of relating to other Veterans and loved ones by improving trust and self-acceptance, identifying personal strengths, restoring appreciation for life, envisioning hope/possibilities going forward, and experiencing spiritual change (accepting grace with new meaning and purpose).

Regardless of approach, recovery from MI may include breaking the silence, naming the pain (lament), taking responsibility in context, confessing/sharing the story (and perceived impact), experiencing compassion, accepting time served (releasing the burden), experiencing forgiveness for and by self or others, and living more in the present with mindful acceptance.

Healing MI is a journey from pain to hope. Victor Frankl survived a World War II concentration camp, after which he wrote poignantly about meaning-making in *Man's Search for Meaning* (2005). Harold Kushner writes in the foreword to Frankl's book:

> *Forces beyond your control can take away everything you possess except one thing, your freedom to choose how you will respond to the situation. You cannot control what happens to you in life, but you can always control what you will feel and do about what happens to you.*

(Kushner, p. X)

Frankl's recipe for meaning-making even during heinous circumstances involved: 1) doing works of significance, 2) sharing love by caring for another person, and 3) maintaining courage through difficult times; he survived his time in a death camp by living these principles. Frankl believed that suffering was meaningless in and of itself; rather, it is given meaning by how we respond to it. Retired Colonel Lisa Carrington Firmin writes about her own and others' military sexual trauma (MST) and pathways to healing and resilience in *Stories from the Front* (Carrington Firmin, 2022). Her exquisite poetry in *Latina Warrior* (Carrington Firmin, 2023) reflects her journey through pain and brokenness to growth and healing after military-related trauma and MI; we aspire to these principles and practices of meaning-making.

Numerous scholarly and biographical resources describe MI, its impact on service members, and promising interventions (Currier et al., 2021; Griffin et al., 2019; Litz et al., 2009; Litz et al., 2015; Maguen et al., 2017; Pernicano et al., 2022; Shay, 1994; Smigelsky et al., 2022; Jones et al., 2021; Tick, 2014; Usset et al., 2021; and Wood, 2016). Several collaborative, integrated models of MI intervention are available within the larger VA that vary by conceptual approach, program components, format, and targeted population. Each has strengths, and some will be described in Chapter 6. Resources are available nationwide and internationally at universities and organizations such as Veterans of America (VOA); all have a place in educating, raising awareness, and healing. Scott Sinkler is creating *Absolutions*, a documentary reflecting pain and healing in Veteran MI (Sinkler, n.d.).

Like the story of the blind men and the elephant, each school of thought touches a different place on the animal. We describe the part we have touched and may be quick to say, *"This* is the elephant!" The descriptions are bound to be very different, given different points of view and types of MI, and in time, Veterans will have access to a variety of evidence-supported interventions that are a good fit to their unique needs and that result in hope and healing. It is not worth arguing over different vantage points when we use different lenses. An elephant is large, and getting the big picture is only possible when we approach the elephant in different ways and do what we can for the elephant to have a better quality of life.

The concepts and stories in this book are not VA-centric and may be helpful to those who recognize themselves, their friends/relatives, their parishioners, or their clients in the chapters. Of course, MI is also experienced by non-Veterans whose core values are violated in person or vicariously: health-care professionals, caregivers, spiritual leaders, first responders, sexual assault survivors, victims of war crimes, those whose children or elderly are harmed by others, survivors of human trafficking, survivors of mass trauma, those betrayed in the workforce, witnesses of natural disaster, immigration workers, and other victims of persecution, betrayal, and inhumanity. That would be a book in and of itself, but the material in this book, and the core themes, may be applied to more than Veterans.

The book is organized around two parts.

Part I: Overview of Moral Injury and the Change Process

The authors begin with an overview of metaphor and storytelling, which are unique ingredients of our program that ground concepts and conceptualization. The next chapters introduce MI and how it overlaps with and differs from PTSD. We describe the spiritual aspects of MI and the chaplain's role in healing. We also provide an understanding of PMIEs and sources of moral pain that, when unresolved, lead to MI. We then introduce stages-of-change group processes and the benefits of group-based MI interventions. Finally, we summarize several treatments being used in MI intervention. Part I is the educational component, setting the stage for Part II–specific activities used in AFT.

Part II: The Healing Process of Compassion, Acceptance, and Forgiveness

Part II parallels the Veteran's journey through healing and includes many rich examples of the healing process from brokenness to restoration. It might be used for self-help, as an adjunct to formal therapy, in a university setting, or as material for a Vet Center group. Chapters 7–14 include some elements and themes from AFT (Pernicano & Haynes, 2023). We personalize this section as if you are someone with MI and refer directly to "you" as a participant. We invite you to read along with the stories and engage in the experiential activities to gain a firsthand understanding of what it means to name the pain, lament, consider appropriate responsibility, confess, receive compassion, accept forgiveness, accept time served, reconnect (to self, other, and divine), and reclaim hope through acceptance and new meaning. The final chapter celebrates Veteran healing through examples of movement from brokenness to restoration. The book's conclusion includes our robust program outcome data and encourages expanded awareness of MI.

Due to the sensitive nature of this material, we suggest you have someone to talk to as needed (pastor, therapist, fellow Veteran, family member, mentor, peer specialist, etc.). Again, the Veterans Crisis Line is available 24/7 at 988, then press 1.

This book honors Veterans who have served our country and experienced pain. We sent young men and women into situations they could not possibly anticipate along with circumstances that would change them forever. It is good to raise awareness and offer Veterans a tool bag to mine for the gold within them (Pernicano, 2019). We hope readers find one or more gold nuggets of their own and finish the book with renewed compassion and new hope and understanding.

References

American Psychiatric Association. (2022). *Diagnostic and statistical manual of mental disorders* (5th ed., text rev.). https://doi.org/10.1176/appi.books.9780890425787

Carrington Firmin, L. (2022). *Stories from the front: Pain, betrayal, and resilience on the MST battlefield*. Blue Ear Books.

Carrington Firmin, L. (2023). *Latina Warrior*. Blue Ear Books.

Currier, J. M., Drescher, K. D., & Nieuwsma, J. (Eds.) (2021). *Addressing moral injury in clinical practice*. American Psychological Association. https://doi.org/10.1037/0000204-000

Griffin, B. J., Purcell, N., Burkman, K., Litz, B. T., Bryan, C. J., Schmitz, M., Villierme, C., Walsh, J., & Maguen, S. (2019). Moral injury: An integrative review. *Journal of Traumatic Stress*, 32(3), 350–362. https://doi.org/10.1002/jts.22362

Haynes, K. N. (2015). *Helping veterans heal from moral injury through faith-based self-forgiveness groups* [Unpublished doctoral dissertation]. Golden Gate Baptist Theological Seminary.

Jones, K. R. S., Rauch, S. A. M., Smith, E. R., Sherrill, A. M., & Eftekhari, A. (2021). Moral injury, posttraumatic stress disorder, and prolonged exposure. In J. M. Currier, K. D. Drescher, & J. Nieuwsma (Eds.), *Addressing moral injury in clinical practice* (pp. 123–141). American Psychological Association. https://doi.org/10.1037/0000204-008

Kushner, H. (2005) (Foreword. In V. E. Frankl. *Man's search for meaning* (p. X). Beacon Press.

Litz, B. (2023). The future of moral injury and its treatment. *Journal of Military, Veteran and Family Health*, 9(2), 1–5. https://doi.org/10.3138/jmvfh.9.2.ed

Litz, B., Lebowitz, L., Gray, M., & Nash, W. (2015). *Adaptive disclosure: A new treatment for military trauma, loss and moral injury*. Guilford Press.

Litz, B. T., Stein, N., Delaney, E., Lebowitz, L., Nash, W. P., Silva, C., & Maguen, S. (2009). Moral injury and moral repair in war veterans: A preliminary model and intervention strategy. *Clinical Psychology Review*, 29, 695–706. https://doi.org/10.1016/j.cpr.2009.07.003

Logan, A. (2023). *Moral injury and post-traumatic growth* [Paper presentation]. South Texas VA Psychology Service, San Antonio, TX.

Maguen, S., Burkman, K., Madden, E., Dinh, J., Bosch, J., Keyser, J., Schmitz, M., & Neylan, T. C. (2017). Impact of killing in war: A randomized, controlled pilot trial. *Journal of Clinical Psychology, 73*(9), 997–1012. https://doi.org/10.1002/jclp.22471

Pernicano, P. (2010a). *Family-focused trauma intervention: Metaphor and play with victims of abuse and neglect.* Jason Aronson.

Pernicano, P. (2010b). *Using metaphor and play in child therapy.* Jason Aronson.

Pernicano, P. (2012). *Outsmarting the riptide of domestic violence: Metaphor and mindfulness for change.* Jason Aronson.

Pernicano, P. (2014). *Using trauma-focused therapy stories: Interventions for therapists, children, and their caregivers.* Routledge. https://doi.org/10.4324/9781003184171

Pernicano, P. (2015). *Metaphors and stories in play therapy.* In O'Connor, K., Schaefer, C. & Braverman, L. *Handbook of play therapy* (2nd ed.). (pp. 259–276). Wiley.

Pernicano, P. (2019). *Using stories, art and play in trauma-informed treatment: Case examples and applications across the lifespan.* Routledge. https://doi.org/10.4324/9781351005302

Pernicano, P. (2021). *Using trauma-focused therapy stories: Interventions for therapists, children, and their caregivers* (Classics ed.). Routledge.

Pernicano, P., & Haynes, K. (2023). *Acceptance & forgiveness therapy: From brokenness to restoration* [Unpublished handbook] (5th ed.). South Texas Veterans Health Care System.

Pernicano, P., & Haynes, K. (2024). *Introduction to acceptance and forgiveness therapy (facilitator & program handbooks)* (2nd ed.). VA Mental Illness Research, Education and Clinical Center. https://www.mirecc.va.gov/visn16/moral-injury-psychoeducation-group.asp

Pernicano, P., Wortmann, J. H., & Haynes, K. (2022). Acceptance and forgiveness therapy for veterans with moral injury: Spiritual and psychological collaboration in group treatment. *Journal of Health Care Chaplaincy, 28,* S57–S78. https://doi.org/10.1080/08854726.2022.2032982

Shay, J. S. (1994). *Achilles in Vietnam: Combat trauma and the undoing of character.* Touchstone.

Sinkler, S. (n.d.). *Absolutions: War and Moral Injury.* https://www.scottsinkler.com/absolutions

Smigelsky, M. A., Trimm, V., Meador, K. G., Jackson, G. L., Wortmann, J. H., & Nieuwsma, J. A. (2022). Core components of moral injury groups co-facilitated by mental health providers and chaplains. *Spirituality in Clinical Practice, 9*(3), 159–174. https://doi.org/10.1037/scp0000297

Tedeschi, R. G., & Calhoun, L. G. (2004). Posttraumatic growth: Conceptual foundations and empirical evidence. *Psychological Inquiry, 15*(1), 1–18. https://doi.org/10.1207/s15327965pli1501_01

Tedeschi, R. G., Park, C. L., & Calhoun, L. G. (Eds.). (1998). *Posttraumatic growth: Positive changes in the aftermath of crisis.* Lawrence Erlbaum Associates Publishers.

Tedeschi, R. G., Shakespeare-Finch, J., Taku, K., & Calhoun, L. G. (2018). *Posttraumatic growth: Theory, research, and applications.* Routledge. https://doi.org/10.4324/9781315527451

Tick, E. (2014). *Warrior's return: Restoring the soul after war*. Sounds True.

Usset, T. J., Butler, M., & Harris, J. I. (2021). Building spiritual strength: A group treatment for posttraumatic stress disorder, moral injury, and spiritual distress. In J. M. Currier, K. D. Drescher, & J. Nieuwsma (Eds.), *Addressing moral injury in clinical practice* (pp. 223–241). American Psychological Association. https://doi.org/10.1037/0000204-013.

Wood, D. (2016). *What have we done: The moral injury of our longest wars*. Little, Brown & Company.

PART I

Overview of Moral Injury and the Change Process

Chapter 1

Moral Pain and Moral Injury

Moral pain arises in many situations, otherwise known as potentially morally injurious events (PMIEs). "The tendency to experience thoughts, feelings, behaviors, and decisions through the lens of morality is a distinguishing attribute of human beings" (Farnsworth et al., 2014, p. 249). Moral injury (MI) develops when there is a seemingly unresolvable dilemma between one's values and something that violates those values. Service members are confronted with morally laden choices that leave them in moral pain for many years following the event(s); they find it difficult to resolve moral emotions such as shame, anger, disgust, and guilt.

According to Currier et al. (2014), PMIEs contribute to mental health (MH) problems among returning Veterans when they are unable to make meaning of the stressors, which arise from acts of "commission or omission, harmful acts perpetrated by comrades, witnessing human suffering, as well as the consequences of violence and injustice" in the area of deployment (p. 2). MI may develop when there is a mismatch between the stressors and Veterans' guiding moral beliefs and values about themselves, the military, and others. One's meaning-making system is *wounded* by stressors that defy previous beliefs and expectations about what is *good* and *right*.

According to Litz et al. (2009), some can assimilate what they do and see in the military, due to training, preparation, warrior culture, their role, rules of engagement, the messages and behavior of peers and leaders, and the acceptance of sacrifice by families and the culture at large. However, "Even prescribed acts of killing or violence may have a delayed but lasting psychosocial-spiritual impact of guilt and shame" (p. 697).

The meaning attributed to a PMIE is a critical element in someone's long-term response, so a shift in meaning may be needed to heal the MI (Bonson et al., 2023; Currier et al., 2014; Farnsworth et al., 2014; Litz et al., 2009). The perception and attributions of PMIEs bring dissonance and an unresolved dilemma based on values, expectations, and appraisal. The response of one's social network may exacerbate the guilt, blame, and judgment of MI.

DOI: 10.4324/9781003494263-3

MI arises after someone has witnessed, experienced (as the target of harm by others), or participated in something that violates core (deeply held) personal, military, spiritual, or religious values. MI stems from violating what a Veteran perceives or believes to be good, fair, and right. MI can also arise following a perceived omission, where a Veteran believes he/she *should* or *could* have stepped up, but instead, he/she observed or stood by while harm was done to others. Using hindsight, Veterans conclude that wrongdoing occurred, and punishment is deserved. MI may arise after sanctioned military action when that action violates the individual's personal or spiritual beliefs or when the action or orders are viewed as immoral. David Wood writes poignantly about combat-related MI from the perspective of an embedded journalist in *What Have We Done: The Moral Injury of Our Longest Wars* (2016).

Potentially Morally Injurious Events

Events that trigger moral pain and MI may be combat-related or non-combat-related. Bonson et al. (2023) look at the salience of event features that may contribute to MI. A person's beliefs about self, others, and the world/humanity develop before entering the military, and premilitary experiences, such as Adverse Childhood Experiences (ACEs) (Felitti et al., 1998), lay the foundation for response to PMIEs. ACEs impact attachment and relational development by altering interpersonal and intrapersonal beliefs. Betrayal of trust, unexpected loss, or unforeseen consequences may activate moral pain. Veterans become morally wounded by such things as sexual trauma, maltreatment of prisoners of war (POWs), humanitarian wrongdoing, threatened retaliation, rescripted cover-ups, non-combat training errors, unintended loss of life (particularly with non-combatants, such as women and children), unreported wrongdoings, unkept promises, abuse of power, ruined reputations, and horrible injustice, among other things.

King et al. (2023) provided an overview of the breadth of PMIEs through interviews with 32 Veterans, in which they asked about types of events committed while stationed in a war zone: witnessed events, events Veterans believed they should have stopped, and events they believed to be morally wrong. In addition to war atrocities, Veterans endorsed 1) fraud, waste, and abuse, 2) animal cruelty, 3) bullying and reputation smearing, 4) infidelity, 5) racism and sexism, 6) morally abhorrent practices, and 7) events outside the military. Many had experienced multiple events as opposed to a single PMIE. In our work, we have encountered these types of PMIEs and more; it behooves us to identify these events and to ensure a wide range of interventions.

Moral Pain

Moral pain is at the root of MI and includes emotions triggered by things most persons would find painful, shocking, or troubling. It is no surprise that the core components of MI have been difficult to define when you consider the many sources of moral pain: 1) actions of the warrior-self in combat, 2) shock of betrayal by those who were trusted, 3) shame at not doing what was called for (omission), 4) guilt for doing things that violated one's core values, 5) spiritual defeat from being part of an "unjust" action, 6) helplessness of witnessing atrocities and being held back by rules of engagement, and 7) horror of the aftermath and unintended harm. Service members may change their views about self, others, and the world/humanity to make sense of the outcome (Bonson et al., 2023). Some Veterans reach a tipping point where they decide that dying is a better alternative than living with moral pain and MI. Here are some examples of pathways to MI:

Veteran Stories of Moral Pain

Jeff could not forgive himself for actions during deployment that resulted in the death and injury of innocents. He struggled with alcohol abuse and had periodic suicidal thoughts. His marriage was over, and he had stopped going to church. He believed God would not love him and that he did not deserve God's love due to his actions in the military. One morning he woke up in the bathtub hung over and saw evidence that he had planned to end his life. He remembered nothing from the night before and realized it was time to get help for his moral injury.

Jim was a convoy driver who, despite misgivings, took the recommended route based on intelligence (intel) and orders. They drove into an ambush and people were killed. He carried guilt and believed tragedy could have been avoided by following his intuition.

A young shepherd boy wandered into the path of a drone-released explosive as it detonated. It was too late to prevent the attack and he suffered serious injuries. Medics provided care and notified his family. They came, but returned home without him, saying a shepherd with one leg was worthless; for them, he was now a liability instead of a financial resource. The drone operator felt responsible for the boy's injury and subsequent abandonment.

A Marine felt guilty when he looked at his 8-year-old son. In the military, while on deployment, he and a battle buddy took potshots at a boy on a bicycle, "just for fun." The memories of that child screaming and riding away stayed with him. He questioned what type of person he was and could not forgive himself.

A female NCO was viciously sexually assaulted in a work trailer by a visiting officer while overseas, and when she reported it, her command ordered her to change her story. The new story was that her broken cheekbone and bruises were due to being thrown from a flipping vehicle. Her command said the other officer was crucial to their mission and would not be reported.

A Vietnam Veteran carried deep guilt over his means of taking out a target in the jungle. He had a clear headshot but reported, "For some reason, I hunted him like an animal, picking him off one shot at a time. I was paying him back for those we lost."

An Army Veteran was troubled by a cover-up of prisoners of war being caged and treated inhumanely during a humanitarian mission. He tried to report it but was threatened by command, and later wondered if he should have done more.

A soldier had been without sleep for three days. His non-commissioned officer (NCO) ordered him to get some sleep and sent someone else out on the mission in his place. That day, his unit was ambushed, resulting in the other soldier's death. "It should have been me," he said. He was not able to shake what he called his survivor guilt.

The NCO training instructor blamed himself for a female's accidental death during martial arts training. She had objected to his belief that females should only train with females and insisted on training with one of the men. She died of a head injury due to a poor landing. He had done nothing wrong, but he felt responsible.

Each of these Veterans carried deep moral pain that led to MI. Most of them came to the Veterans Affairs (VA) for other problems, such as chronic pain, sleep difficulty, suicidal ideation (SI), alcohol abuse, or panic attacks. They had never mentioned these experiences and concluded that there was no path forward. Recognizing and naming the pain and entering treatment are the first steps to healing.

Mike's Story of Moral Pain from Omission

Mike, a medic, was deployed to a location without adequate medical provisions, including lab tests and medications. His team had a very sick soldier with a serious, hard-to-diagnose lung condition who needed additional tests and medications. The team decided to wait until morning to medivac him. His oxygen levels had gone up and down all day, but he seemed stable at the shift's end, and Mike was the medic NCO on night duty. The young man was upright and joking with the staff at shift change. The medic NCO's job was to monitor him every two hours. At 4 AM, he was sleeping soundly, so Mike let him sleep rather than wake him. Around 8 AM the patient tanked and could not be revived, dying before he could be airlifted out. His illness turned out to be an unusual virus that required special tests and care unavailable at the medical site.

The medic's moral pain of "shirking his duty" brought self-blame, regret, and loss of trust in himself because he had not checked on the patient during the night. He didn't notice when the patient's oxygen levels dropped. He wondered if the young soldier might have lived had they airlifted him sooner. He questioned his judgment and that of the team. Others believed there would not have been time or medicine to save him, but he still blamed himself. He was a perfectionist who prided himself on his work ethic and competence. "I was complacent," he said. "It is unforgivable."

After this, Mike viewed himself as selfish, heartless, and, most of all "complacent," which was unacceptable for a very competent young medic with a strong medical code of "do no harm." Spiritually agnostic, Mike did not believe in a higher power. He struggled to accept or forgive himself, yet could see no path forward, as if he had permanently lost his integrity. He drank to excess, became bitter, and used habit-forming medications. He lost his job, withdrew from others, and became suicidal.

Fortunately, Mike brought his pain to the VA and eventually found a path forward through compassion for his imperfection and self-forgiveness. He decided there was no value in continuing his suffering; instead, he would return to his values and choose to live a life that might honor the man who died. Shortly after, Mike visited the man's gravesite, which helped him in his grief. He had suffered and punished himself long enough. He accepted "time served" and planned to make amends and pay it forward. He began a new life, living one day at a time.

Overview of Moral Injury

Hollis et al. (2022) conceptualize MI from psychological, social, and morality perspectives; they conclude, "Moral injury can best be understood as a psychological wound to our basic human needs to feel connected with others" (p. 19). MI disconnects Veterans from relationships (trust), a sense of integrity, and meaning-making or spirituality. MI varies by the type of event as well as the context. Maguen and Litz (2012) indicate that taking a life during Operation Enduring Freedom (OEF) increased the risk of alcohol abuse, anger, relationship problems, and post-traumatic stress disorder (PTSD) diagnosis. Killing non-combatants is more troubling than killing combatants, and for those with MI, re-experiencing (with moral emotions) and avoidance are more common than the hyperarousal of PTSD. There is a link between guilt and suicide; being the agent of killing or failing to prevent death or injury has been associated with general psychological distress and suicide attempts. Guilt may be an important mediator that contributes to SI in Veterans with MI, and the killing of women and children seems to increase guilt.

Research points to an increased risk of suicide for Veterans with MI (Ames et al., 2019). The suicide rate for Veterans is 1.5 times that of non-Veteran adults, with more than 6,000 Veteran suicides each year over the last decade. The majority of suicide deaths occur among those not using VA services during the year before death. Participating in a PMIE (as opposed to betrayal or bystander events) increases grief, guilt, remorse, and SI.

A 2023 article (Maguen et al., 2023) refers to a cross-sectional survey of over 14,000 post-9/11 Veterans to examine the association between MI, MH, and suicide attempts during military service and after separation. Twenty-four percent of women and 41% of men reported witnessing PMIEs; 50% of women and 38% of men reported betrayal; and 24% of women and 21% of men reported participating in or perpetrating PMIEs.

Men and women with MI had somewhat different suicide risks, but all were high. Men with participatory PMIEs were 50% more likely to attempt suicide during service and twice as likely to attempt suicide after separation. Men who endorsed betrayal were almost twice as likely to attempt suicide during service. Women who endorsed betrayal were more than 50% more likely to attempt suicide during service and after separation.

It is important to expand our understanding of protective factors that buffer risks associated with MI. Levi-Belz et al. (2022) report that "self-disclosure (sharing distressing thoughts and emotions) has been recognized as a protective factor against SI in the aftermath of stressful events" (p. 198). They examine the moderating impact of self-disclosure for PMIE exposure and SI in Israeli combat Veterans. The most common PMIEs were seeing morally wrong things, feeling betrayed by leaders who were once trusted, and witnessing others' immoral acts. Those with lower self-disclosure reported higher SI. The writers found that self-disclosure promoted belonging, interpersonal bonding, and support. They concluded that self-disclosure may result in feelings of intimacy and togetherness with other Veterans, thus reducing guilt and shame through reconnection.

Following a PMIE, a conflict emerges between what was done and what, in the Veteran's mind, could, would, or should have been done (Veterans talk of "woulda, coulda, shoulda"). Some feel responsible for and burdened by situations largely beyond their control. They blame themselves for unintended, unanticipated negative consequences. Unprocessed grief and loss contribute to MI: 1) loss of trust in others or the military due to inconceivable betrayal, cruelty, or inaction, 2) loss of trust in self after being rendered helpless to change a tragic outcome, 3) loss of purpose or meaning in the face of vulnerability and inhumanity, 4) loss of self-esteem at one's own *inhumane* emotions or actions, 5) loss of spiritual comfort at feeling abandoned, 6) loss of innocence and overreaching ideals at the hands of immoral leadership, and 7) loss of hope in the face of fallibility, imperfection, or unintended negative outcomes.

MI develops in the context of the Veteran's culture, experiences, family background, spiritual beliefs and practices, conscience, values, interactions, ideals, military intent, and one's role in the event.

Assessing Moral Injury

A variety of measures have been developed, some of which assess the absence or presence of MI, and others that address specific components such as inflexibility, depression, symptoms of PTSD, guilt, forgiveness, healthy functioning, or religious and spiritual stressors (see Chapter 6). Given the association of MI with SI and substance use, Veterans who present with guilt, alcohol-related disorders, PTSD, and SI ought to be screened for MI. Additionally, a PMIE "may trigger dynamic interactions among PTSD, MI-related outcomes, and depression" (Benfer et al., 2023, p. 52).

Houle et al. (2024) reviewed 77 studies representing 42 unique scales assessing moral distress and MI. The writers recommend the Moral Injury Outcome Scale (MIOS; Litz et al., 2022); it captures types of MI (participant, betrayal, witnessed) and subsequent shame and guilt, as well as the impact on functioning. Litz (2023) suggests using this as a screening tool, and although there is no definitive cutoff point, the MIOS can be used in a shared decision-making process with patients about whether MI is a clinical concern. Veterans in acceptance and forgiveness therapy (AFT) scored from the mid-20s to the mid-40s when first assessed. Pernicano (2012) developed a story and drawing task that the writers later modified for Veterans (Pernicano & Haynes, 2023), depicting trauma/impact and hope/healing (Table 1.1).

Moral Injury and Responsibility

Feeling responsible is not the same as *being* responsible, and feelings of regret and grief can be mistaken for guilt. When determining reasonable responsibility, consider the degree of actual control over the situation, the person's intentions, whether the activity was sanctioned, and whether there was time to make other than a split-second decision. Responsibility also considers other factors or persons involved, including enemy forces. Responsibility is not blame; it is a careful examination of the facts and a willingness to take ownership of what is fair and just. It goes beyond military mentality, where blame is often assigned based on military rules about leadership and combat or – at times – a desire for cover-up.

Table 1.1 Likely Impact by Type of Event

Type of Event	Likely Impact	Examples
Betrayal Someone else's actions hurt or betrayed another	• Feelings after betrayal: hurt, angry, grief-filled, fearful, mistrust, helpless, trapped, bitter, angry, vulnerable, sadness, and self-doubt	• Lies/dishonesty/cover-up • Sexual or physical assault • Someone else violated the rules
Involved in Approved Activity with Good Intentions • Action sanctioned by the military; orders followed • What happened violated your personal or spiritual values or beliefs **Bystander Events** • Outside your control • Wrong place/wrong time • Witness • Unanticipated trauma • Aftermath exposure	• Out-of-proportion guilt: you feel responsible, possibly more than you deserve • Self-doubt: you wish you had done more and you second-guess your actions or decisions • You did not consider other factors that affected the outcome • You find it hard to live with yourself • Feelings of bystander: vulnerable, helpless, self-blame, shame, or guilt • Feelings in the aftermath: grief, anger, and helplessness • You might question God or a higher power	• You hit an improvised explosive device (IED), and others were injured • You made a decision that resulted in unintended injury or death • You briefly "froze" and blamed yourself for the outcome • Troubling aftermath (body parts retrieval, carnage, etc.) • Your action was sanctioned, but later, it feels "wrong" or "unforgivable" • Someone made a poor judgment call • Natural disasters like hurricanes and tornadoes • Someone (battle buddy or under your leadership) was severely injured or died (including suicide)

Unapproved Activity with Purposeful Harm		
• You purposefully violated military or personal values, religious beliefs, or standards • Your actions hurt others unnecessarily • You blamed someone else or covered up • Unsanctioned disallowed harm	• Guilt is appropriate • Difficulty forgiving yourself • You rationalized what you did while knowing it was wrong • You likely carry this as a "secret" • Difficulty reconciling what you did then with who you are now	• Violated orders or rules of engagement • Committed physical or sexual assault • Unnecessary harm/cruelty or "overkill" • Illegal actions that hurt others • Did something wrong for your benefit • Retaliated with angry cruelty • Misused power/control/status • Participated in abusive "hazing" or "training" • Revenge or unnecessary kill • Unsanctioned torture or mistreatment of POWs

Source: Pernicano and Haynes (2023).

The Stories to Tell: Types of Moral Injury

For Veterans, MI seems black and white; however, the impact of MI varies by the source, the context, and the Veteran's conclusions about his/her role in the event.

The Moral Injury of Betrayal

John believed in the military and had hoped to make it a career. During a desert training exercise, a training instructor gave alcohol to the troops, then sexually violated John and several others, calling it "hazing." John was reduced to tears, and the instructor mocked him, telling him he was weak and not fit for the military. The instructor said he would write up anyone who reported the "hazing" for underage drinking. John maintained secrecy until he separated and sought help through the VA.

Betrayal is intentional harm that violates trust, honesty, and core values. It is unexpected by the recipient, and the coercive action may carry a threat. The victim of betrayal may be blamed by the perpetrator, the system, and himself or herself. The perpetrator twists facts or demeans the person who has been hurt. The moral pain may be physical, emotional, or spiritual, and betrayal may "break" the person into leaving the military or considering suicide. Betrayal includes such situations as a breach of trust, dishonesty, sexual trauma, racism, cover-up with threat, lack of benevolence in response, and mislabeled hazing. There is often a dilemma of reporting versus not reporting. Betrayal violates the core military values and ideals that were stressed during enlistment and leaves someone stuck and vulnerable in the face of such things as mistreatment of POWs, misogyny, or abuse of military power/structure. The military culture can prevent resolution or lead to retaliation. The perpetrator can be the military as a whole, through a more subtle form of abandonment, as some service members have been traumatized by repeated deployments and labeled as "weak" or inadequate when reaching out for help. Consider Henry's story.

Henry's Story of Betrayal: Thrown in the Landfill

They took my youth, used me up, and then threw me in the landfill. A Marine has to be strong; he has to be able to take it and keep going. They broke me, then sent me to mental health when I wanted to die. They discarded me in the landfill of recruiting. I was weak and useless. I failed at being a Marine.

Henry drank heavily to cope with nightmares and sleep difficulties. He had been sent on seven combat deployments and served in missions where battle buddies did not return. He showed signs of PTSD; before his 8th deployment, Henry privately voiced suicidal thoughts to a peer. A hospital stay became the beginning of the end of his Marine Corps career. In Henry's eyes, leadership ignored his resilience and good record, labeled him a liability, and sent him home to a recruiting job, mocking him for failing as a combat Marine. Shortly after, he was medically discharged.

The stigma of MH ends many strong military careers that could have been saved, and this abandonment is a form of betrayal. It is why so many in the military shun MH and deny symptoms of anxiety, depression, or PTSD. Admitting symptoms becomes a presumed liability, so the military moves them on and out rather than identifying and treating symptoms. The military believes that talking about MI might hurt morale; this belief prevents service members from seeking appropriate help and resolving issues early on. MI contributes to military and Veteran suicide when the individual judges he or she is weak or has failed. Certainly, the military needs to identify potential liability when someone is a danger to himself or others; they also need to recognize the root causes of MI and offer restorative intervention.

Mary's Story of Betrayal: The Father Figure

Mary's Navy team worked hard onboard the ship and partied hard when they were off duty on shore. Drinking is part of the military culture, just as it is part of the culture of young adults pursuing an education or young adults first living independently of their parents. Drinking is culturally accepted, but sexual assault should not be.

Mary's unit had a designated chain of command, and officers were not supposed to "fraternize" with enlistees. Sailors were told to travel in pairs and to escort each other for safety in certain areas. They were not told that harm might well come from within.

Mary traveled with a female friend most nights. One night, her friend was unavailable, and Mary had been drinking with the others at a local bar. She saw an officer she trusted like a father. Indeed, this married man was kind and protective of the women who served under him. She asked him if he would escort her back that night, and he agreed. He did escort her back, but he followed her in, and when she said, "NO!" he became violent. He assaulted her physically and sexually, then told her it was her fault because she asked for it. He said that requesting a ride implied consent. It would be his word against hers, and if she reported it, she would get in trouble for fraternizing with an officer. She remembered another woman charged with that and decided to remain silent. Mary no longer trusted her superiors and felt undeserved shame and self-blame.

The Moral Injury of Participation

When Veterans participate in something that violates core values or results in harm, MI may result, depending on the intentions, the nature of the harm, and any missed opportunities that might have prevented the event. Even with good intentions, things can go wrong, such as training accidents or equipment failure. It is human nature to seek someone to blame or to explain why such terrible things happened. Often, the first finger we point is at ourselves, no doubt reinforced by the military value of taking personal responsibility for outcomes. Many Veterans experience self-doubt as they wonder what they might have done differently.

People join the military for various reasons: some want to protect and preserve safety, while others seek education and experience. In the case of World War II, stopping the Nazi threat was a well-intentioned course of action. However, more recent wars have not been so clear-cut. For instance, some carry guilt from invading Iraq under what seemed to be false pretenses, while others grieve the way we exited Afghanistan as they picture those left behind. Consider the following scenarios, each a form of participation, some by lawful order, some in fun, and some in dishonesty. They are quite different, but each has the potential to arouse moral pain:

- Veterans participated in orders for border separation of women and children.

  Hank said, "I followed orders in my duty assignment. But I can't get the cries of a mother and her baby out of my mind. I pulled an 18-month-old baby from her mother's arms. They took the mother away and locked her in a metal enclosure. I don't know what happened to the baby. I heard later that they sent the mom back, and her baby is still somewhere in the U.S. I won't ever forget my part. I think what we did was morally wrong."

- A young serviceman was not a good swimmer, so when he jumped, in drunken fun, from a bridge into a river, he drowned.

  Perry reported, "I had to identify the body and put it in a refrigerator in the morgue. We knew he was a poor swimmer. I wish we had stopped him."

- An accident where the parachute was not packed properly; someone died during a jump.
- The bombing of a Vietnamese hospital where the Viet Cong held American patients hostage.
- Abusive *hazing* during boot camp.
- Leadership casts blame on the victim to preserve the career of the abuser.
- Accidental deaths of civilians, including children.
- A drone attack that hit the wrong target.
- Faulty intelligence resulted in an ambush.
- Interrogators killed civilians rather than returning them to their villages.
- Longboat operators mowed down civilians on the coast right before exiting Vietnam.
- Witnesses were threatened with harm if they reported wrongdoing.
- A bystander became a party to sexual assault.
- There was a cover-up of an accidental death; those present were told to keep it quiet.
- Service members witnessed the maltreatment of POWs and were threatened to keep silent.

After a PMIE, individuals may ask, "Did I miss something?" or tell themselves, "I should have seen it coming." When we are vulnerable and caught off guard, we wonder why something happened and look for someone to blame. Some factors influence response to PMIEs: military sanction, intentionality, potential at the time for other action, following orders versus violating orders, and degree of predictability / foresight for what happened. The war climate can raise emotions, resulting in quick reactivity or even retaliative rage. Service members may behave unpredictably in the face of loss, grief, high stress, racism, and injustice.

Pete's Story of Participation: Unforgivable Intentional Harm

Pete was a skilled interrogator in Vietnam. He contributed to many missions through skillful interviews and interrogation of villagers. He used unconventional means to gain information, such as taking villagers up in a helicopter with the side door open during an interrogation. Pete returned them to their villages after he got what he wanted. He was well known in the villages and took treats to children and food to families. One week, Pete's unit suffered many losses. Pete's friend was killed by someone who had been working with them and then gave them up. On the day in question, Pete interrogated two villagers, got the info he needed, and on a whim, pushed them out of the helicopter to their deaths. He regretted it immediately as he heard their cries and saw them die. He ended up serving time. He cynically called them "my two best friends. They are always with me, they haunt me in my dreams. They will never let me forget the evil I did. And I will never forgive myself." Pete eventually entered treatment for MI; forgiving himself cleared his soul and saved his life. See Chapter 12 for Pete's depiction of healing.

Philip's Story of Participation: Witnessing the Unthinkable

Part of Navy Seal Training was the swim test. You were thrown into the water in uniform, with your pack on your back. You had to swim to the side with your gear on. Philip watched as his buddy entered the water – and sank. He struggled and could not get back to the surface. As he continued to struggle, Philip asked the instructor if he could enter the water to help. The answer was a sharp, "No! He has to do it to pass this test." After what seemed to be a long time, the training instructor went in the water, pulled Philip's friend out, and began cardiopulmonary resuscitation (CPR). However, it was too late; the man had drowned. Philip had MI over his guilt at not interfering–despite orders to the contrary–as well as observing the cover-up of an "accidental drowning." Philip became a Navy Seal but always regretted not saving his friend's life, even if it meant violating orders.

George's Story of Convoy Action

George had befriended a child who came by the "FOB" (forward operating base). He shared rations and candy and enjoyed the light-hearted banter with the boy. Not long after, George was driving in a convoy. He saw a Taliban soldier carrying a young boy; as he drew nearer, he realized it was his young friend. George wanted to stop or shoot the Taliban soldier. Then the soldier threw the boy into the path of the convoy. The rules were, "Don't stop." The child was hit and died on impact. George knew he had to do what he did, but he blamed himself for participating in the child's death and felt guilty for ever befriending him in the first place.

Mario's Story of Unintended Harm

During the US withdrawal from Afghanistan, Mario's job was to monitor the video feed. "We are responsible for the consequences of our actions. War is not black and white. Sometimes we did more harm than good, and they gave their lives to support American lives. During the withdrawal from Afghanistan, we handed out certificates of appreciation to those who helped in our efforts - America's attempt to feel good when we knew what we were leaving behind. My next feed was a video - a lineup of Afghans in front of a long ditch, holding up their certificates. They were shot and buried in that mass grave."

The Moral Injury of Witnessing or Omission

In the case of omission, a Veteran sees or knows about something, but his/her hands are tied, and perhaps no action is taken. It also can be the case that a service member tries to intervene but is silenced or threatened. This can be the case with POW incidents, observing maltreatment of others outside the wire, observing maltreatment of others during a humanitarian mission/hazing/training incident, and experiencing accidents with cover-ups. MI arises when the witnessing individual wonders, with hindsight, what she should have, could have, or would have done had the opportunity been there.

Polly's Moral Injury of Humanitarian Cover-Up

Polly was sent on a humanitarian mission to intercept refugees, provide blankets, food, and cots, and offer passage to the US. When she arrived, she noticed that the refugees were being kept in cages and treated harshly, in violation of the Geneva Convention. She questioned it, but the NCO threatened her to keep her mouth shut or worse would come to her. The men in the cages were cold at night, poorly fed, and being sent back to certain death, not to the US. She never told anyone what she experienced, but she carried MI of guilt for colluding with the maltreatment. She called herself a "coward," and felt deep shame.

Doug's Moral Injury of Looking the Other Way

Doug saw a young woman go into the Sergeant's office. He heard noises from the room that might have been furniture being shoved around and someone calling out in distress.

The young woman came out, head down, looking somewhat disheveled. Later that day, the Sergeant called everyone together and referred to the woman by name. He called her out for not pulling her weight. He said she was not a team player, and that they should ignore her claims. He wanted them to ostracize her. After the meeting, she asked Doug if she could speak to him. She told Doug she had been sexually assaulted and asked for his support as a witness in reporting it. He denied having witnessed the assault. He said it was her word against the Sergeant's and he could not hear clearly what had been said. Doug felt MI for minimizing what he had heard and seen. The Sergeant eventually got in trouble for another assault, and Doug wondered if he had done enough to help.

Many situations of moral pain and MI remain unresolved because, until recent years, there was no clear differentiation between MI and fear-based PTSD, a topic of our next chapter. There is still controversy over the roots of MI and how to best conceptualize it, given the complex nature of MI and the many components of *the elephant*. Veterans of all ages and combat eras, some in their 60s and 70s, have never heard of MI and are relieved to discover a label for what they experience.

References

Ames, D., Erickson, Z., Youssef, N. A., Arnold, I., Adamson, C. S., Sones, A. C., Yin, J., Haynes, K., Volk, F., Teng, E. J., Oliver, J. P., & Koenig, H. G. (2019). Moral injury, religiosity, and suicide risk in U.S. veterans and active duty military with PTSD symptoms. *Military Medicine, 184*(3–4), e271–e278. https://doi.org/10.1093/milmed/usy148

Benfer, N., Vannini, M. B., Grunthal, B., Darnell, B., Zerach, G., Levi-Belz, Y., & Litz, B. T. (2023). Moral injury symptoms and related problems among service members and veterans: A network analysis. *Journal of Military, Veteran and Family Health, 9*(2), 54–71. https://doi.org/10.3138/jmvfh-2022-0040

Bonson, A., Murphy, D., Aldridge, V., Greenberg, N., & Williamson, V. (2023). Conceptualization of moral injury: A socio-cognitive perspective. *Journal of Military, Veteran and Family Health, 9*(2). https://doi.org/10.3138/jmvfh-2022-0034

Currier, J. M., Holland, J. M., & Malott, J. (2014). Moral injury, meaning-making, and mental health in returning veterans. *Journal of Clinical Psychology, 71*(3), 229–240. https://doi.org/10.1002/jclp.22134

Farnsworth, J. K., Drescher, K. D., Nieuwsma, J. A., Walser, R. B., & Currier, J. M. (2014). The role of moral emotions in military trauma: Implications for the study and treatment of moral injury. *Review of General Psychology, 18*(4), 249–262. https://doi.org/10.1037/gpr0000018

Felitti, V. J., Anda, R. F., Nordenberg, D., Williamson, D. F., Spitz, A. M., Edwards, V., Koss, M. P., & Marks, J. S. (1998). Relationship of childhood abuse and household dysfunction to many of the leading causes of death in adults: The adverse childhood experiences (ACE) study. *American Journal of Preventive Medicine, 14*(4), 245–258. https://www.ajpmonline.org/article/S0749-3797(98)00017-8/pdf

Hollis, J., Hanna, P., & Perman, G. (2023). Recontextualising moral injury among military veterans: An integrative theoretical review. *Journal of Community & Applied Social Psychology, 33*(1), 85–101. https://doi.org/10.1002/casp.2643

Houle, S. A., Ein, N., Gervasio, J., Plouffe, R. A., Litz, B. T., Carleton, R. N., Hansen, K. T., Liu, J. J., Ashbaugh, A. R., Callaghan, W., Thompson, M. M., Easterbrook, B., Smith-MacDonald, L., Rodrigues, S., Bélanger, S. A., Bright, K., Lanius, R. A., Baker, C., Younger, W., Bremault-Phillips, S., Hosseiny, F., Richardson, J. D., & Nazarov, A. (2024). Measuring moral distress and moral injury: A systematic review and content analysis of existing scales. *Clinical Psychology Review, 108*, 102377. https://doi.org/10.1016/j.cpr.2023.102377

King, H. A., Perry, K. R., Ferguson, S., Chicken, B. L., Jackson, G. L., Lynch, C., Woolson, S. L., Wortmann, J. H., Nieuwsma, J. A., & Parry, K. J. (2023). Identifying potentially morally injurious events from the veteran perspective: A qualitative descriptive study. *Journal of Military, Veteran and Family Health, 9*(2), 27–39. https://doi.org/10.3138/jmvfh-2022-0049

Levi-Belz, Y., Shemesh, S., & Zerach, G. (2022). Moral injury and suicide ideation among combat veterans: The moderating role of self-disclosure. *Crisis: The Journal of Crisis Intervention and Suicide Prevention, 44*(3), 198–208. https://doi. org/10.1027/0227-5910/a000849

Litz, B. T. (2023). The future of moral injury and its treatment. *Journal of Military, Veteran and Family Health, 9*(2), 1–5. https://doi.org/10.3138/jmvfh.9.2.ed

Litz, B. T., Plouffe, R. A., Nazarov, A., Murphy, D., Phelps, A., Coady, A., Houle, S. A., Dell, L., Frankfurt, S., Zerach, G., & Levi-Belz, Y. (2022). Defining and assessing the syndrome of moral injury: Initial findings of the moral injury outcome scale consortium. *Frontiers in Psychiatry, 13*(923928). https://doi.org/10.3389/ fpsyt.2022.923928

Litz, B. T., Stein, N., Delaney, E., Lebowitz, L., Nash, W. P., Silva, C., & Maguen, S. (2009). Moral injury and moral repair in war veterans: A preliminary model and intervention strategy. *Clinical Psychology Review, 29*, 695–706. https://doi. org/10.1016/j.cpr.2009.07.003

Maguen, S., Griffin, B. J., Vogt, D., Hoffmire, C. A., Blosnich, J. R., Bernhard, P. A., Akhtar, F. Z., Cypel, Y. S., & Schneiderman, A. I. (2023). Moral injury and peri- and post-military suicide attempts among post-9/11 veterans. *Psychological Medicine, 53*(7), 3200–3209. https://doi.org/10.1017/S0033291721005274

Maguen, S., & Litz, B. (2012). Moral injury in veterans of war. *PTSD Research Quarterly, 23*(1), 1–6. https://vva1071.org/uploads/3/4/4/6/34460116/moral_injury_in_ veterans_of_war.pdf

Pernicano, P. (2012). The cracked glass bowl. In *Outsmarting the riptide of domestic violence: Metaphor and mindfulness for change* (pp. 141–144). Jason Aronson.

Pernicano, P., & Haynes, K. (2023). *Acceptance & forgiveness therapy: From brokenness to restoration* [Unpublished handbook] (5th ed.). South Texas Veterans Health Care System.

Wood, D. (2016). *What have we done: The moral injury of our longest wars.* Little, Brown & Company.

Chapter 2

PTSD and Moral Injury: Overlapping Symptoms and Different Meanings

Veterans and others may have confusion over moral injury (MI) and post-traumatic stress disorder (PTSD), which develop and are activated in different ways. MI, unlike PTSD, is not a formal "diagnosis" although the two conditions may overlap. Both PTSD and MI might be considered traumatic in that the events are shocking, troubling, and hard to put out of your mind; however, the roots of PTSD and MI are somewhat different.

About the time Jonathan Shay (1994) coined the term "moral injury," social psychologist Ronnie Janoff-Bulman (1992) wrote about two differing routes to trauma: the terror of one's vulnerability and the horror of one's immorality. Individuals with PTSD experience a wide variety of symptoms after exposure to a life-threatening event that shatters assumptions about safety and well-being (Friedman, 2023). MI, the second horror, is based on shattered assumptions about values, goodness, and worth (Janoff-Bulman, 2013). Let's consider the roots of both PTSD and MI, as Veterans may have one or both conditions.

PTSD may be diagnosed when symptoms arise after a traumatic, adverse, life-threatening event that involves actual or threatened death or injury or a threat to the physical integrity of self/others (i.e., sexual violence). The event is called a Criteria A stressor, as described in the *Diagnostic and Statistical Manual* (American Psychiatric Association, 2013). PTSD symptoms may also arise following indirect exposure, which includes learning about the violent or accidental death or perpetration of sexual violence to a loved one.

Those who develop PTSD report symptoms of high arousal, startle response, and fear. These arise from the adrenaline survival system, designed to protect us and ensure survival, much like a radar tornado warning system. After trauma, the person's *radar for danger* is set too high, and a *tornado warning* might be triggered at the first sign of rain (Pernicano, 2014). PTSD impacts several areas of the brain, including the amygdala (which activates the alarm), the prefrontal cortex (reduced ability to plan, focus, and concentrate), and the hippocampus (memory difficulties). In other words, Veterans with PTSD continue to react for safety and survival, long after the traumatic event has passed.

Some situations that meet Criteria A may also result in MI, such as witnessing the unintended death of women or children, experiencing a sexual assault, or causing

DOI: 10.4324/9781003494263-4

death due to negligence; these horrific situations also violate core values and are morally troubling. Some Veterans report situations that are not life-threatening, which do not meet Criteria A, and we do not diagnose PTSD. These situations may stem from experiences that violate core values and are morally reprehensible, so MI results.

Regarding PTSD symptoms, evidence-based therapies such as prolonged exposure (PE; Foa et al., 1991, 2019) and written exposure therapy (WET; Sloan & Marx, 2019) reduce arousal, anxiety, startle response, and avoidance of situations that resemble the stressor. There are established interventions to help with nightmares and improve sleep. Veterans with MI may dwell on often unpreventable negative outcomes, presume moral responsibility when they were not culpable, or believe they could, would, or should have engaged in other actions that would have changed the outcome. Cognitive processing therapy (CPT; Resick & Schnicke, 1992, 2017) allows Veterans to modify inaccurate or distorted cognitions that result in negative emotions, self-blame, and faulty assumptions about what happened and who is responsible.

Cognitively focused interventions for PTSD may not adequately address moral pain, injustice, breach of trust, grief from loss, spirituality (meaning/purpose), and legitimate wrongdoing or guilt-worthy actions. Moral pain differs from the high arousal that occurs in the face of a near-death experience. In MI, the negative cognitions of guilt, shame, and betrayal are not always stuck points because they do not necessarily arise from inaccurate self-/other-condemning beliefs regarding culpability (Litz, 2023). These may respond to a forgiveness process of intentional amends, restitution, serving, and caring for others (Barnes et al., 2019; Litz et al., 2022; Litz, 2023; Pernicano & Haynes, 2023; Pernicano et al., 2022). Those with guilt or spiritual wounds may respond to adaptive disclosure (Gray et al., 2021), building spiritual strength (BSS, Usset et al., 2021), or the impact of killing (Burkman et al., 2021). Practices found within acceptance and commitment therapy (ACT, Walser & Wharton, 2021) help Veterans become more mindfully centered in the present, and meaning-making is important for those who were betrayed or who violated their core values. Those with grief and regret benefit from a process of lament, and those who were betrayed find validation and release of inner pain.

Research suggests that MI and PTSD may have different neurobiological roots and the underlying neurobiology of PTSD may be affected by the nature of the index trauma (Barnes et al., 2019; Moll et al., 2002; Ramage et al., 2016). PTSD and MI have been described as often co-occurring yet mechanistically different (Barnes et al., 2019). Studies of combat-related PTSD have reported that 25–34% of those with combat-related PTSD also have moral injuries, and the rate is higher in those with PTSD, betrayal, and participatory guilt (Barnes et al., 2019). MI arises out of military situations but also among first responders, police, health-care providers, and civilians.

Ramage et al. (2016) indicate that the brain processes danger-based and non-danger-based traumas differently. Danger-based PTSD triggers brain areas involved in fear-freeze-flight-fight. The neurobiology of fear does not adequately explain the impact of non-fear-based trauma. Non-danger-based trauma (MI) is processed in different brain locations than fear-based PTSD, and emotions of disgust, anguish, guilt, shame, or sadness are common.

Moll et al. (2002) have studied moral emotions and the roots of MI and PTSD. Moral processing involves prefrontal brain regions, and negative self-evaluations are associated with negative moral emotions. Moral emotions differ from basic emotions because they are intrinsically interpersonal, and MI arises from painful interpersonal violations (by self or others). Attachment-based loss may trigger moral emotions where trust and security are threatened. Veterans experience attachment disruption when someone they trusted in the military violates their trust or intentionally hurts them. As in childhood attachment disruption, the recipient may point the finger at himself or herself, associating the harm with worthlessness and viewing it as loss or abandonment.

The Same but Different

Some symptoms of PTSD resemble those seen in MI, yet the root causes of the symptoms are different. Metaphorically speaking, the roots of PTSD are deeply embedded in life-or-death situations that startle and prompt quick action to survive. MI roots include shame, regret, grief, perceived weakness, vulnerability and powerlessness, apathy, anger and bitterness, and guilt. MI says, "You are worthless," and is deeply rooted in unforgiveness, hopelessness, and the soil of "woulda, coulda, shoulda."

Jerry, an African-American Army Reserves Specialist (E4) in the Infantry branch, was scheduled to deploy. Two non-commissioned officer (NCO) training instructors had recently returned from deployment and had become bitter, angry, and disillusioned. One day, Jerry was in the shower after working out. He felt hands push him from behind. Before he knew what happened, he was face down on the floor with two strong men behind him. The sexual assault was brutal, and the attackers disappeared before he could identify them. He did not report it, and he suffered from symptoms of PTSD: nightmares, intrusive memories, avoidance of public places, and discomfort being touched. He also developed MI at the betrayal by those he trusted: "I am weak," he said. "I should have seen them coming, and with my black belt, I should have been able to fight them off. If I can't deal with this, how will I deal with combat?!" He needed treatment for PTSD symptoms and for MI, one focused on trauma symptoms and the other on his betrayal by those he trusted that brought undeserved shame and the misguided perception that he was weak.

Some symptoms seem the same until you examine the roots. Veterans with PTSD or MI may become isolated and avoid connecting with others and doing things they used to enjoy. Veterans with PTSD may avoid persons, places, or situations that remind them of the trauma out of fear for their safety. Veterans with PTSD avoid higher-risk situations such as crowds and imagine what *could* happen because they believe that the world is dangerous. They scope out escape routes and have well-developed safety and protection plans for family and personal safety (home alarms, weapons, escape plans, and periodic nightly patrols). Veterans with PTSD may avoid talking about the military or specific missions because it raises anxiety or triggers panic attacks. They avoid movies or TV shows about the military because these trigger nightmares and memories of the trauma.

Veterans with MI may also avoid others but less so much out of fear. Their avoidance may be out of lost hope, shame, disillusionment, and loss of trust in self or humanity. Those with MI judge that no one else would understand or accept what happened. They develop a life of secrecy and don't want to discuss the military or specific missions. Many "hide the real me" from others; the self they see in the mirror is shattered or monstrous.

Veterans with PTSD or MI may experience increased negativity or anger. Veterans with PTSD believe that the world is *unsafe* and take extra safety precautions to protect and defend themselves and their families from harm. Veterans generalize times in combat zones or deployments to their current lives; they misread cues from others, seeing others as insurgents. Sometimes their experiences and nightmares reinforce their beliefs about safety, and they replay situations that involve inescapable danger. Many Veterans with PTSD are irritable when they feel out of control, and anger is easily triggered when they feel vulnerable, pressured, or afraid. Due to the high nervous system arousal associated with PTSD, Veterans react to perceived threats with high baseline arousal and stress hormones (cortisol, adrenaline). Poor sleep, with interruptions, such as nightmares, can result in fatigue and irritability with poor mood regulation. PTSD-related anger is part of the fight-flight-freeze-fawn response.

Veterans with MI develop hopeless, negative thinking. They think the world *should be safe*; those you trust *should* have your back and come through under stress. They become bitter over negative outcomes that *could have* been prevented with proper action or planning. They may judge that they have *failed* or that what happened is *unspeakable* or *unforgivable*. They lose faith and trust in themselves and others. They may have nightmares about being helpless or having failed. Veterans with MI may report depressive symptoms (low energy, tearfulness, depressed mood, negative thinking, self-blame, poor motivation, short fuse, irritability, or over-sensitivity). Veterans with MI often have unresolved grief or loss displayed as a negative mood. Sleeplessness may result from rumination (going over and over things in one's mind), which results in fatigue, poor focus and concentration, and negative mood. The use of alcohol or drugs to sleep or suppress feelings contributes to mood changes. Veterans with MI can become very angry or bitter over things that *should not* (in their opinion) have happened, and they experience moral outrage, righteous indignation, and a desire for justice or retaliation.

Kelly had been treated for PTSD and was finishing up that process. She had served as a medic, and after her second deployment, she started having nightmares about explosions. She had saved many badly wounded soldiers and civilians, but many others had died from explosive and burn injuries. One of her battle buddies had died - Kelly had been unable to save her. They had limited medical resources in the field. She was sleeping better after her PTSD treatment. Still, she found herself thinking more about a young girl who had been brought in after being sexually assaulted by her uncle, and Kelly was part of the medical team who treated her injuries. The man who brought her in was waiting for her, to take her back to her home. Per protocol, the medical team was only allowed to provide medical care. Kelly felt guilty: "I pray for her and can't stop thinking about her pain. I wish I could have done more. I sent her back to the place where she was hurt. I should have been able to protect her." Kelly's doctor realized Kelly had MI from that experience and sent her to the chaplain to begin processing it.

According to military rules of engagement, Kelly did nothing wrong. However, she valued protecting children, and this experience violated those values.

See Chapter 6 for a brief description of some of the programs available for healing from MI, as there are different pathways to restoration. Guiding Veterans toward appropriate resources and intervention will allow them to address their roots and establish healthy pathways forward. A key feature of our own program for healing is the use of story and metaphor. As discussed in the next chapter, stories are powerful in introducing themes and guiding change.

References

American Psychiatric Association. (2013). *Diagnostic and statistical manual of mental disorders: DSM-5™* (5th ed.). American Psychiatric Publishing, Inc. https://doi.org/10.1176/appi.books.9780890425596

Barnes, H. A., Hurley, R. A., & Taber, K. H. (2019). Moral injury and PTSD: Often co-occurring yet mechanistically different. *The Journal of Neuropsychiatry and Clinical Neurosciences*, 31(2), 98–103. https://doi.org/10.1176/appi.neuropsych.19020036

Burkman, K., Maguen, S., & Purcell, N. (2021). Impact of killing: A treatment program for military veterans with moral injury. In J. M. Currier, K. D. Drescher, & J. Nieuwsma (Eds.), *Addressing moral injury in clinical practice* (pp. 203–221). American Psychological Association. https://doi.org/10.1037/0000204-012

Foa, E., Hembree, E. A., Rothbaum, B. O., & Rauch, S. (2019). *Prolonged exposure therapy for PTSD: Emotional processing of traumatic experiences - therapist guide* (2nd ed.). Oxford University Press. https://doi.org/10.1093/med-psych/9780190926939.001.0001

Foa, E. B., Rothbaum, B. O., Riggs, D. S., & Murdock, T. B. (1991). Treatment of posttraumatic stress disorder in rape victims: A comparison between cognitive-behavioral procedures and counseling. *Journal of Consulting and Clinical Psychology*, 59, 715–723.

Friedman, M. J. (2023). *History of PTSD in veterans: Civil war to DSM-5*. U.S. Department of Veterans Affairs National Center for PTSD. https://www.ptsd.va.gov/understand/what/history_ptsd.asp

Gray, M. J., Binion, K., Amaya, S., & Litz, B. T. (2021). Adaptive disclosure: A novel evidence-based treatment for moral injury. In J. M. Currier, K. D. Drescher, & J. Nieuwsma (Eds.), *Addressing moral injury in clinical practice* (pp. 183–201). American Psychological Association.https://doi.org/10.1037/0000204-011

Janoff-Bulman, R. (1992). *Shattered assumptions: Towards a new psychology of trauma*. Free Press.

Janoff-Bulman, R. (2013, April 9). *Shattered assumptions: Toward an understanding of trauma [poster presentation]*. VA National Chaplain Center, Hampton, VA.

Litz, B. T. (2023). The future of moral injury and its treatment. *Journal of Military, Veteran and Family Health, 9*(2), 1–5. https://doi.org/10.3138/jmvfh.9.2.ed

Litz, B. T., Plouffe, R. A., Nazarov, A., Murphy, D., Phelps, A., Coady, A., Houle, S. A., Dell, L., Frankfurt, S., Zerach, G., & Levi-Belz, Y. (2022). Defining and assessing the syndrome of moral injury: Initial findings of the moral injury outcome scale consortium. *Frontiers in Psychiatry, 13*(923928), 1–16. https://doi.org/10.3389/fpsyt.2022.923928

Moll, J., de Oliveira-Souza, R., Eslinger, P., Bramati, I., Mourao-Miranda, J., Andreiuolo, P., & Pessoa, L. (2002). The neural correlates of moral sensitivity: A functional magnetic resonance imaging investigation of basic and moral emotions. *Journal of Neuroscience, 22*(7), 2730–2736. https://doi.org/10.1523/JNEUROSCI.22-07-02730.2002

Pernicano, P. (2014). *Using trauma-focused therapy stories: Interventions for therapists, children, and their caregivers*. Routledge.

Pernicano, P., & Haynes, K. (2023). *Acceptance & forgiveness therapy: From brokenness to restoration* [Unpublished handbook] (5th ed.). South Texas Veterans Health Care System.

Pernicano, P. U., Wortmann, J., & Haynes, K. (2022). Acceptance and forgiveness therapy for veterans with moral injury: Spiritual and psychological collaboration in group treatment. *Journal of Health Care Chaplaincy, 28*(sup1), S57–S78. https://doi.org/10.1080/08854726.2022.2032982

Ramage, A. E., Litz, B. T., Resick, P. A., Woolsey, M. D., Dondanvill, K. A., Young-McCaughan, S., Borah, A. M., Borah, E. V., Peterson, A. L., & Fox, P. T. (2016). Regional cerebral glucose metabolism differentiates danger- and non-danger-based traumas in post-traumatic stress disorder. *Social Cognitive and Affective Neuroscience, 11*(2), 234–242. https://doi.org/10.1093/scan/nsv102

Resick, P. A., Monsoon, C. M., & Chard, K. M. (2017). *Cognitive processing therapy for PTSD: A comprehensive manual*. The Guilford Press.

Resick, P. A., & Schnicke, M. K. (1992). Cognitive processing therapy for sexual assault victims. *Journal of Consulting and Clinical Psychology, 60*(5), 748–756. https://doi.org/10.1037/0022-006X.60.5.748

Shay, J. (1994). *Achilles in Vietnam: Combat trauma and the undoing of character*. Atheneum Publishers/Macmillan Publishing Co.

Sloan, D. M., & Marx, B. P. (2019). *Written exposure therapy for PTSD: A brief treatment approach for mental health professionals*. American Psychological Association. https://doi.org/10.1037/0000139-000

Usset, T. J., Butler, M., & Harris, J. I. (2021). Building spiritual strength: A group treatment for posttraumatic stress disorder, moral injury, and spiritual distress. In J. M. Currier, K. D. Drescher, & J. Nieuwsma (Eds.), *Addressing moral injury in clinical practice* (pp. 223–241). American Psychological Association. https://doi.org/10.1037/0000204-013

Walser, R. D., & Wharton, E. (2021). Acceptance and commitment therapy: Using mindfulness and values in the treatment of moral injury. In J. M. Currier, K. D. Drescher, & J. Nieuwsma (Eds.), *Addressing moral injury in clinical practice* (pp. 163–181). American Psychological Association. https://doi.org/10.1037/0000204-010

Chapter 3

Meaning-Making Through Story and Metaphor

As the book's title suggests, metaphor and story play an important role in fostering connection and healing. Moral injury (MI) disconnects Veterans from relational trust/ attachment, values, self-esteem, spiritual purpose and meaning, and overall well-being. Stories help make new connections – within the self and between the Veteran and others – and aid meaning-making to envision a path forward. Memorable stories, like a ladder leading out of a pool of quicksand, propel us in new directions. Stories remove the terror of being seen by others the way we see ourselves; they are integral to healing.

Story and metaphor ground each phase of acceptance and forgiveness therapy (AFT), offering Veterans the means to process traumatic memories, new ways of looking at things, and possible pathways forward. Metaphors and stories take the listener to a place where painful memories are activated and re-experienced and then to new realms of discovery and healing. Pernicano (2019, p. 16) describes metaphor as "a universal shorthand or Morse code" that sends a complete message in a few words. Metaphors are helpful when words fail, and many Veterans have not yet found the words to describe their memories and pain following trauma-related MI.

Listening to a story is a cognitive task; however, as Veterans *join the story* and then find themselves *in the story,* metaphor and story have the potential to elicit a right brain, experiential *aha moment* with a shift in meaning. Peterson and Fontana (1991) suggest that listeners often visualize their associations while hearing a story, then access memories from personal experiences, in essence, joining the story.

Story and metaphor convey meaning, plant seeds of new understanding, and put the past in context. Metaphor, a form of universal language, activates emotion, fosters identification, and enhances self-understanding (Pernicano, 2014, 2019, 2021). Crenshaw (2014, p. x), points out that metaphor is "right-hemisphere dominant but links to and is integrated with the language-based activity of the left hemisphere." This integration creates "coherence, meaning, and well-being" (Crenshaw, p. x). According to Lawrence et al. (2006), storytelling is at the heart of all therapy. Pernicano (2019) adds that stories become catalysts, entranceways to new possibilities, and tools for change or acceptance. She describes the salience of language in therapy, where clients' words carry layered meanings. They test the waters as they go, ensuring safety before plunging into the depths, often revealing the complete story only over time.

DOI: 10.4324/9781003494263-5

Carl Jung (1968) described a universal language of art and symbols that reside in a non-conscious part of us. Memories may emerge in dreams or nightmares before they come to the understanding mind. Stories and art reflect meaning-making, and later in the book, we will share some Veteran metaphors and drawings representing their moral pain, forgiveness, and healing. A picture speaks a thousand words and expresses emotions that might lay dormant and unspoken. A carefully selected story awakens the past and allows the Veteran a new means of "speaking" to his or her pain and envisioned healing.

Metaphors and stories have been used in several approaches, including Ericksonian hypnosis, narrative therapy, mindfulness, and cognitive behavioral therapies. Erickson has been named the first advocate of using stories and metaphors in therapy. He believed stories could influence our understanding by providing new information, arousing emotions, and creating new experiences at a less conscious level of awareness (Pernicano, 2019). "Stories move the listener to a vulnerable, receptive state of readiness, a readiness to be open and shift one's inner state of mind and emotion" (p. 13). Veterans become more aware of their inner strengths and resources through Erickson's tools of humor, imagery, flexibility, persuasion, metaphor, reframing, relabeling, and indirect suggestion to introduce choice and guide inevitable change. What has been described as a corrective emotional experience offers growth, new perspective, and healing from the inside out.

Pernicano (2010, p. 1) described *The Magic of Metaphor* as a cross-theoretical tool to seed possibilities, offer meaning, present alternative views, restructure cognition, and reframe narrative history. Stories and their characters serve as models, teach values and skills, and provide insight on both a conscious and nonconscious level. Story characters may resemble the listener in some way, such as with personal characteristics, life struggles, and thought patterns. The story theme may parallel some aspect of the person's life, model insight, or solve a problem. A message is packaged and received in a way that is more palatable than direct feedback from a therapist. Stories gently open up unrecognized, not fully conscious emotional material (Pernicano, 2019).

Stories also enable empathy and foster connection with others. Perhaps most importantly, story and metaphor contribute to meaning-making, and MI is a condition that alters one's meaning-making about self, others, spirituality, and the military. Stories can mirror a Veteran's inner experience and offer a lens for a new point of view. Smigelski et al. (2022) note the difference between sharing one's story of MI in a group (a relational process) and completing a trauma narrative during exposure therapy (to reduce anxiety) or identifying stuck points in an index trauma (a cognitive intervention).

The Science of Storytelling and Metaphor

There is science behind storytelling. For example, brain scans suggest that when we tell stories, our brains become more active in language processing areas. Storytelling can also activate mirroring, a process where one person's brain activity is essentially copied in someone else's brain and the other person responds to the connection, such as during parent–infant interactions of gazing, smiling, and babbling back and forth. A good storyteller engages the other person, and the other person feels very attuned, i.e., connected and understood. Researchers suggest that when we are *told* a story, it is as if we are *there* (Suzuki et al., 2018). Stories and metaphors *light up* parts of the brain we would use if we lived out the story events, such as our senses and emotions.

The Veteran joins and becomes part of the story when the theme and metaphors trigger memories of a Veteran's lived experiences. Suzuki et al. (2018) refer to the research of Uri Hasson from Princeton who demonstrated that the brains of the teller and listener can be in sync for emotion and meaning when the story is understood. Emotions and thoughts related to the story are activated in the storyteller and transmitted to the reader. It is as if the listeners' brains connect to the storyteller's brain. The brain recognizes the similarity between a story and a lived experience, and the subsequent emotions can parallel what was felt earlier in time. It is truly *almost like being there.*

Suzuki et al. (2018) describe *The science and power of storytelling*: "Skilled storytelling helps listeners understand the essence of complex concepts and ideas in meaningful and often personal ways" because of shared understanding (p. 9468). Coulson and Lai (2016), editors of 15 articles on *The Metaphorical Brain*, state, "Metaphor is increasingly viewed as a central feature of higher cognition and abstract thought" (p. 1). Their work suggests that the right cerebral hemisphere (RH) "plays a crucial role in understanding metaphor, not literal language."

Faust and Kennett (2014) remind us that in communication, the left hemisphere (LH), the home of literal language, lacks the creativity and flexibility of the RH. Creativity is about creating something novel and useful, and metaphors convey explicit and implicit emotions through symbolic associations, in only a few words, such as, "The classroom was a zoo." The creative brain gets the message, while the literal brain might picture a classroom full of elephants, zebras, and monkeys.

Psychologist Valentina Stoycheva (2020) describes the moment something clicks into place using a metaphor in therapy. She suggests that the metaphor strikes a chord and is understood as more than spoken words. Metaphors organize our experiences through their conceptual meaning. Metaphors can evoke memories, feelings, images, and experiences previously hidden from awareness (Stoycheva, 2020). Metaphors convey complex and abstract concepts; they facilitate the assimilation of new knowledge and understanding. Khatin-Zadeh et al. (2023) suggest that metaphorical embodiment allows us to understand concepts in non-literal ways.

Metaphors and stories are experienced with strong emotion and sensory components when they resemble an emotionally laden, deeply personal situation for the listener. The process might resemble a flashback or a brief dissociative response to a trigger. The narrated story triggers and becomes the Veteran's story, and the individual is pulled into an altered trance-like state dominated by the RH. The Veteran re-experiences what happened in response to the story. Veterans often report strong painful emotions after listening to *The Cracked Glass Bowl* story (Pernicano, 2012) as they picture themselves as the main character and draw themselves as a bowl that feels *broken, damaged, or changed.*

Storytellers embed details in the narrative that take listeners down a path of *being there* unlike listening for facts or details. The *aha* of metaphor and story helps Veterans construct a new narrative and – early on – weigh the risks and benefits of change. Metaphors and stories help Veterans resolve the dissonance between what they aspired to (grounded in values and meaning-making) and what they experienced or engaged in that violated those values. Metaphors are memorable and facilitate experiential learning. Veterans spontaneously use metaphors once introduced: "I want to find my ladder" or "You all are helping me cut my rope." It is common for Veterans' eyes to light up as they connect with a story or metaphor and see something from a new perspective.

Veterans revisit, challenge, and broaden their original stories of moral pain and their role in it; over time, they use a new lens to review and release the past. They develop a new story of self-acceptance as their pain and stories are heard and accepted, especially by other Veterans. There is some relief, and perhaps even joy, when a Veteran expects rejection and scorn yet instead is offered empathy, compassion, and forgiveness.

Foley (2016) studied how Veterans use metaphors to describe experiences of post-traumatic stress disorder (PTSD) and the implications for social work practice. Many Veterans with PTSD also report MI. Foley pointed out the importance of understanding military culture and that care providers and Veterans may use metaphors to describe painful experiences when there are no words. Metaphors can be provider- or client-elicited. His work revealed that Veterans use metaphors to describe the impact of trauma, cultural components, symptom management, and the process of integration. In AFT, Veterans create metaphors during a lament process; they also use metaphors to envision forgiveness (of self or other), which allows some creativity and psychological distance.

The military has metaphors of its own, some of which do not facilitate healing. Metaphors like "warriors" or "fortress" convey stoicism and unrealistic strength; *fearless* combatants are expected to contain their emotions. Military culture makes it more difficult for a Veteran to seek help. Metaphors such as surviving a storm, becoming a new creation, bearing battle scars, reweaving a tapestry, and releasing burdens from a rucksack help Veterans reframe MI as they apply the metaphors to their lives.

A powerful metaphor can quickly shift someone's point of view. Let's close this chapter with a metaphor that cuts to the truth when a Veteran reports guilt or shame following a military sexual trauma (MST). MST (non-consensual sexual activity) occurs in all service branches; it is opportunistic, predatory behavior, often between unequal ranks. The targeted individual may be doing their job, sleeping, showering, working out, consuming alcohol, or engaging in off-duty relaxation. These are normal parts of military culture and should not be feared. After all, fellow service members are trusted to *have your back*. When the offender (someone trusted) strikes, the Veteran is caught off guard and freezes in shock or fear, and the assault takes place. Later, the targeted person may blame himself or herself and wonder if they sent the wrong message or missed warning signs.

Gina, a private in basic training, blamed herself for her sexual assault. She said she was "in the wrong place at the wrong time." She wondered if the non-commissioned officer (NCO) had interpreted her freeze response as consent. The following story helped her, and other survivors of MST see predatory behavior through a new lens:

> *Consider the National Geographic special on lions in Africa. The film opens with a herd of beautiful gazelles running, jumping, and playing together on the grass. The camera pans to a lion, crouched down close to the ground, hidden in the tall grass. The lion is on the hunt for fresh meat. He is arrogant, confident, and knows what he is doing. Lions are predatory and when they are hungry, they prepare for the kill. Some of the older gazelles catch the scent of the lion and scamper away. A small unsuspecting gazelle knows nothing of lions and playfully tracks a beautiful butterfly, chasing it a few feet from the herd. The opportunistic, predatory lion pounces and takes her down. No regrets. He was hungry. Any gazelle would do. He is a serial predator. The next day or the day after that, the lion will again be on the prowl.*
>
> *No one would blame a gazelle for the lion's predatory behavior.*

References

Coulson, S., & Lai, V. T. (2016). Editorial: The metaphorical brain. *Frontiers in Human Neuroscience, 9*, 699. https://doi.org/10.3389/fnhum.2015.00699

Crenshaw, D. (2014) Foreword. In J. M. Mills., & R. J. Crowley, *Therapeutic metaphors for children and the child within* (2nd ed.) (Foreword, p. x). Routledge.

Faust, M., & Kennett, Y. N. (2014). Rigidity, chaos and integration: Hemispheric interaction and individual differences in metaphor comprehension. *Frontiers in Human Neuroscience, 8*(511), 1–10. https://doi.org/10.3389/fnhum.2014.00511

Foley, P. S. (2015). The metaphors they carry: Exploring how veterans use metaphor to describe experiences of PTSD. *Journal of Poetry Therapy, 28*(2), 129–146. https://doi.org/10.1080/08893675.2015.1011375

Jung, C. (1968). *Man and his symbols*. Dell Publishing.

Khatin-Zadeh, O., Farsani, D., Hu, J., Eskandari, Z., Zhu, Y., & Banaruee, H. (2023). A review of studies supporting metaphorical embodiment. *Behavioral Science, 13*(585), 1–13. https://doi.org/10.3390/bs13070585

Lawrence, M., Condon, K., Jacobi, K., & Nicholson, E. (2006). Play therapy for girls displaying social aggression. In C. E. Schaefer & H. G. Kadusob (Eds.), *Contemporary play therapy: Theory, research, and practice*. Guilford Press.

Pernicano, P. (2010). *Family-focused trauma intervention: Metaphor and play with victims of abuse and neglect*. Jason Aronson. https://doi.org/10.1111/j.1475-3588.2011.00617_7.x

Pernicano, P. (2012). The cracked glass bowl. In *Outsmarting the riptide of domestic violence: Metaphor and mindfulness for change* (pp. 141–144). Jason Aronson.

Pernicano, P. (2014). *Using trauma focused therapy stories: Interventions for therapists, children, and their caregivers*. Routledge/Taylor & Francis. https://doi.org/10.4324/9781003184171

Pernicano, P. (2019). *Using stories, art and play in trauma-informed treatment: Case examples and applications across the lifespan*. Routledge/Taylor & Francis. https://doi.org/10.4324/9781351005302

Pernicano, P. (2021). *Using trauma-focused therapy stories: Interventions for therapists, children, and their caregivers (Classic ed.).* Routledge/Taylor & Francis.

Peterson, R., & Fontana, L. (1991). Utilising metaphoric storytelling in child and youth care work. *Journal of Child & Youth Care, 5*(2), 53–58. https://cyc-net.org/cyc-online/cycol-0706-peterson.html

Smigelsky, M. A., Trimm, V., Meador, K. G., Jackson, G. L., Wortmann, J. H., & Nieuwsma, J. A. (2022). Core components of moral injury groups co-facilitated by mental health providers and chaplains. *Spirituality in Clinical Practice, 9*(3), 159–174. https://doi.org/10.1037/scp0000297

Stoycheva, V. (2020). Are metaphors your secret magic wand in therapy? Why metaphors work and how they can be useful in therapy. *Psychology Today.* https://www.psychologytoday.com/us/blog/the-everyday-unconscious/202001/are-metaphors-your-secret-magic-wand-in-therapy#:~:text=In%20therapy%2C%20metaphors%20can%20be,were%20previously%20hidden%20from%20awareness.

Suzuki, W. A., Feliú-Mójer, M. I., Hasson, U., Yehuda, R., & Zarate, J. M. (2018). Dialogues: The science and power of storytelling. *The Journal of Neuroscience: The Official Journal of the Society for Neuroscience, 38*(44), 9468–9470. https://doi.org/10.1523/JNEUROSCI.1942-18.2018

Chapter 4

Dealing with the Spiritual in Moral Injury

"Why does this group have a chaplain in it? Is this a religious group?" Veterans sometimes ask questions like this, out of fascination or caution. The wounds of moral injury (MI) are psychological and spiritual, and because of this, acceptance and forgiveness therapy (AFT) includes collaborative facilitation, with a chaplain and mental health (MH) provider. Veterans in the military may seek counsel from a chaplain when confused about the validity of military intentions, the morality of killing in war, the desire for forgiveness, or other trials of life. They seek comfort when faced with moral pain. Healing from MI involves an examination of one's values and meaning-making regarding why something happened and who is responsible. Veterans approach chaplains as spiritual guides, seeking answers to questions about higher power and violations of core values. As such, MI calls for psychological and spiritual healing. Services for MI might be described as spiritual (meaning-making for purposeful living) but not necessarily religious, as MI crosses schools of thought and touches persons with differing religious views.

Currier et al. (2021) note that when polled, most Americans claim to be religious and that the fastest growth among younger Americans is the claim to be spiritual but not religious. They suggest that religion refers more to institutions and traditions while the word *spiritual* encompasses individualized experiences. They also conclude that Americans may use the terms interchangeably when discussing morality; religion and spirituality are both important. Callaghan (2023) notes the aversion of some Veterans to anything religious. Focusing on spirituality rather than religion offers inclusivity and eliminates unnecessary roadblocks to care.

The Veterans Affairs (VA) defines spirituality as "that which gives meaning, purpose, and hope in life" (Department of Veterans Affairs, 2019, p. 5). Meaning, purpose, and hope all interface with MI. Carey et al. (2016) more specifically describe spirituality as "that aspect of humanity that refers to the way individuals seek and express meaning and purpose and the way they experience their connectedness to God [we would use the more inclusive phrase, 'the divine'], to self, to others, to nature, and to the significant or sacred" (p. 1221). In addition to meaning and purpose, the authors note the importance of relational connection, which restores trust and reduces the isolation they experience. Frankl (1962) connects meaning-making to increasing connection, displaying love, helping others, and engaging in meaningful, purposeful activities.

DOI: 10.4324/9781003494263-6

Carey et al. (2016) provide a wide-scope review of MI and spiritual care. They note that the term *spiritual injury* was coined by Gary Berg, a VA chaplain, as early as 1992. Spiritual injury, a subset of MI for those with a theistic religious belief, has been defined by Berg (2011, np) as "a response to an event caused by self, or an event beyond our control, that damages our relationship with God, self, and others, and alienates us from that which gives meaning to our lives" (also see Carey, p. 1221). Fuson (2013) describes how a person with spiritual injury struggles with "understanding how his or her view of faith, spirituality, relationship with God, and God's involvement in one's life can be true given the horrific experiences observed. A person suffering from spiritual injury may be doubting that God is trustworthy" (p. vi).

More generally, spirituality deals with universal human themes such as meaning-making and the purpose of life, while religion features the beliefs and practices of a specific faith group. Spirituality may draw from archetypal or universal themes of moral goodness. There are common emotions elicited in the face of inhumanity or moral code violations, such as guilt, shame, and rage, all of which may manifest through MI. To some extent, cultural definitions of right and wrong contribute to moral pain. Religion may speak to these emotions but along a set line of beliefs and practices common to specific people. Religious views may be harmful or helpful in addressing MI, depending on a person's spiritual development and specific belief structures (Pernicano et al., 2022). Spiritually focused MI programs tend to use a broader, more inclusive spiritual framework focused on practices such as forgiveness and meaning-making (Pernicano et al., 2022).

MI recovery often includes a *higher power* concept similar to that in 12-step groups, i.e., reliance on a power greater than oneself for healing. Within VA programming, other Veterans become a higher power similar to how Alcoholics Anonymous group members provide for the alcoholic newcomer (Alcoholics Anonymous, 2014). We use the term *benevolent other* to encourage Veterans to see themselves through the eyes of someone who can love them unconditionally. Benevolent means good, kind, and humane. When you can see yourself through someone else's benevolent eyes, they become a mirror in which your goodness is reflected. Veterans choose a wide variety of benevolent others, including someone within the military chain of command (i.e., a respected sergeant major), a relative or friend, an MH provider, a religious leader, or a spiritual being. The benevolent other is someone who cares about them unconditionally and appreciates their inherent worth apart from their MI. Veterans move toward self-forgiveness when they experience grace and acceptance from benevolent others.

The Role of Chaplain

The chaplain serves as the primary spiritual resource in the military as well as in the VA (Department of Veterans Affairs, 2019). In some VAs, a designated chaplain joins an MH provider to co-facilitate MI interventions. A chaplain is a clergyperson who serves the members of an organization outside a traditional religious faith setting. Chaplains do not proselytize (push their own beliefs on those they serve), which frees Veterans to adhere to their worldviews of spirituality and religion.

Everyone in the organization becomes part of a chaplain's *parish*, regardless of their religious faith or lack thereof. Chaplains are most prevalent in the military, prisons, hospices, and larger hospital settings (both VA and civilian). However, they also serve among police and firefighters, Veteran service organizations, sports teams, businesses, biker organizations, and any other setting valuing a person of faith to care for its members. Carey et al. (2016) note the various categories of chaplain service, characterized by the World Health Organization, as assessment, ministry support, counseling, education, ritual, and worship.

In the military, chaplains are considered special staff officers, the eyes and ears of the commander who provides the commander with broad feedback, and offers informal, undocumented, and usually unlicensed counseling to those in need. Chaplains also provide optional chapel and religious rites to those requesting, per the chaplain's faith tradition, and they provide training on a variety of morale-related subjects such as suicide prevention, relationship enrichment, and more. Senior military chaplains provide technical supervision of junior chaplains although chaplains usually report directly to their commander or deputy commander. Within the rank and file, military chaplains are best known and treasured for their privileged communication status, protecting with absolute confidentiality the sanctity of their conversations with service members and their families, similar to how a Roman Catholic priest holds confidential the rite of confession.

Veterans see chaplains as approachable for private, non-judgmental conversations. Within the VA, chaplains are integrated into multidisciplinary teams that work together on behalf of the Veteran's needs. VA chaplains balance the spiritual needs and privacy concerns of the Veteran with the need-to-know of the treatment team members.

Chaplains serving in the VA and other larger hospital systems in America complete Clinical Pastoral Education (CPE); they learn various clinical skills such as active listening and unconditional positive regard. CPE also focuses on personal awareness and growth, as chaplains learn to reflect on their clinical experiences and grow in self-awareness. Chaplains are trained to serve in a pluralistic environment, i.e., how to be true to one's faith tenets yet also available to anyone, regardless of religious orientation (Nieuwsma et al., 2021). Perhaps most applicable to MI, CPE chaplain residents learn to sit with discomfort instead of trying to *fix* the patient.

Some chaplains receive additional training and certification in MH-related areas. Since 2014, VA Integrative Mental Health (IMH) has offered an intensive training program for selected military and VA chaplains that, since 2020, is included in an optional Doctor of Ministry program. In 2021, this program was broadened to include chaplains outside VA and military settings. Participating chaplains, regardless of work setting, become enabled to work in MH settings through understanding therapy models and the roles of MH professionals. They are well-trained to work collaboratively with MH providers to provide supportive care for MI.

Smith-MacDonald et al. (2018) indicate that MH chaplains offer a level of expertise and a complementary skill set to not only their patients but also the interdisciplinary teams with which they serve. Such embedded MH chaplains can bridge patients to MH services, facilitate spiritual/religious coping and grounding, reconcile worldviews, and foster reconciliation with self, others, and/or a higher power. The authors also note that the MH chaplain can care for the rest of the treatment team as well, helping to prevent burnout and compassion fatigue.

Smigelsky et al. (2022) indicate that the gold standard for the facilitation of MI groups is a board-certified MH chaplain and a licensed MH professional familiar with and appreciative of chaplaincy. Each has an appreciation of the other's discipline while practicing within the scope of their training and expertise. However, not all Veterans come to the VA, and not all VAs have teams available for MI services. Historically, some Veterans have been more comfortable with a member of the clergy than with an MH professional, due to military stigma, cultural background, family history, and other reasons (Wang et al., 2003). It is important to have a variety of caregiving professionals educated about MI and equipped to offer information, comfort, and healing.

Treatment Roots of AFT

In 2008, VA Mental Health and Chaplaincy (later renamed Integrative Mental Health) was established to foster the collaborative work of MH providers and chaplains. In the years to follow, Pernicano and Haynes worked closely with this program office to help disseminate MI interventions across the VA.

The early roots of AFT date back to a 2014 MI group developed and led by Chaplain Haynes, as part of his Doctor of Ministry project (2015). He had worked with hundreds of service members and Veterans who felt betrayed or unforgivable. Veterans with post-traumatic stress disorder (PTSD) also reported deep spiritual or moral wounds. Haynes (2015) offered MI group intervention, with faith-based stories as case examples, incorporating various psychological/spiritual healing models; this contributed to self-forgiveness. Veterans grew spiritually as they began to identify with a loving (rather than judging) higher power. The State Self-Forgiveness Scale (Wohl et al., 2008) and the Loving and Controlling God Scale (Benson & Spilka, 1973) suggested there were spiritual benefits of group intervention for MI.

This early MI work was lauded by the VA with Diffusion of Excellence "Shark Tank" designation in 2016 and included in the VA Under Secretary for Health's Book of Best Practices (Shulkin et al., 2017); a "Best Practice" award was given by the VA National Chaplain Center in 2017.

Veteran suicide was found to be related to MI (Ames et al., 2019), and military and Veteran suicides were at an all-time high when Haynes began his work, thus elevating VA interest in all MI work. Haynes' early work in MI included stories with predominant themes of guilt, shame, forgiveness, and restoration from the Jewish and Christian scriptures. In 2018, Pernicano offered to help develop and co-lead a group that would be spiritually inclusive, broaden the use of stories, and incorporate spirituality focused on purpose and meaning. The authors, and others, viewed MI as a psycho-spiritual condition that would benefit from psychological and spiritual interventions (Litz et al., 2009; Pernicano et al., 2022; Wortmann et al., 2017). AFT (Pernicano & Haynes, 2023) integrated psychology and spirituality and replaced the biblical case studies with metaphorical/therapeutic stories adapted from the psychologist's previous publications (Pernicano, 2010a, 2010b, 2012, 2014). Even the most battle-hardened Veterans related to the stories and the meaning within, finding those gold nuggets spoken of earlier. De-identified Veteran examples were incorporated into AFT to help group members relate to and identify with concepts as they were introduced. Thus, the new curriculum transformed from religious lite to spiritual but not religious, accessible to many more Veterans.

Nieuwsma et al. (2021) argue for the inclusion of a chaplain or other spiritual care provider with the MH provider in MI groups, for several reasons: to offer a moral authority that may have been avoided in the practice of psychology, to meet the preference of some Veterans for ministry professionals over MH providers, and to offer practical advantages, such as more time available for patients at high risk for suicide. Swift et al. (2012) state, "When spiritual care is well integrated and effective, the patient's ability to cope, find meaning, and be supported during a crisis is enhanced" (p. 185).

With co-facilitation, there is an opportunity to debrief, check one's reactions, and review the group process. Through consultation and collaboration, facilitators reduce defensiveness, discuss countertransference, and stay focused on Veteran needs; it is also a good model for training interns, fellows, and residents. MI work can be painful and stressful, and there is a risk of vicarious traumatization should someone choose to go it alone.

The availability of co-facilitators (chaplains and mental providers) may be limited in some community settings. It is better to offer some help than none at all. At a minimum, we suggest a team of facilitators who have received some training/coaching in this kind of work and who appreciate both the psychological and spiritual aspects of MI recovery. Depending on the setting, we also recommend spiritual inclusivity and clear communication in advertising when that is not the case. For instance, a Christian church may want to offer a group that is more closely linked to the Christian faith, but they must advertise it as such. Alternatively, a Christian church may choose to offer a community group open to all Veterans regardless of religious faith and advertise the group as spiritual but not religious. Facilitators must think through their approach and communicate it when seeking referrals, registering Veterans, and familiarizing themselves with the group process introduced in Session 1.

One final consideration for the spiritual care provider is sensitivity to both Eastern and Western spirituality through words of acceptance, grace, unconditional love, compassion, health, and well-being rather than a religious approach that judges or condemns, even if well-intended. Many Veterans with MI already engage in guilt and blame, judging themselves as unworthy. Pastoral judgment or focusing on rules at the expense of the relationship can damage someone who already feels hopeless and unforgivable. Clinical, board-certified chaplains are trained to honor and speak to the individual spirituality of the client, regardless of the chaplain's particular faith. The authors encourage spiritual care providers to build up the Veteran rather than draw attention to the Veteran's shortcomings. Veterans carry more than a fair share of guilt and shame, usually more than would be called for given their circumstances. They lack an objective viewpoint that regardless of their story, they are more than their MI, carry inherent worth as human beings, have caring hearts with good intentions, and can move toward health and wholeness. Thus, we advise spiritual care providers to steer clear of doctrine, correction, and condemnation and to offer care within the Veteran's belief systems with affirmation and unconditional positive regard. When a Veteran expresses self-hate or spiritual condemnation (i.e., "God will never forgive me"), we affirm the positive, redirect the negative, and suggest an open mind to other possibilities.

Of course, MH providers need to be aware of how their spiritual beliefs and practices influence care for Veterans. Currier et al. (2021) warn against spiritually grounded MH providers or psychologically minded chaplains blurring their boundaries and functioning outside their scope of practice. Both types of providers would be wise to know their limitations and refer when warranted.

Inclusive Spirituality

Veterans with MI may be atheist, agnostic, Christian, Jewish, Buddhist, Muslim, "spiritual but not religious," Unitarian, or other. Because MI often results from a violation of core values, judgment, guilt, emotional pain, and hopelessness block acceptance and forgiveness. Spiritual components of compassion, grace, and forgiveness can relieve the pain of guilt, injustice, and wrongdoing. Although not initially intended, the phases of AFT resemble the four steps of forgiving noted by Tutu and Tutu (2015): telling the story, naming the hurt, granting forgiveness, and renewing or releasing the relationship. Many spiritual practices incorporate shared rituals that allow persons to address wrongdoing (confession), betrayal (comfort), and guilt (forgiveness) in the presence of non-judgmental, forgiving others. Persons who engage in regular worship practices often find comfort in a shared ritual that infuses hope. Private spiritual practices such as prayer or meditation encourage the release of pain and instill hope.

As mentioned earlier, negative religious coping styles or beliefs (such as "deserving judgment, punishment, or damnation") contribute to blame, guilt, grief, and blocked forgiveness. MI often contributes to the loss of spiritual purpose and meaning. In healing from MI, meaning-making may include practices such as: 1) processing morally injurious events more objectively, 2) engaging in lament (Chapter 8), 3) taking appropriate responsibility for what happened (Chapter 9), 4) practicing confession and forgiveness (Chapter 10), and 5) restoring worth and acceptability in the eyes of self and others (Chapters 11–13).

Meaning-Making Through Stories

Stories and metaphors are spiritually universal, powerful tools to introduce and seed new ways of thinking. The reader will be introduced to several stories in Part II that illustrate spiritual relinquishment in response to pain. Listening to stories and telling one's own story, along with healing rituals, incorporates Veteran spirituality without the confines of religion.

> Edward recently told his story, wrote down what he wanted to release, then dissolved his paper into the warm water. He teared up as it disappeared and said, "It's gone. It's really gone. This is special. It is a spiritual moment. I feel lighter. You are my witnesses. You heard my confession. Now I can let it go. I can become a new creation. Thank you for listening."

The stories embedded in AFT guide Veterans to process MI and to be absolved through the compassion of others. Smigelsky et al. (2022) note that optionally sharing one's story and receiving the affirmation of the group are core components of collaborative MI interventions across the VA. The Wounded Warrior Project (www.woundedwarriorproject.org) describes the benefits of Veterans sharing their stories and ways in which to do so as a meaning-making process. Tick, in *Warrior's Return: Restoring the Soul After War* (2014), points out that the deaths of one's friends and all others have to mean something; to heal, they must be made meaningful.

Spiritual Ritual and Meaning-Making

Ritual is used in most spiritual practices as a meaningful, shared experience. Ritual helps turn words into inner meaning and locks in truth in a way that mere conversation cannot. Smigelsky et al. (2022) describe ritual as a core component of MI treatments. Ritual is a component of meaning-making, and military rituals instill military values, truths, and expectations. When those are violated, new rituals, with spiritual components, can help restore what was lost and rebuild trust and hope. As stated earlier, a universal aspect of spirituality is meaning-making, particularly in adversity. Meaning-making after MI includes formulating assumptions about why something happened (i.e., being punished), assigning blame based on hindsight, using faulty "what-if thinking," and making attributions about the worth of self or others (Kopacz et al., 2019). Meaning-making after highly stressful events has far-reaching effects on MH outcomes (Park, 2005) and influences MI in military populations (Kopacz et al., 2019).

Conclusion

MI is a psycho-spiritual state of being. A spiritual but not religious approach connects Veterans from a variety of backgrounds and belief systems. Collaborative group facilitation, with an MH professional and MH-trained chaplain or other clergy member, is optimal; yet appreciation across disciplines will allow a variety of providers to give excellent Veteran care. Spiritual facets of compassion, acceptance, forgiveness, grief work, meaning-making, stories, and rituals contribute to healing MI. One former participant recently said, "First you heal spiritually with forgiveness, Then you heal your mind and body. Science with spirituality - it gives you back your life."

References

Alcoholics Anonymous (2014). *Many paths to spirituality.* https://www.aa.org/sites/default/files/literature/assets/p-84_manypathstospirituality.pdf

Ames, D., Erickson, Z., Youssef, N. A., Arnold, I., Adamson, C. S., Sones, A. C., Yin, J., Haynes, K., Volk, F., Teng, E. J., Oliver, J. P., & Koenig, H. G. (2019). Moral injury, religiosity, and suicide risk in U.S. Veterans and active duty military with PTSD symptoms. *Military Medicine, 184*(3–4), e271–e278. https://doi.org/10.1093/milmed/usy148

Benson, P., & Spilka, B. (1973). God image as a function of self-esteem and locus of control. *Journal for the Scientific Study of Religion, 12*(3), 297–310. https://doi.org/10.2307/1384430

Berg, G. (2011). Spiritual assessment manual. https://spiritualassessment.com/manual

Callaghan, W. (2023). Critical intercession for non-religious Canadian veterans on the intersections of moral injury, religion, and spirituality. *Journal of Military, Veteran and Family Health, 9*(2), 91–95. https://doi.org/10.3138/jmvfh-2022-0046

Carey, L. B., Hodgson, T. J., Krikheli, L., Soh, R. Y., Armour, A. R., Singh, T. K., & Impiombato, C. G. (2016). Moral injury, spiritual care and the role of chaplains: An exploratory scoping review of literature and resources. *Journal of Religious Health, 55*, 1218–1245. https://doi.org/10.1007/s10943-016-0231-x

Currier, J. M., Carroll, T. D., & Wortmann, J. H. (2021). Religious and spiritual issues in moral injury. In J. M. Currier, K. D. Drescher, & J. Nieuwsma (Eds.), *Addressing moral injury in clinical practice* (pp. 53–70). American Psychological Association.

Department of Veterans Affairs (2019). VHA Directive 1111(1), *Spiritual and Pastoral Care in the Veterans Health Administration*.

Frankl, V. (1962). *Man's search for meaning: An introduction to Logotherapy*. Beacon Press.

Fuson, J. E. (2013). A pastoral counseling model for leading post-combat Christian soldiers experiencing spiritual injury to spiritual health through examining the biblical concepts of evil, pain, abandonment, and forgiveness [Doctoral dissertation, Biola University]. ProQuest Dissertations; Theses Global Database.

Haynes, K. N. (2015). *Helping veterans heal from moral injury through faith-based self-forgiveness groups* [Unpublished doctoral dissertation]. Golden Gate Baptist Theological Seminary.

Kopacz, M. S., Lockman, J., Lusk, J., Bryan, C. J., Park, C. L., Sheu, S. C., & Gibson, W. C. (2019). How meaningful is meaning-making? *New Ideas in Psychology, 54*, 76–81. https://doi.org/10.1016/j.newideapsych.2019.02.001

Litz, B. T., Stein, N., Delaney, E., Lebowitz, L., Nash, W. P., Silva, C., & Maguen, S. (2009). Moral injury and moral repair in war veterans: A preliminary model and intervention strategy. *Clinical Psychology Review, 29*, 695–706. https://doi.org/10.1016/j.cpr.2009.07.003

Nieuwsma, J., Smigelsky, M. A., Wortmann, J. H., Haynes, K., & Meador, K. G. (2021). Collaboration with chaplaincy and ministry professionals in addressing moral injury. In J. M. Currier, K. D. Drescher, & J. Nieuwsma (Eds.), *Addressing moral injury in clinical practice* (pp. 243–260). American Psychological Association. https://doi.org/10.1037/0000204-014

Park, C. (2005). Religion as a meaning-making framework in coping with life stress. *Journal of Social Issues, 61*(4), 707–729. https://doi.org/10.1111/j.1540-4560.2005.00428.x

Pernicano, P. (2010a). *Family-focused trauma intervention: Metaphor and play with victims of abuse and neglect*. Jason Aronson.

Pernicano, P. (2010b). *Using metaphor and play in child therapy*. Jason Aronson.

Pernicano, P. (2012). *Outsmarting the riptide of domestic violence: Metaphor and mindfulness for change*. Jason Aronson.

Pernicano, P. (2014). *Using trauma focused therapy stories: Interventions for therapists, children, and their caregivers*. Routledge/Taylor & Francis.

Pernicano, P., & Haynes, K. (2023). *Acceptance & forgiveness therapy: From brokenness to restoration* [Unpublished handbook] (5th ed.). South Texas Veterans Health Care System.

Pernicano, P., Wortmann, J., & Haynes, K. (2022). Acceptance and forgiveness therapy for veterans with moral injury: Spiritual and psychological collaboration in group treatment. *Journal of Health Care Chaplaincy, 28*(1), 557–578. https://doi.org/10.1080/08854726.2022.2032982

Shulkin, D., Elnahal, S., Maddock, E., & Shaheen, M. (Eds.). (2017). *Best Care everywhere*. Department of Veterans Affairs.

Smigelsky, M. A., Trimm, V., Meador, K. G., Jackson, G. L., Wortmann, J. H., & Nieuwsma, J. A. (2022). Core components of moral injury groups co-facilitated by mental health providers and chaplains. *Spirituality in Clinical Practice, 9*(3), 159–174. https://doi.org/10.1037/scp0000297

Smith-MacDonald, L. A., Morin, J. S., & Brémault-Phillips, S. (2018). Spiritual dimensions of moral injury: Contributions of mental health chaplains in the Canadian armed forces. *Frontiers in Psychiatry, 9*(592), 1–7. https://doi.org/10.3389/fpsyt.2018.00592

Swift, C., Handzo, G., & Cohen, J. (2012). Healthcare chaplaincy. In M. Cobb, C. M. Puchalski, & B. Rumbold (Eds.), *Oxford Textbook of spirituality in healthcare* (pp. 185–90). Oxford University Press.

Tick, E. (2014). *Warrior's return: Restoring the soul after war.* Sounds True Adult.

Tutu, D., & Tutu, M. (2015). *The book of forgiving: The fourfold path for healing ourselves and the world.* Ed. D. Abrams. HarperCollins.

Wang, P. S., Berglund, P. A., & Kessler, R. C. (2003). Patterns and correlates of contacting clergy for mental disorders in the United States. *Health Services Research, 38*(2), 647–673. https://doi.org/10.1111/1475-6773.00138

Wohl, M. J. A., DeShea, L., & Wahkinney, R. L. (2008). Looking within: Measuring state self-forgiveness and its relationship to psychological well-being. *Canadian Journal of Behavioural Science/Revue canadienne des sciences du comportement, 40*(1), 1–10. https://doi.org/10.1037/0008-400x.40.1.1.1

Wortmann, J. H., Eisen, E., Hundert, C., Jordan, A. H., Smith, M. W., Nash, W. P., & Litz, B. T. (2017). Spiritual features of war-related moral injury: A primer for clinicians. *Spirituality in Clinical Practice, 4*(4), 249–261. https://doi.org/10.1037/scp0000140

Chapter 5

Forgiving Self and Others

Psychiatrist Jonathan Shay (1994), who first coined the term "moral injury" (MI), began his definition with the word "betrayal" (p. 3). Psychologist Brett Litz and colleagues (2009) expanded Shay's definition of betrayal by others to include the possibility of betrayal by self. Dr. Edward Tick (2014) describes the Greek meaning of the word "trauma" as a "puncture wound" or "wound that pierces" (p. 17). A person with MI carries a deep, piercing sense of betrayal, by self, others, an institution, a higher power, or a combination of these, depending on the story. Acceptance allows one to make peace with the past, not approving what happened but accepting that it did happen; however wrong it was, no amount of anger, rage, worry, despair, or shame will change that. Without acceptance, one remains *stuck* in *what if?* thinking, condemned to live in the past, and missing out on the present. Since betrayal is at the heart of MI – betrayal by self, others, or a higher power – forgiveness is part of the healing.

There is often a misunderstanding about forgiveness. Some believe it condones or excuses the wrong action. Some mistake it for reconciliation, whereas forgiving another requires no contact with the offender. Some believe in "forgive and forget," or "If I still remember the offense, I must not have forgiven it."

What is forgiveness? First, on an individual basis, it is a choice; no one can force forgiveness on you; it is up to you whether to pursue it. Next, forgiveness might be considered a decision to let go of resentment and not get even. In recent years, forgiveness research has grown significantly (Worthington & Wade, 2020). Webb et al. (2017) define it as a "deliberate, volitional process involving a fundamental shift in affect, cognition, and/or behavior in response to negative feelings regarding an acknowledged offensive experience, without condoning, excusing, or denying the transgression(s)–at a minimum, an absence of ill will toward an offender" (p. 220). Forgiveness benefits the one injured when it is paired with responsibility and accountability to allow a path forward. Purcell et al. (2018) speak of forgiveness in the context of MI as a "process of emotional growth, release, and transformation that can facilitate reconciliation in the aftermath of a significant moral violation. It is an active, morally engaged process that requires both acceptance and change" (p. 3). We describe other-forgiveness as letting go of the deep anger, bitterness, and desire for retaliation that ties up energy and prevents living in the present.

DOI: 10.4324/9781003494263-7

Self-forgiveness is a unique form of forgiveness and has been researched extensively in mental health (MH) circles (Cornish & Wade, 2015; Enright, 1996; Hall & Fincham, 2005; Macaskill, 2012; McConnell & Dixon, 2012). It is defined by Webb et al. (2017) as a "deliberate, volitional process initiated in response to one's negative feelings in the context of a personally acknowledged self-instigated wrong, that results in ready accountability for said wrong and a fundamental, constructive shift in one's relationship to, reconciliation with, and acceptance of the self through human connectedness and commitment to change" (p. 221). This definition includes a willingness and commitment to change for the better. Self-forgiveness recognizes the oxymoron, "Although we are flawed, we are also capable of seeking virtue and goodness" (Worthington & Griffin, n.d., p. 62). We all make mistakes. There are times when we are not our best selves. We hurt ourselves and others, and our imperfections bring pain and regret. No matter how big the wrongdoing (and MI seems big even if it's not), it does not have to define the whole person. In healing from MI, the individual realizes he or she is more than the MI and can address guilt and wrongdoing through compassion, forgiveness, and making amends.

Some Veterans understand forgiveness better by contemplating what it is *not*; forgiveness is not forgetting although, as burdens are released, it makes the recall less painful. The process of forgiveness requires time to weigh and engage in it. Forgiveness is the opposite of bitterness, revenge, self-righteousness, and denial. Forgiveness does not pardon, excuse, or condone the wrongdoing, nor diminish the seriousness of the offense. It does not demand or even include reconciliation with the offender, which in some cases would be ill-advised and in other cases impossible. The beautiful thing about forgiveness is that it can be accomplished by just one person, the one who was hurt, whereas reconciliation (a separate process after forgiveness) requires the cooperation of both the offended and the offender.

Forgiveness benefits the one forgiving in many ways. Naming the pains suffered and fostering compassion for persons lightens the mental, emotional, and spiritual load. It contributes to better physical health with an improved immune system and a reduced risk for cardiovascular problems. It reduces rumination (replaying negative thoughts in our head) and decreases a stress hormone that affects overall health and sexual performance. When appropriate, forgiveness coupled with reconciliation builds healthier relationships (Toussaint et al., 2015; Tutu & Tutu, 2015).

Compassion as a Pathway to Forgiveness

Compassion for self and others is a primary pathway to acceptance and forgiveness. *The Greater Good Magazine* at Berkeley (Keltner, 2024) has a series describing the benefits of compassion and forgiveness. Compassion means to suffer together; in the face of another's suffering, we feel compelled to relieve their pain. Keltner points out that compassion goes beyond empathy, or feeling someone else's feelings; compassion arouses a desire to help. When we experience compassion, we may become altruistic and engage in kind, selfless behavior. Compassion can be a way to see oneself and others from a new perspective. Scientific evidence reveals that when we feel compassion, our heart rate slows, and oxytocin (a bonding hormone) increases. Regions of the brain associated with empathy, caregiving, and pleasure are activated. It is not surprising that these areas are also the ones that activate (with glucose metabolism) in MI. Acceptance and forgiveness therapy (AFT) activates compassion and empathy for self and others and affirms positive shared values (Pernicano & Haynes, 2023).

Forgiveness conveys worth and restores value and integrity. Choosing to leave an emotional prison is easier with the compassionate support of others. Many initially view what has happened as unforgivable, inhumane, or deserving of permanent judgment. Offering alternatives to that view commutes the life sentence, converting it to a compassionate release and an opportunity to live to honor the past and make the world a better place.

Punitive Versus Healthy Response to Guilt

Purcell et al. (2018) state that to pursue forgiveness,

> There must be some wrong to forgive, and this is often ambiguous. In combat, violent actions that are considered immoral in most other contexts become, instead, one's duty. These actions become, also, the basis for protecting oneself and one's fellow soldiers from grave harm. Often, warriors must make split-second decisions—for instance, to shoot or not to shoot—with life-or-death consequences. Those decisions are often fraught with moral complexity and are made under intense pressure. In these contexts, right and wrong are by no means black-and-white. (p. 2)

Veterans often carry inappropriate guilt for things beyond their control. Emotional reasoning tells the Veteran, "Because I *feel* guilty, I must *be* guilty." Many Veterans treat guilt as the "go-to" emotion when they have trouble processing other difficult emotions such as sadness, frustration, and anger. The military culture's emphasis on assigning blame, top-down, unwittingly reinforces this mentality. Consider the following cases:

> Victor's battle buddy and close friend was killed by a sniper while lying next to Victor. The horror of seeing his friend's head explode and realizing it could have been him resulted in post-traumatic stress disorder (PTSD). He also reported MI due to survivor guilt, because his friend left behind a young wife and three small children

while Victor was single with no family. Victor began to examine factors that may have contributed to his friend's death, some beyond his control and others for which he held himself responsible; for example, Victor knew his friend was not adequately concealed but didn't warn him. He began working on self-forgiveness and to grieve the factors over which he had no control.

Andy sought to explain in his mind the brutal sexual assault onboard the ship that left him with PTSD and its accompanying nightmares, flashbacks, etc. Andy also carried MI as he faulted himself for not doing more to stop the attack and came to judge anyone in authority as untrustworthy since his attackers included non-commissioned officers (NCOs) in his chain of command. Andy's treatment included cognitive methods to challenge the stuck points that "I was weak," and "All authority figures are untrustworthy." He realized he had been caught off guard and outnumbered by people larger than himself. He had been betrayed by people who outranked him and abused their authority; also by fellow sailors he had trusted. Andy became more willing to forgive his perpetrators (release his shame and bitterness) as he pursued restorative justice, advocated for a change in the military culture, and helped other Veterans in similar situations.

For many Veterans, self-forgiveness begins with objectively clarifying their responsibility, going beyond the guilt they have carried to make meaning of what happened. Later in this book, Chapter 9 clarifies guilt and responsibility, while Chapter 10 provides tools and a healthy process of working through legitimate guilt. Intentional wrongdoing, betrayal by others, and overwhelming grief at inhumanity need pathways to resolution. As Purcell et al. (2018) note, we offer Veterans the opportunity to "make a cognitive reappraisal that eases guilt, shame, and suffering" (p. 2). Through this process, some Veterans find no moral failure in themselves. Yet, for others, there is work to do toward healing.

In these cases, Purcell et al. (2018) concur that "guilt is, in fact, an important precursor to the transformational experience of authentic self-forgiveness" (p. 3). A punitive response to guilt does not have a pathway to peace, as it often transforms into shame, a rejecting, judgmental view of the self. A healthy response to guilt guides Veterans toward compassion and self/other healing through restorative forgiveness. Punitive response to guilt interferes with acceptance, meaning-making, amends-making, and personal growth; this contributes to and exacerbates MI. Veterans with MI often report self-other blame or condemnation with no way out.

Purcell et al. (2018) suggest that the core components of the self-forgiveness process (accepting responsibility, cultivating self-compassion, making amends, and reconstructing an intact moral identity) are "near-universal steps on the pathway through and beyond moral guilt" (p. 4). Most go into the military believing in "the sanctity and dignity of human life" (p. 4), and we invite them to recognize and *confess* violations of core values and engage in reparative actions when desired.

A story of self-forgiveness by Pernicano (2023) refers to accepting grace or time served granted by a *benevolent judge* in the courtroom of acceptance and forgiveness. Forgiveness does not remove responsibility for amends or restitution, and it prepares the person for the journey forward. Enright (1996) describes self-forgiveness as "a willingness to abandon self-resentment in the face of one's acknowledged objective wrong, while fostering compassion, generosity, and love toward oneself" (p. 116). Griffin et al. (2018) described two processes essential for self-forgiveness: a reorientation toward positive values and a restoration of personal esteem. Later, Griffin et al. (2021) noted that both must be present for genuine self-forgiveness. Alternatively, "to accept responsibility and seek to atone for a perceived transgression by denigrating oneself is self-punishment, and to maintain a positive sense of self-esteem by deflecting responsibility for one's actions is self-exoneration" (page 78). We would label these alternative actions as "cheap" or "pseudo-" forgiveness.

Forgiving Others

For the Veteran wronged by someone else, metaphor can be a conceptual first start. The Veteran can choose a metaphor such as finding an antidote to the poison inside, the poison being bitterness or revenge fantasies (see Chapter 10 for forgiveness metaphors). One who survives betrayal needs to realize that it is not their fault; changes are needed in the military system, with pathways to restorative justice. We can encourage Veterans to speak up (use their voice), educate others, or help someone in honor of their story. In helping others, we find a path toward our healing. Like the 12th step of recovery in a 12-step program, sharing one's story often helps others and contributes to the recovery of the one sharing.

Of course, long before step 12, other important forgiveness-related steps aid in MI recovery. These may involve completing a moral inventory (confession), making an honest appraisal of self, connecting with a higher power (and other healthy relationships), and making amends to those who have been hurt, including the Veteran. Purcell et al. (2018) note that "embarking on a journey of authentic self-forgiveness unlocks the possibility of re-engagement in one's life and one's community after moral injury" (p. 4). Forgiveness unexpectedly brings life again!

In addition to forgiving themselves or others, some Veterans work on "forgiving" their higher power; what happened was seen as "God's will." Usually, this becomes a process of "acceptance" more than "forgiveness," as these Veterans blamed God for nearly unspeakable evils they encountered. They reach a point of acceptance and move forward through spiritual meaning-making. Some Veterans develop a stronger faith that will withstand future storms of life. Some Veterans give up on their childhood faith. Some Veterans become believers for the first time. Some view certain life events as unrelated to God, attributing negative outcomes to human error or free will. Others see the divine as a loving, benevolent figure who understands their grief and pain and walks with them through the valley. As facilitators, we respect and accept all spiritual/religious views regardless of their pilgrimage and help them live their best life possible.

Understanding Cultural and Religious Traditions

The spiritual components of MI – guilt, shame, and loss of meaning (see Chapter 4) – respond to intentional practices of confession and forgiveness. Forgiveness is not a sign of weakness; some say that only the strong can truly forgive. We seek to understand cultural differences among Veterans because different faith practices give unique meaning to suffering and healing. All worldwide religions encourage the practice of forgiveness (Toussaint & Worthington, 2017); cultures have different traditions and practices for forgiveness and accepting responsibility for wrongdoing. Forgiveness may be sought through rituals of confession, compassion, and some form of action or ritual that brings justice including an apology, making amends, or restitution. Overall, forgiveness practices are ways of confronting injustice.

Joo et al. (2019) reflect that different forgiveness practices in East Asian and Western cultures reflect differences in cultural values and priorities. In their study, Japanese participants focused more on re-establishing relationship harmony (for the sake of the relationship) through rational and cognitively driven decisional forgiveness, with less emphasis on emotional forgiveness (feeling better). In China, a slight might be overlooked for the sake of the relationship rather than create conflict. Relational forgiveness focuses more on reconciliation and restitution; it is done to preserve social harmony. Worldwide, sharing a meal is a common ritual of reconciliation, as eating together symbolizes union among people.

Western cultures are more individualistic in forgiveness practices; they focus more on self-enhancement (emotional forgiveness within the individual) than the relationship between the forgiver and transgressor. Individualistic cultures use forgiveness to relieve a burden, do the right thing, or clear their conscience.

According to Park (2020), African cultures like Ghana are more collectivist, and forgiveness maintains or restores social harmony. Terms refer to letting go of or forgiving a transgression. There is often a physical display such as kneeling and showing submission toward the transgressed. It is not enough to apologize – you must show you are sorry. The person responsible for the harm offers an apology and restitution. The focus is on responsibility and making wrongs right by repairing and rebuilding relationships.

Tutu and Tutu (2015) wrote about apartheid and the desire to pursue forgiveness instead of revenge to find peace as a nation. In Rwanda and Uganda, people have risen above anger, pain, and loss to seek ways to rebuild themselves and their communities (Clark, 2024). Clark and his colleagues are working on a project about "finding forgiveness within ourselves" (p. 3) through interviews with atrocity perpetrators, victims, and those who rescued others.

Worthington et al. (2007) discuss decisional forgiveness, where the individual no longer wishes to avoid or retaliate against the transgressor. Worthington's REACH model has been shown to work in both Western and Eastern cultures; it works best "when the transgressor and the transgressed share a belief system" (Park, 2020, p. 6). Forgiveness focuses on commonalities in values and pursues conditions for peaceful coexistence through reconciliation with self, others, or higher power. It is a decision to let go of the desire for revenge and ill will toward someone who wronged you; it is part of the grief process in acknowledging pain and loss.

Religions' Aspects of Forgiveness and Compassion

An artificial intelligence (AI) blog (Level Super Mind, 2023) offers an overview of religious practices of forgiveness, gratitude, and compassion. In most religions, compassion is seen as a "powerful force that binds humanity together" (AI Blog, 2023, np). Compassion comes from empathy, or understanding the pain of others, and compassion includes a desire to alleviate that pain. Gratitude, a universal sentiment of profound thankfulness and appreciation, is also a quality that helps with forgiveness. It transcends cultural and religious differences and fosters calm, positivity, and relational connections.

Christian

Christian teachings focus on love, kindness, and forgiveness through actions and prayer. In the Christian tradition, God does not change hearts through punishment or retribution. Like a human parent, God teaches, directs, and offers restoration through love, unexpected mercy, and grace. Love restores wholeness and transforms the human heart. In the Bible, people are transformed amid guilt and expectation of punishment. In Christianity, compassion is to be extended toward all neighbors and marginalized persons, with love, humility, gentleness, and patience.

Buddhism

Buddhism stresses that forgiveness can shed light through meditation and insight, thus liberating us from suffering and harm. *Khanti* or *ksanti* is the Buddhist concept of patience, forbearance, and tolerance: the capacity to let go of interpersonal resentment and cultivate qualities of acceptance and forgiveness. Forgiveness means giving up all hope for a better past and offers a way to move on. In Buddhist philosophy, forgiveness ends suffering and brings dignity and harmony into our lives. Forgiveness is fundamentally for our own sake and for our MH; mindfulness practices guide us toward compassion. Compassion, or *karuna*, helps oneself and others be happy.

Sikhism

Guru Arjan Dev Ji describes forgiveness as a practice of fasting, good conduct, and contentment. Kabir says that God resides in forgiveness. It instills inner peace and tranquility as a remedy to anger through compassion. Meditation is the medium to replace anger and ego with forgiveness and compassion.

Judaism

Judaism emphasizes *teshuva* or repentance, which includes expressing sorrow or regret with emotional awareness of the need for forgiveness. In Jewish tradition, forgiveness includes atonement, and *Yom Kippur* is the Day of Atonement when Jews strive to perform *teshuva*. Judaism advises against vengeance or bearing grudges, and on *Yom Kippur*, Jewish people ask for forgiveness from God and their fellow human beings. In Judaism, God is compassionate, and we are to be the same, being kind by helping others and being fair.

Islam

Forgiveness is a prerequisite and pathway for genuine peace. The Quran says to show forgiveness, speak for justice, and avoid the ignorant. The Prophet of Muhammad taught that the true meaning of strength is to control your anger and to forgive; God is said to love the just. Forgiveness is an imitation of Allah's love, mercy, and justice. Before embarking upon a *hajj* pilgrimage to Mecca, Muslims follow Allah's example by visiting others to ask for forgiveness for any wrongdoing. In Islam, Rahmah means being compassionate, kind, and caring to everyone and everything created by God.

Hinduism

This faith teaches that everything and everyone is connected; being kind and compassionate to all living beings is dear to God.

Commonalities Among Traditions and Religions

Several cultural and religious traditions speak to *restorative justice* and *peacemaking*. Restorative justice focuses on responsibility and accountability and is a relational process that seeks to repair harm; justice seeks to heal, not to punish. Justice seeks to transform broken lives and relationships. Justice is not getting even, and it seeks restorative action. The authors do not discuss faith directly in AFT; however, Veterans may share their faith views in the context of guilt and forgiveness, and we stress the importance of honoring all traditions. Veterans draw on their unique spiritual beliefs and practices in pursuit of healing.

As Victor's story provided earlier indicates, some Veterans examine their actions and responsibilities and experience a shift from guilt to grief. They are freed to engage in healthy grieving activities rather than unrelenting self-punishment for situations beyond their control. For instance:

A sergeant major named Harold carries a list of the fallen Marines under his command in Vietnam. Every Memorial Day he burns the list in a ritual designed to commit these Marines to his higher power, and every Veterans Day he rewrites the list and tucks it in his wallet. He knows he did his best for his Marines; he realizes that punishing himself is an unhealthy option. The best he can do is live the life given to him and honor his fallen Marines however he can. He has moved from unhealthy guilt to healthy grief.

Veterans dealing with perceived or actual betrayal by others or their higher power did nothing wrong and are encouraged toward restorative justice and self-compassion, not self-forgiveness. Sometimes betrayal is by one's country or at the hands of military leadership; it leaves a bitter taste to be lured into service under false pretenses, in the name of justice when there is no justice to be found, or collectively part of violence, then seeing the aftermath of inhumanity that destroys homes and lives. Veterans feel betrayed when they are part of actions that topple one dictator only to leave a void in which something worse arises. Responsibility must be born at higher levels and by larger social networks that blame Veterans for their well-intentioned service. To some degree, we are all complicit when we remain uninformed, rigidly partisan, or *blissfully* ignorant of wrongdoing.

Survivors of military sexual trauma (MST), regardless of how they may *feel*, are not responsible for the assault against them; that responsibility belongs solely to their attacker and, sometimes, to the military leadership that looks the other way, creates a false story of what happened, or blames the recipient. Too often leadership colludes with and condones wrongdoing that is life-changing for the one who was harmed. Speaking about self-forgiveness in such a case could compound harmful feelings of self-blame (Cornish & Wade, 2015).

However, it has been suggested that we may have difficulty living a full life until we become willing to forgive the harm done to us, not by condoning but by releasing what we carry, pursuing restorative justice peacefully, and moving beyond retaliation or revenge (Tutu & Tutu, 2015). Forgiving those who betrayed your trust is difficult, yet the alternative – carrying bitterness, pain, or desire for revenge – can be personally harmful.

Forgiving – particularly when the person and the offense seem *unforgivable* – seems a bridge too far. The survivor may need to focus in the near term on self-care and compassion. Healing involves accepting what cannot be changed (the event or events), knowing it was not their fault, and pursuing restorative justice. As we will discuss later in the book, forgiving is not condoning, or letting someone off the hook. Taking the hook out of yourself frees you to live a life less encumbered.

Effective, researched forgiveness models include Enright's (2001) PROCESS model, Worthington's (2001) REACH forgiveness model, and Luskin's (2003) *Forgive for Good* model. Wade et al. (2014) found over 50 published and unpublished reports of interventions designed to promote forgiveness.

Desmond Tutu and his daughter Mpho Tutu (2015) offer a cohesive model of forgiving others in their work, *The Book of Forgiving*, reminding us that we are all broken, and in our brokenness, we hurt others. Archbishop Tutu won the Nobel Peace Prize in 1984 and received the Presidential Medal of Freedom in 2009. He was appointed chair of South Africa's Truth and Reconciliation Commission and suggested the importance of forgiveness after the civil conflict and oppression of apartheid. Tutu and Tutu (2015) recognized that when we do not forgive, we remain bound to the person who harmed us. We reside in a self-imposed prison with a life sentence of emotional pain, such as in Pernicano's story of *Time Served* (2023). Forgiveness is for ourselves, not for others, as it releases us from those spiritual chains. Tutu and Tutu note that we all carry the potential to hurt others although they believe that no one is born evil. While the contributions of nature and nurture are debatable; the roots of hurting others can stem from childhood abuse. Narcissistic, antisocial practices may seem normal to those whose narcissism is rewarded and antisocial behaviors are condoned. Faulty, insecure attachment may damage the capacity for empathy and put children at risk of poor relationship connections.

Tutu and Tutu (2015) offer a *prayer before the prayer* for the one who finds it difficult to pursue forgiveness. This prayer acknowledges a step before forgiveness, a desire for the *willingness* to forgive. This prayer normalizes hesitation and doubt at being ready to forgive, juxtaposed with a desire to reach that point. Willingness may be the first step to lighten the load of pain that we carry.

The Worthington REACH Model for Emotional Self-Forgiveness

Dr. Everett Worthington's REACH model (2001 and Worthington & Griffin, n.d.) targets self- and other-forgiveness. Worthington's story stems from family tragedy/losses with moral pain. His mother was brutally murdered during a theft in 1996. Worthington flew to the scene the next day after his brother discovered their mother's body. In the weeks to follow, Worthington felt ruminating anger and then experienced a turning point through his Christian faith: he realized he was spending every waking moment plotting revenge, thus becoming in his estimation little better than the murderers. He developed the REACH model for forgiving others, described in Chapter 10. Worthington's full model includes seven steps involving both the "head" (decisional forgiveness) and the "heart" (emotional forgiveness).

Years later, Worthington was concerned about his brother Mike's undiagnosed post-traumatic stress disorder (PTSD), stemming from discovering their mother's body. Worthington urged his brother to seek help, and Mike "blew it off," later taking his own life. Worthington regretted their final conversation and his less than adequate, "whatever" rebuff to his brother's dismissal of help. He sank into despair over failing to help his brother, especially given his MH experience. He applied the REACH model of forgiving others to his self-forgiveness and found peace through the process (Worthington & Griffin, n.d.).

Worthington & Griffin (n.d.) point out the difficulties of self- and other-forgiveness. We know our hidden motives better than the motives of others. We have high standards for ourselves and blame ourselves more than others. Sometimes when someone lets us down or hurts us, we want the other person to be sorry or to suffer. We believe wrongdoing must be "punished," and we may take matters into our own hands as judge and jury.

Our hearts may block us from pursuing forgiveness for ourselves or others – this can feel like a drawbridge pulled up tight. Willingness, perhaps, is letting down the drawbridge. The first step toward forgiveness might be to consider what that word means to you and what willingness would entail. In Chapter 10, we offer various metaphors for forgiveness that may help readers envision a personal path forward.

References

Clark, P. (2024). *The complexity of forgiveness and reconciliation in central Africa. Fetzer Institute.* https://fetzer.org/blog/coplexity-forgivness-and-reconciliation-central-africa

Cornish, M. A., & Wade, N. G. (2015). A therapeutic model of self-forgiveness with intervention strategies for counselors. *Journal of Counseling & Development, 93*(1), 96–104. https://doi.org/10.1002/j.1556-6676.2015.00185.x

Enright, R. D. (1996). Counseling within the forgiveness triad: On forgiving, receiving, forgiveness, and self-forgiveness. *Counseling and Values, 40*(2), 107–126. https://doi.org/10.1002/j.2161-007X.1996.tb00844.x

Enright, R. D. (2001). *Forgiveness is a choice: A step-by-step process for resolving anger and restoring hope.* American Psychological Association.

Griffin, B. J., Cornish, M. A., Maguen, S., & Worthington, E. L. Jr. (2021). Forgiveness as a mechanism of repair following military-related moral injury. In J. M. Currier, K. D. Drescher, & J. Nieuwsma (Eds.), *Addressing moral injury in clinical practice* (pp. 71–86). American Psychological Association. https://doi.org/10.1037/0000204-005

Griffin, B. J., Worthington, E. L. Jr., Davis, D. E., Hook, J. N., & Maguen, S. (2018). Development of the self-forgiveness dual-process scale. *Journal of Counseling Psychology, 65*(6), 715–726. https://doi.org/10.1037/cou0000293

Hall, J. H., & Fincham, F. D. (2005). Self-forgiveness: The stepchild of forgiveness research. *Journal of Social and Clinical Psychology, 24*(5), 621–637. https://doi.org/10.1521/jscp.2005.24.5.621

Joo, M., Terzino, K. A., Cross, S. E., Yamaguchi, N., & Ohbuchi, K. (2019). How does culture shape conceptions of forgiveness? Evidence from Japan and the United States. *Journal of Cross-Cultural Psychology, 50*(5), 676–702. https://doi.org/10.1177/0022022119845502

Keltner, D. (2024). *What is compassion?* Greater Good Magazine, Berkeley.edu: Greater Good Science Center. https://greatergood.berkeley.edu/article/item/the_compassionate_species

Level Super Mind (2023). *Are there religions that despise forgiveness?* https://level.game/blogs/stories-of-forgiveness-and-religious-teachings-across-all-religions?srsltid=AfmBOorOdTexjkWdRtlopiqWLcByZ3qe6LJvGPx2tmJe4LBXJIDF6sXo&lang=en

Litz, B. T., Stein, N., Delaney, E., Lebowitz, L., Nash, W. P., Silva, C., & Maguen, S. (2009). Moral injury and moral repair in war veterans: A preliminary model and intervention strategy. *Clinical Psychology Review, 29*(8), 695–706. https://doi.org/10.1016/j.cpr.2009.07.003.

Luskin, F. (2003). *Forgive for good: A proven prescription for health and happiness.* HarperOne.

Macaskill, A. (2012). Differentiating dispositional self-forgiveness from other-forgiveness: Associations with mental health and life satisfaction. *Journal of Social and Clinical Psychology, 31*, 28–50. https://doi.org/10.1521/jscp.2012.31.1.28

McConnell, J. M., & Dixon, D. N. (2012). Perceived forgiveness from God and self-forgiveness. *Journal of Psychology and Christianity, 31*(1), 31–39.

Park, W. (2020). *What other cultures can teach us about forgive*ness. https://www.bbc.com/future/article/20201109-what-other-cultures-can-teach-us-about-forgiveness

Pernicano, P. (2023). *Time served* [Unpublished story]. In P. Pernicano, & K. Haynes (2nd ed.). *Introduction to acceptance and forgiveness therapy (facilitator & program handbooks).* Mental Illness Research, Education and Clinical Center, Houston, TX (MIRECC VISN 16). https://www.mirecc.va.gov/visn16/moral-injury-psychoeducation-group.asp

Pernicano, P., & Haynes, K. (2023). *Acceptance & forgiveness therapy: From brokenness to restoration* [Unpublished handbook] (5th ed.). South Texas Veterans Health Care System.

Purcell, N., Griffin, B. J., Burkman, K., & Maguen, S. (2018). "Opening a door to a new life": The role of forgiveness in healing from moral injury. *Frontiers in Psychiatry, 9*(498). https://doi.org/10.3389/fpsyt.2018.00498

Shay, J. (1994). *Achilles in Vietnam: Combat trauma and the undoing of character.* Scribner.

Tick, E. (2014). *Warrior's return: Restoring the soul after war.* Sounds True.

Toussaint, L. L., & Worthington, E. L. Jr (2017). Forgiveness. *The Psychologist, 30,* 28–33. British Psychological Society. https://www.bps.org.uk/psychologist/forgiveness

Toussaint, L. L., Worthington, E. L., Jr., & Williams, D. R. (Eds.). (2015). *Forgiveness and health: Scientific evidence and theories relating forgiveness to better health.* Springer Science + Business Media. https://doi.org/10.1007/978-94-017-9993-5

Tutu, D., & Tutu, M. (2015). *The book of forgiving: The fourfold path for healing ourselves and the world.* D. Abrams (Ed.). Harper.

Wade, N. G., Hoyt, W. T., Kidwell, J. E., & Worthington, E. L. (2014). Efficacy of psychotherapeutic interventions to promote forgiveness: A meta-analysis. *Journal of Consulting and Clinical Psychology, 82*(1), 154–170. https://doi.org/10.1037/a0035268

Webb, J. R., Bumgarner, D. J., Conway-Williams, E., Dangel, T., & Hall, B. B. (2017). A consensus definition of self-forgiveness: Implications for assessment and treatment. *Spirituality in Clinical Practice, 4*(3), 216–227. https://doi.org/10.1037/scp0000138

Worthington, E. L. Jr (2001). *Five steps to forgiveness: The art and science of forgiving.* Crown.

Worthington, E. L. Jr., & Griffin, B. J. (n.d.). *Moving forward: Six steps to forgiving yourself and breaking free from the past.* [Online workbook] (2nd ed.). Virginia Commonwealth University. https://forgiveself.com/workbooks/20150903%20Self-Forgiveness%20Intervention%20Workbook.pdf

Worthington, E. L., & Wade, N. G. (Eds.). (2020). *Handbook of forgiveness* (2nd eds.). Routledge/Taylor & Francis Group.

Worthington, E. L., Witvliet, C. V. O., Pietrii, P., & Miller, A. J. (2007). Forgiveness, health, and well-being: A review of evidence for emotional versus decisional forgiveness, dispositional forgivingness, and reduced unforgiveness. *Journal of Behavioral Medicine, 30,* 291–302.

Chapter 6

Models of Healing for Moral Injury

Veterans can be metaphorically uprooted by life's experiences that bring pain, loss, grief, and burdensome responsibility. Roots must be protected and strengthened for a plant to survive the winter and make it to spring. People need nurture, compassion, and emotional sustenance to recover from moral injury (MI). Veterans sometimes consider giving up when they see their roots weakening and no longer find purpose or meaning in their lives. However, a plant that has died down to the ground may still have life in its roots and emerge in the spring with proper care. Services for MI target the roots, so Veterans may survive and one day thrive. MI has roots in loss and "disconnect" (spiritual, within the self, between Veteran and others) that result in:

+ guilt;
+ shame;
+ hate and bitterness;
+ hopelessness;
+ vulnerability;
+ abandonment, deceit, and mistrust;
+ injustice;
+ desire for revenge;
+ inadequacy or "not enough"; and
+ perceived failure.

Different types of MI call for unique forms of healing. Depending on the roots, healing may involve an apology (from the general community for what the Veteran has suffered and what he/she was called to do), grief work (to mourn rather than to carry false guilt and to learn to hope again), restitution and amends (to ease one's conscience), confession and forgiveness (to restore self-acceptance and perceived worth), and positive engagement with others (to restore trust and community).

DOI: 10.4324/9781003494263-8

Stages of Change in MI

Healing from MI is a work in progress, and it takes time to put the pieces back together after trust is broken and hopes and ideals are shattered. Veterans have hidden their cracks for many years, unable to conceive of becoming whole again. Pursuing healing involves commitment, planning, and practice. It is valuable to consider change from the view of Prochaska and DiClemente (1982) who developed the transtheoretical stages of change. Veterans are at different stages in the change process when they seek help. This model has evolved through studies on behaviors like smoking, using drugs/alcohol, or exercising. Healing from MI is a process of individual decision-making and intentional change. Change takes place one step at a time, and during the process, Veterans experience changes in thoughts/beliefs, feelings, perceptions, attitudes, and behaviors.

The first stage of change is called *precontemplation*. At this stage, the person may be unaware that his or her behavior is problematic or produces negative consequences. Educational services may be helpful during this stage. The person with MI may feel "stuck" in an attitude of blame or hopelessness. The Veteran may not yet have a word to describe his/her moral pain and may avoid thinking and talking about what happened, wishing it would go away.

> *Greg had been drinking more since he retired six months ago. During his last deployment, he was driving in a convoy when a bomb exploded, resulting in injuries. He wondered if it was his fault but was told to get over it and snap out of it. He did not like civilian life. He snapped at his wife and kids. He was written up at work for being late, and he got defensive when his boss told him to improve his attitude toward customers. "They are a bunch of complainers; they can kiss my ass." His wife suggested he go to Veterans Affairs (VA) or talk to someone. She told him he had changed. He blew her off and thought, "She doesn't understand. I'm not crazy." Greg was in the Precontemplation stage.*

When Veterans reach the *contemplation* phase, they may be aware of problems associated with MI and feel stuck, but they are unsure what to do next. A Veteran may feel disconnected from friends and family and want a better quality of life and then read about MI and identify with other Veteran stories. Veterans weigh the pros and cons of getting help during contemplation. *Thinking about change is part of the change process.* Veterans at this stage may doubt that change is possible or worry about the consequences of opening up painful memories. Those seeking help for MI usually start with education to decide if they might have it. They would like to return to "normal" even though they have no idea what that is or how to do it. A partner or spouse may encourage the Veteran to seek help for the family's sake or the relationship. Someone with MI may put off getting help because he/she doesn't want to open that can of worms. But carrying around MI is a heavy load. The person ponders whether to stay where he/she is or to seek help, and s/he stays in contemplation until the benefits of getting help outweigh the pain of staying the same.

Joe's therapist was treating him for post-traumatic stress disorder (PTSD). Joe made progress but was stuck in what he called guilt. He thought a lot about a burned-out car with a family inside. He dreamed about them and wondered why he had been sent to Iraq after 9-11. I'm a bad person," he said. "I never did anything I wasn't ordered to do, but they lost their lives, and I'll never get over it." His therapist thought Joe might have MI and recommended some reading material. Joe reviewed the material and saw himself in it – guilt, sleep problems, sadness and regret, unworthiness, self-blame – yes, all of those. And he didn't know that there was a term for it. "How is moral injury different from my PTSD?" he asked. His therapist noted that Joe had completed Cognitive Processing Therapy as well as Prolonged Exposure and he still struggled with these other issues. Maybe those other issues needed a different type of intervention so that Joe could forgive himself and come to terms with his MI. Joe weighed the pros and cons of seeking help for MI. He didn't want to think or talk about the MI, but his guilt and stress interfered with his focus at work. He feared losing control of his emotions if he opened up that can of worms, but perhaps the worms were already crawling into his sleep. Joe went to the VA and met with a chaplain about MI. He realized he had nothing to lose and much to gain if it helped.

The next phase of change is *determination*. At this stage, the pros of changing outweigh the cons, and the person enters into a change process. This shift happens when the Veteran wants a better quality of life and is convinced it might help try something new. As the Veteran joins a class or begins therapy, small changes seem encouraging, and the Veteran continues to move forward. Being around others with MI reminds the Veteran that he/she is not alone. Veterans may seek Veterans Affairs (VA) peer support, volunteer for a service project, or join a Wounded Warrior program. They get approval at work for the time needed to attend a treatment group. Contemplation has shifted into determination, or planned change.

Jean waited several months after a sexual assault, then went to talk to a military chaplain. Her performance had suffered, and she was uncomfortable working around the non-commissioned officer (NCO) who had given her alcohol and targeted her. She blamed herself for not seeing it coming and being in the wrong place at the wrong time. She pointed the finger at herself – her clothing, her drinking, her friendly manner – and she felt stupid and naïve that she had been so trusting. She was embarrassed that they had written her up for fraternizing and underage drinking when the NCO got a slap on the wrist. The female chaplain was a kind listener, genuinely concerned about Jean's well-being, and able to question her self-blame. She reminded Jean that the NCO was at fault and the military had betrayed her trust. Jean could report the sexual assault - she decided to do so. In the meantime, Jean worked with the chaplain to heal her MI.

Once a Veteran starts treatment or does something new to resolve MI, he/she is at the *action* stage of change. *Action commits the person to an ongoing change process.* Someone in the action stage has a plan, believes it will work, trusts those in charge, and is all in. At this stage, a Veteran is willing to keep an open mind and do things to heal from MI. Being in the action stage does not mean there is no anxiety or misgiving. Feelings remain painful, but they no longer keep the person stuck. Action starts with the willingness to pursue change.

In the fourth session, John shared, "I'm so relieved to have a name for what I'm experiencing: 'moral injury.' And to know I'm not alone. I don't know yet how life can get better, but for the first time, I think there is a chance it could get better. I'm doing the homework, because I want to get better. I have to get better! Thank you for having this group and doing this work. I know many Veterans who could benefit from being here, and I'm spreading the word!"

Benefits of Group Format for MI Recovery

So why do we do this work in groups, especially when most Veterans are very private and tell us they hate talking in groups? Military service is structured around group interactions, and Veterans have been members of many types of military groups. The groups are nested, increasing in size, from the smallest unit of the team or section to the squad (two teams comprising 8–11 members) and so on. The average size of an MI therapy group is about eight members or a small squad. Military training and service are conducted in groups that are supposed to be trustworthy and reliable, *have your back*, and *be there for you*. Military training includes rituals and structures designed to instill military expectations, values, and beliefs, including obedience to the chain of command, adherence to rules of engagement, protection of the group over the individual, and responsibility for negative outcomes ("The buck stops here"). For many, the military discouraged or failed to offer processing and debriefing after potentially morally injurious experiences (PMIEs). Some military-entrenched beliefs may contribute to MI, such as "Emotions are weak," "It's just good old boys having good old fun," and "Never betray a brother." MI, especially betrayal, ostracizes or separates the Veteran from his/her group. Many PMIEs occur in relational or interpersonal contexts, and the experiences violate core attachment and trust. Some of the most painful situations faced by Veterans are perpetrated or prolonged by military personnel, policies, or practices that preclude justice and healing. The imposed silence afterward may be coercive and affect many areas of Veterans' lives.

The Shay Center developed and piloted an evidence-based small group model, resilience strength training (RST); Jonathan Shay led the planning team for this program and was an advisor throughout its pilot phase. This peer-facilitated program was piloted through two Veterans of America (VOA) affiliates from 2017 to 2019. The program targets problems related to Veteran MI, including self-concept, social alienation, reduced self-regulation, and a changed view of the world. Barth et al. (2020) describe the program and the outcome study. It incorporates a "military squad model of group trust and bonding to address problems specific to moral injury" (p. 101). The program targets the collapse of meaning-making or faith, lost trust, self-isolation, and relationship failure in those with MI. Interventions develop self-calming, communication skills, and self-esteem. Pre-post measures reflected post-traumatic growth, meaning in life, propensity to trust, dispositional optimism, positive attitudes toward themselves, personal self-esteem, better sleep quality, and decreased dependence on alcohol. Improvement was still evident six months later. Establishing a peer-supported community with shared experiences was instrumental "in mitigating the negative impacts of MI" (Barth et al., 2020, p. 109).

VA MI services are offered individually and in group formats with chaplains, mental health (MH) providers, peer supports, trained residents, and fellows. The group process restores those with interpersonal trauma, and the relationships that develop become the basis for new trust in self and others. Education and skills-based services are also available at some locations. There are some pitfalls for Veterans being seen by less-trained persons (risks related to MH conditions) or those who might unintentionally judge or express punitive religious attitudes about Veterans' moral pain. Likewise, pitfalls arise when those who, with good intentions, too easily dismiss Veterans' possible wrongdoing, saying such things as "Don't worry about it – it was in a war setting!"

Effective listeners or helpers respond with empathy, compassion, and grace as Veterans share vulnerability, pain/bitterness, regret, and perceived guilt. As noted earlier, trained peer support specialists become helpful role models with whom Veterans identify and gain trust in small-group RST interactions (Barth et al.).

In group intervention, a process emerges that allows the group to work cohesively toward change. Irving Yalom wrote his first book, *The Theory and Practice of Group Psychotherapy*, in 1970. Now in its fifth edition, this book is considered one of the ten most influential psychiatric publications of its time. Yalom identified several healing-type factors that can be observed in process groups, including stages in the group process that emerge during the interpersonal process. These elements transform the group into a compassionate source of healing. Group therapy is not individual therapy times ten; it is an interpersonal, synergetic change process through member interactions.

Facilitators, educators, or therapists in group and individual settings become catalysts for change and mirrors for unconditional positive regard. First, Veterans discover hope through education about MI and word-of-mouth encouragement from other Veterans. Reading this book might be a good first start for someone wanting to learn more about MI. If you work with Veterans or live with one, remember that it feels risky for them to open up the MI – "can of worms." Many Veterans carry moral pain and MI for a long time, and it is not helpful to try to push them from contemplation into determination. Once a Veteran seeks help, hope is instilled by validation and empathic listening. It does not help to rescue, minimize, or rationalize what the Veteran has been going through. The Veteran is on a healing journey to a self-identified destination, even when he/she is not yet sure where that is. Hope also arises through information-gathering and thoughtful contemplation, raising positive expectations, challenging negative preconceptions, and anticipating the benefits of therapy or other MI services.

A group factor that emerges among Veterans is *universality*. Veterans initially feel alone and unique in their pain and distress, while they work their way through contemplation. Hearing that other Veterans have had similar experiences brings identification and relief. Educational groups impart information and allow Veterans to get their feet wet before taking the plunge. Facilitators convey information that helps Veterans understand the symptoms of MI and clear up misconceptions. Didactic information provides structure, and Veterans "recognize" themselves in the information shared.

Wanting to help and offer advice is natural, but each Veteran needs to experience and process pain. Group members may offer one another advice or compare stories, in a show of empathy; however, this also may be a defensive form of avoidance. Advice-giving is sometimes more in the eye of the giver than in the need of the recipient. Facilitators may get the urge to jump in with reassurance or to help the Veteran justify what he or she is trying to come to grips with. Group members need time to sit with their emotions, sometimes in painful silence, because empathy does not equate to fixing or giving advice. Long ago, a wise group therapist said, "Let the group do the work, let the process emerge, and let the patient work through his/her struggle." It reminds one of watching a butterfly struggle to release itself from the cocoon. You must resist the urge to help because it weakens the wings that need to experience struggle before release. We can model empathy and compassion through listening and attunement and acknowledge that struggle is unique to the person, with different views of spirituality and pathways to restoration.

In some ways, a therapy group resembles a family unit: authority/parental figures, sibling-like relationships with peers, sharing of strong emotions/personal experiences, intimacy, and negative/competing feelings. Coed facilitators pull for parental identification, and members may display behaviors they show in their families (dependence, defiance, appeasing, wariness, splitting, competition, envy, gaining allies, etc.); this is to be expected. Veterans test the waters in sharing memories and emotions, and in doing so, they re-establish trust in others and come to appreciate relationships that cross culture, socio-economic status, military history, age, and gender. In time, healing becomes a shared process.

Those involved in the healing process model vulnerability, self-disclosure, and openness. As Veterans realize the complexity of MI, including shared responsibility, they become more open-minded with themselves and others. Members come to see the importance of interpersonal relationships, and through sharing, they may have what is referred to as a corrective emotional experience or post-traumatic growth. The group encourages members to form satisfying relationships that are free of distortion. Veterans gradually risk new ways of being with others through disclosure, trust, and emotional sharing. Yalom reminds us that interactions correct previous misconceptions and interpersonal distortions, and healing transfers to the Veteran's social environment.

Example of Group Process in Forgiveness Work

George had deep guilt over killing a man in Vietnam. It was a legitimate "kill or be killed" moment, and he did not hesitate. George was a practicing Catholic, and he had nightmares about the man he had killed. He thought about the man's family and started wondering if God would forgive him for killing someone. He could not bring himself to confess to a priest, but he heard a priest say that killing in war was a sin. He stopped going to church and started believing he might be unforgivable.

He was unsure that the group would help him, but he worked very hard and was moved to tears by the caring of the other group members. He bonded tightly with them and told them he cared. He encouraged them to forgive themselves. One day, George looked up and said, "I need to do what I am asking you to do - to accept time served and forgive myself for what I did over 50 years ago. I do not deserve life in prison." He wept as he engaged in a ritual of release, sending his pain into healing waters. The group members showed empathy and compassion for George; they understood his pain at what war had taken from him. Grief and loss are normal, but George did not need to carry guilt and blame as if his military experience defined the whole of who he was. The group members expressed caring for George. His self-blame would not honor those who died, nor allow him to live his "best self" going forward. A few weeks later, George mentioned that his wife liked the new George. "I went to church with her," he said. It had been many years since he had gone to church. His relationships in the group had become a mirror of empathy and compassion. What he saw reflected in their eyes and hearts changed his heart and life.

Cohesiveness is an important factor that emerges in groups where members become accepting of one another and increasingly supportive. Sharing your story with others before there is cohesiveness can be ill-advised. Early in our work, we allowed this to happen once, as an anxious Veteran dumped his story on the group in our first session before we knew how to redirect. The result was confusion, fear, and anxiety all around: other group members seemed to wonder if they were supposed to share but were terrified to match his level of transparency before trust had been established. The Veteran did not understand why he was the only one sharing and felt somewhat rejected by the group. We contacted him after the group and encouraged him to stick with it, as trust would naturally develop and others would share. He learned that members open up and relate more deeply to others as cohesiveness grows. Signs of cohesiveness include self-disclosure, risk-taking, and offering constructive feedback. Group activities that encourage emotional vulnerability (usually ones that involve risk-taking) promote this. The acceptance and forgiveness therapy (AFT) curriculum (Pernicano & Haynes, 2023) is designed to facilitate appropriate sharing in greater ways as the group progresses, and this process and the reasoning behind it are explained in our initial session.

Venting and catharsis are not sufficient for change although strong displays of emotion may pull Veterans out of overly cognitive, rational states and shift them into experiencing grief and loss. Some forms of sharing are not helpful when sharing becomes a form of bitter trauma-dumping, and the atmosphere becomes competitive around whose situation is worse. Veterans with MI come to realize that life can be unfair and unjust, that there are times in our lives when we are not our best selves (and act in ways contradictory to our values), and that pain and death are part of life. Sharing *is* helpful as Veterans claim reasonable responsibility for some decisions, those over which they had some control, and begin to grieve what they cannot change. Veterans struggling with MI may say, "Let me have my pain. There is no value in easy/cheap forgiveness." The grief process is part of the restoration; however, wallowing in pain and engaging in self-punishment serves no real purpose. There are better avenues to healing.

A cohesive group becomes concerned when someone misses the group, and they may check on one another. Veterans in cohesive groups are surprised to discover that they connect with those of different age groups, cultures, races, wars, politics, ethnic backgrounds, ranks, military service experience, and gender, and they come to see ways they are "the same" in their moral pain and MI. Cohesiveness is a matter of commitment and investment in one another's well-being, where they put aside their differences with empathy and compassion.

Example of a Cohesive Group

A virtual moral group had been meeting together for about eight weeks, and the members varied widely by age, race, military background, gender, and life experience:

- *One member was a male E6 (staff sergeant) who was angry and wanted revenge on those who had betrayed him. He had been blamed for the wrongdoing of others, and he was passed over for promotion.*
- *The next member was an educated black female NCO who had been sexually assaulted. When she reported it to her female commander, the woman asked, "What did you do to encourage him?" She was reassigned and her colleagues retaliated against her.*

- *The other woman in the group was a white female Army Veteran who lived marginally and had a rough life growing up on a pig farm. She had a long career as a medic, but her career ended when she reported wrongdoing by a powerful male on base. She had done the right thing but paid for it with her reputation as rumors flew. She had gone through enough and quietly retired and retreated. She went to work on the family farm and struggled with the betrayal by the Army she had served so well.*
- *The last member was a soft-spoken older Muslim gentleman, Mr. M., who was seeking forgiveness in his heart for those who racially attacked him. He was quiet in the group and kind to the other members. He did not like himself for what was in his heart and wanted to be less angry.*

The group members accepted one another and did not judge or compare. After several sessions, each member told his or her story and noted ways that healing was taking place. Each listener weighed in with affirmation at hearing the stories of others.

The female medic who had been betrayed was quiet in the group, and when she spoke, she did not mince words. She was direct and to the point in her communication. We sometimes wondered what she would say next, but the other group members were protective and kind toward her. They saw she had a caring heart, and she voiced empathy for other group members in her unique way.

After each person shared, Mr. M. nodded and said, kindly, "I am sorry that happened to you. You did not deserve it and it was wrong. Tonight, I will pray for you. I will pray for each of you that you might find peace." The members were surprised and touched by his compassion for them.

The other man said, "You are amazing. I am struggling with my anger and wanting to get even, and you want to forgive those who hurt you! I would like to be more like you!"

The black female NCO tearfully shared about her betrayal through sexual assault and the command's disregard. There was total silence until the male E6 said, with heat in his voice, "I would have been proud to have you serve with me. I wish I had been there – I would like to jump his as#. I'm so sorry that happened to you, and justice was not served."

Then the medic looked at her colleague and said, matter-of-factly, with a dry chuckle, "We should stop issuing guns to women in the service." We didn't know where she was going with this. She continued, with a smile, "We should issue them knives like this during basic training." She showed them a picture of her hog knife, used to castrate hogs. "You give each of them a knife and show them how to use it, so they can use it on anyone who bothers them, just like I use it on the hogs. That'll stop them. I wish I could take care of them for you."

Yes, there was a moment of somewhat shocked silence, then laughter, and the other woman leaned in and smiled. "I am grateful for your words," she said. "I would be glad to have you by my side in the face of any threat!"

Veterans' protective responses to one another come in many forms: mother bear, fatherly empathy, or hog knife bearer. Even though her words were packaged differently and lacked eloquence, her unfiltered empathy and compassion were felt by all group members; her spontaneous and passionate version of imagined justice hit home.

Veterans establish connections with one another through their common values, training, and military experiences. We need to provide a sanctuary for healing, where they feel understood and safe to share their stories of pain and find hope. Persons with sound moral values, a strong sense of personal responsibility, or high positive expectations for the military are troubled by things that violate those values. And those who entered the military with values of youthful idealism and desire to help/serve are deeply wounded by a military (and the public) that has let them down.

Confessing genuine wrongdoing and guilt-worthy actions in the presence of compassionate, forgiving others can propel Veterans into self-forgiveness, with restitution and making amends. Confessing the deep pain of betrayal and injustice brings release. The compassion and empathy from like-minded others are validating and restorative. As Smigelsky et al. (2022) conclude, the vulnerability of group members, coupled with the acceptance of other members, counteracts the shame individuals bring to the group.

Distinct Models of Healing

Farnsworth et al. (2014) point out that interventions may be beneficial when they arouse positive emotions such as compassion, elevation, and pride; this counteracts or balances out moral emotions of guilt, shame, and blame. Compassion is a reaction to suffering that triggers a desire to help. Directing compassion at oneself has been described as "being touched by and open to one's own suffering, without avoidance or disconnect" (Farnsworth et al., p. 257).

Treatments vary, with some considered evidence-based from randomized clinical trials; some with pre-post data and manuals; and some less replicable due to a less consistent format. There are different views about capturing changes in MI, and measurements vary from program to program. Treatments also differ by modality (group or individual), length (number of sessions), degree of cross-discipline collaboration, individual's status (active duty or Veteran), type of MI (combat and non-combat; participant, witness, or survivor), and targeted change (different conceptual views of MI).

Interventions for MI may include one or more of the following: developing compassion (through forgiveness and self-acceptance), engaging in meaning-making (often through telling one's own story), reframing or challenging a Veteran's thinking or assignment of responsibility, developing a new narrative (with forgiveness, empathy, and acceptance), and "normalizing" the Veteran's response to what he or she experienced. A Veteran's assigned blame and presumed responsibility may overlook the context or details that affected the outcome. It is freeing to lighten the load of guilt and blame through self-compassion in the presence of a caring "other."

Some treatments are MI-dedicated versions of existing therapies, such as cognitive behavioral therapies, cognitive processing therapy (CPT, Resick & Schnicke, 1992, 2016), prolonged exposure (PE) therapy (Foa et al., 1991, 2019), or acceptance and commitment therapy (Hayes et al., 2012). Borges et al. (2020) note that some Veterans report that MI is not sufficiently identified nor discussed during therapies for PTSD such as CPT or PE, that the therapeutic relationship is key to facilitating or inhibiting the discussion of MI, that PE and CPT may have a limited impact on MI symptoms, and lastly, that some Veterans struggle to cope with MI after completing those treatments. Jones et al. (2022) note the need for more evidence-supported interventions uniquely designed for MI that include a multidisciplinary psycho-social-spiritual approach.

While not necessarily multidisciplinary, some therapies were designed specifically with MI in mind. These include building spiritual strength (Harris et al., 2011; Usset et al., 2021), adaptive disclosure (Gray et al., 2012; Gray et al., 2021), and impact of killing (Burkman et al., 2021; Maguen et al., 2017). Currier et al. (2021) dedicate several chapters to several existing therapies and interventions for MI in their primer for clinicians. Jones et al. (2022) summarize many of these treatment approaches and their benefits.

Chaplain-specific interventions tend to be less structured and formalized; however, Drescher et al. (2018) note routine chaplain interventions that help those with MI, including pastoral/therapeutic presence, therapeutic interventions, pastoral care, therapeutic exercises, and therapeutic process. Ames et al. (2021) provide a structured chaplain intervention for Veterans with moral injury and PTSD. Carey et al. (2016) describe categories of chaplain service characterized by the World Health Organization – including assessment, ministry support, counseling, education, and ritual and worship – and how each addresses MI.

In 2019, VA Integrative Mental Health (IMH) formed a Dynamic Diffusion Network (DDN) with 12 paired chaplains and MH providers at VA sites. Each team offered a different model of MI intervention or suicide prevention effort. The purpose of the DDN was to generate, measure, enhance, and disseminate quality MI care and suicide prevention activities (Smigelsky et al., 2020). No doubt countless other VAs have delved into MI work apart from those involved in the DDN; we appreciate their efforts on behalf of Veterans. As part of the DDN, the authors refined and trained other sites in AFT (Pernicano et al., 2022). The DDN and IMH worked closely with specific MI teams and programs: 1) the Philadelphia VA (Moral Engagement Group curriculum; Antal et al., 2022), with a strong emphasis on community responsibility and reconciliation; 2) the Muskogee, OK and Durham, NC VAs with continued refinements to their Reclaiming Experiences and Loss (REAL) MI curriculum (Smigelsky et al., 2022); and 3) the Portland, Oregon VA (Rebecca Morris, Jaimie Lusk, and Stephanie Rodriguez), with their unique version of acceptance and commitment therapy for MI). See also Cenkner et al. (2021) for a description of a pilot study of chaplain/psychology intervention at the Philadelphia VA. These treatment interventions are available through training for teams of chaplains and MH providers in VA settings.

In Part II of this book, we invite you to journey with us through acceptance and forgiveness, our model of healing MI. We will share painful yet inspiring Veteran stories and artwork that reveal how Veterans move from pain to restoration and will invite you, the reader, to participate personally in the exercises they complete. Part II of the book is rich with examples of "doing" that will guide you to understanding MI pain and recovery. After all, survival alone is never enough; it leaves one fragile and prevents growth. Recovery lets you thrive and, as your roots heal, then grow new fruit.

References

Ames, D., Erickson, Z., Geise, C., Tiwari, S., Sakhno, S., Sones, A. C., Tyrrell, C. G., Mackay, C. R. B., Steele, C. W., Van Hoof, T., Weinreich, H., & Koenig, H. G. (2021). Treatment of moral injury in US veterans with PTSD using a structured chaplain intervention. *Journal of Religion and Health, 60*, 3052–3060. https://doi.org/10.1007/s10943-021-01312-8

Antal, C. J., Yeomans, P. D., Denton-Borhaug, K., & Hutchinson, S. A. (2022). A communal intervention for military moral injury. *Journal of Health Care Chaplaincy, 28*(sup1), S79–S88. https://doi.org/10.1080/08854726.2022.2032981

Antal, C. J., Yeomans, P. D., East, R., Hickey, D. W., Kalkstein, S., Brown, K. M., & Kaminstein, D. S. (2023). Transforming veteran identity through community engagement: A chaplain–psychologist collaboration to address moral injury. *Journal of Humanistic Psychology, 63*(6), 801–826. https://doi.org/10.1177/0022167819844071

Barth, T. M., Lord, C. G., THakkar, V. J., & Brock, R. N. (2020). Effects of resilience strength training on constructs associated with moral injury among veterans. *Journal of Veteran Studies, 6*(2), 101–113. https://doi.org/10.21061/jvs.v6i2.199

Borges, L. M., Bahraini, N. H., Holliman, B. D., Gissen, M. R., Lawson, W. C., & Barnes, S. M. (2020). Veterans' perspectives on discussing moral injury in the context of evidence-based psychotherapies for PTSD and other VA treatment. *Journal of Clinical Psychology, 76*(3), 377–391. https://doi.org/10.1002/jclp.22887

Burkman, K., Maguen, S., & Purcell, N. (2021). Impact of killing: A treatment program for military veterans with moral injury. In J. M. Currier, K. D. Drescher, & J. Nieuwsma (Eds.), *Addressing moral injury in clinical practice* (pp. 203–221). American Psychological Association. https://doi.org/10.1037/0000204-012

Carey, L. B., Hodgson, T. J., Krikheli, L., Soh, R. Y., Armour, A., Singh, T. K., & Impiombato, C. G. (2016). Moral injury, spiritual care and the role of chaplains: An exploratory scoping review of literature and resources. *Journal of Religious Health, 55*, 1218–1245.https://doi.org/10.1007/s10943-016-0231-x

Cenkner, D. P., Yeomans, P. D., Antal, C. J., & Scott, J. C. (2021). A pilot study of a moral injury group intervention co-facilitated by a chaplain and psychologist. *Journal of Traumatic Stress, 34*(2), 367–374. https://doi.org/10.1002/jts.22642

Currier, J. M., Drescher, K. D., & Nieuwsma, J. (Eds.). (2021). *Addressing moral injury in clinical practice*. American Psychological Association. https://doi.org/10.1037/0000204-000

Drescher, K. D., Currier, J. M., Nieuwsma, J. A., McCormick, W., Carroll, T. D., Sims, B. M., & Cauterucio, C. (2018). A qualitative examination of VA chaplains' understandings and interventions related to moral injury in military veterans. *Journal of Religion and Health, 57*(6), 2444–2460. https://doi.org/10.1007/s10943-018-0682-3

Evans, W. R., Smigelsky, M. A., Frankfurt, S. B., Antal, C. J., Yeomans, P. D., Check, C., & Bhatt-Mackin, S. M. (2023). Emerging interventions for moral injury: Expanding pathways to moral healing. *Current Treatment Options in Psychiatry, 10*, 431–45. https://doi.org/10.1007/s40501-023-00303-8

Farnsworth, J. K., Drescher, K. D., Nieuwsma, J. A., Walser, R. B., & Currier, J. M. (2014). The role of moral emotions in military trauma: Implications for the study and treatment of moral injury. *Review of General Psychology, 18*(4), 249–262. https://doi.org/10.1037/gpr0000018

Foa, E., Hembree, E. A., Rothbaum, B. O., & Rauch, S. (2019). *Prolonged exposure therapy for PTSD: Emotional processing of traumatic experiences - therapist guide* (2nd ed.). Oxford University Press.

Foa, E. B., Rothbaum, B. O., Riggs, D. S., & Murdock, T. B. (1991). Treatment of posttraumatic stress disorder in rape victims: A comparison between cognitive-behavioral procedures and counseling. *Journal of Consulting and Clinical Psychology, 59*, 715–23.

Gray, M. J., Binion, K., Amaya, S., & Litz, B. T. (2021). Adaptive disclosure: A novel evidence-based treatment for moral injury. In J. M. Currier, K. D. Drescher, & J. Nieuwsma (Eds.), *Addressing moral injury in clinical practice* (pp. 183–201). American Psychological Association. https://doi.org/10.1037/0000204-011

Gray, M. J., Schorr, Y., Nash, W., Lebowitz, L., Amidon, A., Lansing, A., Gray, M., Schorr, Y., Nash, W., Lebowitz, L., Amidon, A., Lansing, A., Maglione, M., Lang, A. J., & Litz, B. T. (2012). Adaptive disclosure: An open trial of a novel exposure-based intervention for service members with combat-related psychological stress injuries. *Behavior Therapy, 43*(2), 407–415. https://doi.org/10.1016/j.beth.2011.09.001.

Harris, J. I., Erbes, C. R., Engdahl, B. E., Thuras, P., Murray-Swank, N., Grace, D., Ogden, H., Olson, R. H. A., Winskowski, A. M., Bacon, R., Malec, C., Campion, K., & Le, T. (2011). The effectiveness of a trauma focused spiritually integrated intervention for veterans exposed to trauma. *Journal of Clinical Psychology, 67*, 425–438. https://doi.org/10.1002/jclp.20777

Hayes, S. C., Strosahl, K. D., & Wilson, K. G. (2012). *Acceptance and commitment therapy: The process and practice of mindful change* (2nd ed.). Guilford Press..

Jones, K. A., Freijah, I., Carey, L., Carleton, R. N., Devenish-Meares, P., Dell, L., Rodrigues, S., Madden, K., Johnson, L., Hosseiny, F., & Phelps, A. J. (2022). Moral injury, chaplaincy and mental health provider approaches to treatment: A scoping review. *Journal of Religion and Health, 61*(2), 1051–1094. https://doi.org/10.1007/s10943-022-01534-4

Jones, K. R. S., Rauch, S. A. M., Smith, E. R., Sherrill, A. M., & Eftekhari, A. (2021). Moral injury, posttraumatic stress disorder, and prolonged exposure. In J. M. Currier, K. D. Drescher, & J. Nieuwsma (Eds.), *Addressing moral injury in clinical practice* (pp. 123–141). American Psychological Association. https://doi.org/10.1037/0000204-008

Maguen, S., Burkman, K., Madden, E., Dinh, J., Bosch, J., Keyser, J., Schmitz, M., & Neylan, T. (2017). Impact of killing in war: A randomized, controlled pilot trial. *Journal of Clinical Psychology, 73*, 10. https://doi.org/10.1002/jclp.22471

Norman, S. (2022). Trauma-informed guilt reduction therapy: Overview of the treatment and research. *Current Treatment Options in Psychiatry, 9*(3), 115–125. https://doi.org/10.1007/s40501-022-00261-7

Pearce, M., Haynes, K., Rivera, N. R., & Koenig, H. G. (2018). Spiritually integrated cognitive processing therapy: A new treatment for post-traumatic stress disorder that targets moral injury. *Global Advances in Health and Medicine, 7*, 1–7. https://doi.org/10.1177/2164956118759939

Pernicano, P., & Haynes, K. (2023). *Acceptance & forgiveness therapy: From brokenness to restoration* [Unpublished handbook] (5th ed.). South Texas Veterans Health Care System.

Pernicano, P. U., Wortmann, J., & Haynes, K. (2022). Acceptance and forgiveness therapy for veterans with moral injury: Spiritual and psychological collaboration in group treatment. *Journal of Health Care Chaplaincy, 28*(sup1), S57–S78. https://doi.org/10.1080/08854726.2022.2032982

Prochaska, J. O., & DiClemente, C. C. (1982). Transtheoretical therapy: Toward a more integrative model of change. *Psychotherapy: Theory, Research & Practice, 19*(3), 276–288. https://doi.org/10.1037/h0088437

Pyne, J. M., Sullivan, S., Abraham, T. H., Rabalais, A., Jaques, M., & Griffin, B. (2021). Mental health clinician community clergy collaboration to address moral injury symptoms: A feasibility study. *Journal of Religion and Health, 25*(1), 1–19. https://doi.org/10.1007/s10943-021-01257-y

Resick, P. A., Monson, C. M., & Chard, K. M. (2016). *Cognitive processing therapy for PTSD: A comprehensive manual.* Guilford Press.

Resick, P. A., & Schnicke, M. K. (1992). Cognitive processing therapy for sexual assault victims. *Journal of Consulting and Clinical Psychology, 60*(5), 748–756. https://doi.org/10.1037/0022-006X.60.5.748

Smigelsky, M. A., Malott, J., Parker, R., Check, C., Rappaport, B., & Ward, S. (2022). Let's get "REAL": A collaborative group therapy for moral injury. *Journal of Health Care Chaplaincy, 28*(sup1), S42–S56. https://doi.org/10.1080/08854726.2022.2032978

Smigelsky, M. A., Nieuwsma, J. A., Meador, K., Vega, R. J., Henderson, B., & Jackson, G. L. (2020). Dynamic diffusion network: Advancing moral injury care and suicide prevention using an innovative model. *Healthcare, 8*(3), 100440. https://doi.org/10.1016/j.hjdsi.2020.100440

Smigelsky, M. A., Trimm, V., Meador, K. G., Jackson, G. L., Wortmann, J. H., & Nieuwsma, J. A. (2022). Core components of moral injury groups co-facilitated by mental health providers and chaplains. *Spirituality in Clinical Practice, 9*(3), 159–174. https://doi.org/10.1037/scp0000297

Starnino, V. R., Sullivan, W. P., Angel, C. T., & Davis, L. W. (2019). Moral injury, coherence, and spiritual repair. *Mental Health, Religion & Culture, 22*(1), 99–114. https://doi.org/10.1080/13674676.2019.1589439

Usset, T. J., Butler, M., & Harris, J. I. (2021). Building spiritual strength: A group treatment for posttraumatic stress disorder, moral injury, and spiritual distress. In J. M. Currier, K. D. Drescher, & J. Nieuwsma (Eds.), *Addressing moral injury in clinical practice* (pp. 223–241). American Psychological Association. https://doi.org/10.1037/0000204-013

Wachen, J. S., Evans, W. R., Jacoby, V. M., & Blankenship, A. E. (2021). Cognitive processing therapy for moral injury. In J. M. Currier, K. D. Drescher, & J. Nieuwsma (Eds.), *Addressing moral injury in clinical practice* (pp. 143–161). American Psychological Association. https://doi.org/10.1037/0000204-009

Walser, R. D., & Wharton, E. (2021). Acceptance and commitment therapy: Using mindfulness and values in the treatment of moral injury. In J. M. Currier, K. D. Drescher, & J. Nieuwsma (Eds.), *Addressing moral injury in clinical practice* (pp. 163–181). American Psychological Association. https://doi.org/10.1037/0000204-010

Yalom, I. D. (1970). *The theory and practice of group psychotherapy.* Basic Books.

PART II

The Healing Process of Compassion, Acceptance, and Forgiveness

Chapter 7

Beginning the Journey of Acceptance and Forgiveness

Models for healing moral injury (MI) are each based on the targeted population and the conceptual approach. The authors developed acceptance and forgiveness therapy (AFT) as a spiritual (meaning-making), interpersonal, and psychological treatment process for MI (Pernicano et al., 2022; Pernicano & Haynes, 2023). This book is not intended as a treatment process or therapy; what follows might be considered a form of self-help. Yet this book is not only about AFT. It is also about raising awareness and helping Veterans *hold the pain they carry* in new ways, with compassion, acceptance, and forgiveness, through reconnection with self, others, values, and spirituality. To heal from MI, Veterans begin to accept the past that cannot be changed and recognize the whole of who they are rather than being defined by the most painful moments of their lives.

Through acceptance and forgiveness, Veterans form new connections and discover something precious within them, like gold, that emerges as they make sense of the pain and suffering and begin to develop a new life story.

Even though there is no one conceptual view of MI, here are a few premises:

♦ Moral pain arises in the face of something that violates core values (military, spiritual, and personal) and deeply held beliefs about what is morally right and just.
♦ Moral pain is not transient; it is deep and earthquake-like shattering, metaphorically speaking.
♦ A conflict, or dissonance, develops in the Veteran's mind between what occurred and what the Veteran thinks should or could have happened.
♦ The person believes that wrongdoing occurred even though his or her perception may be personally biased, filtered, or incomplete.
♦ Whether MI develops depends on whether the conflict gets resolved. Some Veterans resolve moral pain through 12-step programs, spiritual practices, community service, or mindful acceptance. As the wound heals, it leaves a scar, a reminder of the previous injury.
♦ Veterans with MI may feel broken, damaged, or changed by what happened.

DOI: 10.4324/9781003494263-10

- ◆ Veterans with MI may believe that they or others lack worth, and are unforgivable, with no pathway to redemption and hope.
- ◆ There are different types of moral pain. For example, perceived "wrongdoing" may result in the belief of being unforgivable; the aftermath of combat may result in viewing the world as a horrible place; and betrayal by those you thought you could trust may result in later mistrust of others.
- ◆ MI leaves one *stuck* and perhaps inflexible concerning daily living. Someone might feel stuck emotionally (mood), physically (sleep and energy), cognitively (negative thinking), interpersonally (connections with others), or spiritually (lost hope, purpose, or meaning).
- ◆ MI services and interventions target different types of "stuck-ness" and aspects/types of MI.
- ◆ Healing from MI involves understanding the impact, grieving losses, restoring connections, confessing one's pain, and, eventually, accepting, forgiving, and making new meaning out of the past.
- ◆ Compassion (suffering with oneself or others) leads to empathy and contributes to forgiveness. Compassion becomes possible when we realize and accept human imperfection, i.e., fallibility with worth and value. Both truths contribute to healing.
- ◆ Healing from MI may involve atonement, restitution, or the pursuit of justice. These help restore moral integrity for the individual and the community. Atonement can create a path forward from the past that cannot be changed.
- ◆ Healing may result in post-traumatic growth or a restored sense of self as worthy and viewing connections with others as possible.
- ◆ Being more at peace with self, others, and the world motivates Veterans toward compassion, gratitude, and the desire to "do good" by helping others.
- ◆ Healing is a process, and those pursuing it are a work in progress.
- ◆ Healing from MI is done through education, experiential learning, establishing trust, group or individual processing, self-disclosure, and application through practice.

As noted in Chapter 3, Pernicano began writing and using therapeutic stories in trauma-informed treatment with adults and children in 1978 and became interested in Milton Erickson's methods of metaphor, storytelling, seeding possibility, reframing, and shifting perception. As Veterans identify with story themes and discover commonalities through self-disclosure, they realize they are not alone in their pain.

Veteran stories, poetry, and artwork reveal a journey from pain to hope and healing that includes: 1) remembering and grieving the injury (feeling and naming the pain and expressing lament), 2) clarifying guilt versus grief (appraising the responsibility for what happened and considering the context), and 3) experiencing hope and healing (forgiving self/others through acceptance, compassion, acknowledgment of "time served," and discovering a path forward).

Part II walks the reader through the phases of the AFT healing process. The first stories are about becoming stuck and the burdens of carrying moral pain. At this stage, Veterans might access education about MI or go through a four-week educational program (Pernicano & Haynes, 2024). Veterans with MI put their lives on hold after the military because their views of themselves, others, and the military have changed. Veterans move from pre-contemplation to contemplation as they discuss how they are stuck and burdened; they consider the benefits of seeking help for MI.

The next healing phase is about naming and processing the pain of MI. We tend to bury, lock up, or avoid talking about shame, guilt, and associated grief. We may associate what happened with our worth and value; at some level, the memory becomes *who I am*, with shame and regret. For others, the memory is *not me* or *never again*. MI is an invisible wound, deep and hard to face. Those with MI wonder what others will think about them and fear judgment. Many enter treatment when the wound is raw, painful, or festering. The stories and drawings built into AFT help Veterans ease into naming the pain during early recovery.

The next phase of healing is that of processing guilt and evaluating responsibility. In this phase, Veterans build cohesiveness with others who suffer with them. They begin to see their situation through a broader lens. As Veterans process guilt and responsibility, they confess and begin to choose healthier ways of dealing with guilt and pain; this prepares Veterans to forgive themselves or others. The forgiveness process includes a ritual of compassion and release, which moves them toward restoration and growth.

The final phase is *restoring the whole*; Veterans find hope and new meaning through shared stories and acceptance. Metaphors and stories of moving out of brokenness remind us that healing is about becoming whole again, by putting our pieces back together. Retired Air Force Colonel Lisa Carrington Firmin pursued her whole through writing poetry (2023), and she has told the stories of Veterans who suffered military sexual trauma (MST) in *Stories from the Front: Pain, Betrayal, and Resilience on the MST Battlefield* (2022). Healing may involve creating meaning out of suffering (Frankl, 2006), forgiving oneself and others (Worthington, 2006; Worthington & Griffin, 2013), and restoring humanity (Desmond & Mpho Tutu, 2014).

Healing from MI is done within oneself and in relationships with others. Our story does not end when we have healed our brokenness and put our pieces back together. The journey continues, and we are part of a greater whole. In *No Man Is an Island* (1955), contemplative monk Thomas Merton indicates that love can be kept only by giving it away. He reflects that loving ourselves is not about what we get but rather about what we can give to others. As Veterans begin to see themselves as part of a larger creation or purpose, they discover something greater than themselves and reconnect to self, others, faith, and community. There is a path forward as they make meaning of their lives through compassion and good intentions.

Should you think, "I'm not ready to talk about what happened in the military," we understand. Veterans may fear they can't handle it or will be triggered emotionally. You might think about the stages of change described in Chapter 6. Thinking about change is part of change. Are you OK where you are? Are you willing to try something new? Would you be OK taking one step in a new direction? You may continue in the contemplation stage while you weigh the pros and cons of staying where you are. Certainly, you are not alone in your misgivings and concerns. If you have MI and are willing to try something new, be sure you have someone to encourage you on this journey. Dealing with MI is a process, and everyone with MI needs a starting point.

> *A nine-year-old boy once spent all summer trying to jump off the high dive at the neighborhood pool. His goal was to accomplish this before he turned ten. So far, each time he climbed the ladder and stepped out on the board, his courage spurted out like a lit match in the wind. His mother would give him a high-five, and he would look down on the water from the end of the board and count to three. Then he would call out, "Mom, I can't do it," and climb back off the high-dive.*
>
> *One day at the pool he started to cry. "Mom, I really want to jump off the high dive. I'm almost ten, and I feel like a failure. But I'm so afraid. I shake. I feel my heart pounding. I think I'm going to throw up. I don't know what to do."*
>
> *His mother hugged him and said, "It's OK to be afraid. We're all afraid sometimes. The solution is to push through it until the fear goes away. You can carry your fear with you and jump. Go out on the board, be afraid, and jump."*
>
> *He looked at her in astonishment. "Mom, I was waiting for the fear to go away. I thought I had to conquer my fear before I jumped."*
>
> *"Nope," she said. "Get to the end of the board, be afraid, and jump."*
>
> *This time he climbed up, went to the end of the board, looked over for the high-five, quivered and shook, and jumped.*
>
> *"I did it!" he exclaimed as he surfaced. He had pushed into and through his fear. His fear of the high dive eventually lessened, and he had learned something important. Fear chases you, walks with you, pounds in your heart, sits in your gut, and even talks to you in your head until you freeze and stop in your tracks. You can stare back at it, square in the face. Be afraid and jump.*

Metaphorically speaking, stories allow us to get our feet wet before plunging into the deep end, but at some point, we can jump into deeper waters. There may be deep waters for you as you read about Veteran MI, but you will be relieved and perhaps better for taking the plunge, and we will cheer you on and celebrate your courage.

As we begin Part II, we invite you to apply the concepts to your life. We all know what it means to be betrayed or to feel unresolved guilt or painful responsibility. Readers can participate through the stories and exercises or share them with others. Perhaps readers will find a gold nugget in these pages or think about someone you know who is struggling with moral pain. Welcome to the community of fallible, imperfect, and yet valuable human beings (Worthington & Griffin, 2013). We have been on our journey since 2018, and there is much to learn. Go at a pace that you can tolerate and be in a place of compassion for yourself. Some of the material could potentially arouse moral pain (shock, disgust, sadness, horror, and grief), so take a break if you are stirred or triggered. These are real stories of Veteran pain. If you find yourself in a place of hurt and darkness, care for yourself and move toward the light.

Phases of Acceptance and Forgiveness
Early Phase: Becoming Stuck

Veteran

I'm stuck, Doc. I retired from the military two years ago, and nothing is the same. I can't sleep. In my dreams, I see people I killed. They had family and kids, like I do. I saw some pretty terrible things. I did some terrible things. And I got so good at it that I liked it. I was mad as hell. They (the military) liked who I became and turned me into a fighting monster. That isn't who I was before the military. Now I wonder who I am. I yell at my wife and kids, and I don't hang out with my friends. I'm not the monster; or am I? Who am I?

Therapist

Do you want to talk about it?

Veteran

I'm not ready, Doc. Maybe later. Let's just work on my sleep and my depression.

Many Veterans feel stuck emotionally when deciding whether to pursue healing. Pernicano (2012) described being caught by an ocean riptide. The strong current is hidden and pulls the swimmer slowly out to sea without the person realizing the strength of its pull. If you fight it, it wears you out, and you might drown. If you freeze and float, it pulls you out to sea, and you might drown. If you outsmart it, you swim or move sideways in the water until you are out of its grip. Freeze, fight, and flight do the same thing; they exhaust or isolate you from humanity until you lose your bearings and stop trying.

The quicksand of MI is the freeze of survival, trying to stay afloat, without a path forward. Quicksand is very watery sand that looks like regular sand but is not. It is a mix of sand and water that gives way when you step on it. Quicksand has strong suction and pulls you under a little at a time. If you struggle or fight against it, it sucks you down, and you can't release yourself. When you want to escape quicksand, stop fighting it and float on your back as if treading water. You can only float until your energy and hope give out, or until you find a means out. Veterans living with moral pain and MI are stuck in the pain. *Staying in pre-contemplation or contemplation is a little like floating in quicksand.*

Floating in Quicksand: A Story of Feeling Stuck

(Pernicano, 2020)

There once was a man floating in quicksand, out in the middle of nowhere, keeping his head above water and trying to survive. He had not seen the quicksand in time to stop his fall. He regretted falling in, wishing he could retrace his steps and avoid this dilemma. He said to himself, "It's my fault. I wasn't paying close enough attention." But what was done was done; now, he was resigned to staying afloat as best he could. He knew not to struggle or panic because that might pull him under. Perhaps help would come.

No one had passed by since he fell in, and he was starting to lose hope. He feared he would get sucked under when his strength gave out.

Then came a voice, "Hey, there, what's going on down there?" Someone had finally come upon him!

The man replied in an annoyed voice, "Isn't it obvious?! I'm floating in quicksand, treading water, keeping myself alive! Might you give me a hand?"

The stranger pondered as he viewed the situation. "Yes, I can give you a hand. Or you can carefully turn yourself around and use the rope ladder behind you."

Hmmm. He had not noticed that solution. He was probably not the first to face the quicksand dilemma if a rope ladder was directly behind him.

Life is a little like that; something unexpected happens and you find yourself stuck. You might be frozen in fear or unable to move. You can survive by floating in quicksand, but if you are ready to move in a new direction, you might carefully turn around to find a whole new point of view.

Veterans may feel stuck for a long time before seeking help because of what they tell themselves when they are in the contemplation stage, such as:

♦ It's not that bad – it could be worse (it is that bad, and you don't have to wait for it to get worse because by then you might get fired from a job, lose your marriage, or even consider ending your life).

♦ I can do it myself (but if you could, by now you would have).

♦ It is weak to ask for help (actually, this is military lore and not true. It takes strength to admit imperfection and ask for help).

♦ It will go away on its own in time (probably not).

♦ I don't deserve to get better (everyone deserves a path to healing).

♦ I'm afraid of what will be left if I let this go (you have carried it for so long!).

♦ I might fall apart or get worse if I talk about this (and you might feel relieved and get better. The only way to heal pain is to move through it).

Many things get in the way of healing, such as avoidance, a busy schedule, "what-if" thinking, or ambivalence. It is important to stop saying, "I can't." Eventually, we weigh the risks and possible benefits of resolving MI versus staying the same. If you are stuck in MI, you might ask yourself if what you are doing is helping or resolving the pain of MI. Hanging out at the Veterans of Foreign Wars (VFW) and drinking with a group of bitter, angry Veterans are not likely to heal your pain, nor is spending long nights alone in your room away from family and friends. We encourage you to weigh your options and plan to live your best self, whatever that entails.

Others may see the Veteran's MI before the Veteran does, and they might point out changes in the Veteran's moods, attitudes, or behaviors. During pre-contemplation, a Veteran may not notice changes in himself/herself. He or she might think others should change, as in, "Leave me alone," "Quit nagging me," and "My way or the highway." Veterans may eventually seek help out of loneliness, emotional pain, loss of loved ones, or recognition that attempts to feel better are not working, such as risk-taking, denial, substance abuse, or gambling.

Once someone realizes there is a problem, he or she enters *contemplation*, a phase where the person admits to a problem, and feels stuck, but is not ready to do anything about it yet, like my son on the high dive. We fear the risk of vulnerability and doubt that relief or healing is possible.

We all feel stuck at one point or another, with or without MI. Your quicksand is unique to you; it might be a difficult relationship, a painful life change, or a past regret. We encourage the reader to take a few minutes to complete the following worksheet about being stuck. Floating in quicksand is like trying to paddle a river without a paddle. Either way, if you don't find a solution, you might drown. Consider how you might be stuck and what you have already tried to feel better. The following worksheet may be helpful for those in pre-contemplation or contemplation.

Quicksand Worksheet
(Pernicano, 2019)

Identify the areas where you became stuck after the moral injury and give an example.

Avoidance

I avoid thinking and talking about my moral injury. I avoid reminders of my moral injury.

_____

Disconnecting from Others

I don't fit in anymore. I distance myself from others. I do not let others get close to me.

_____

Dealing with Emotions

I keep my feelings to myself. I pretend to be happy, but I'm not. I do not know how to express my feelings. I sometimes think that feelings are a sign of weakness.

_____

Loss of Interest

I stopped doing things I used to enjoy. I have become a loner.

_____

Substance Abuse or Misuse

After my moral injury, I increased the use of drugs or alcohol to forget, cope, or sleep.

_____

Spiritual/Faith

I lost my faith or stopped/changed worship practices. I feel punished or betrayed by a higher power. I have lost meaning and purpose in life.

_____

Self-Esteem

I lost respect for myself, or I think less of myself. I no longer trust myself to do "good" or "right."

_____

Anger and Blame

I am angry and lack patience. I resent what happened and find myself quick to blame myself or others.

_____

Trust

I lost faith in others and no longer trust people to do "good" or "right."

_____

Guilt

I blame myself for what happened and feel guilty for my actions.

_____

Carrying Burdens from the Past

When you become stuck, you have fewer resources for coping, and your quality of life may suffer. Chronic stress can be damaging to health and emotional well-being, and MI is a form of chronic stress. Metaphorically speaking, it is like trying to hike with a rucksack full of heavy rocks. Many Veterans with MI feel burdened and weighed down. They find themselves moving very slowly when they would prefer to run. Feeling burdened increases stress and may trigger the immune system into a survival response or a chronic stress reaction.

Douglas Bremner (2005) writes about the effects of chronic stress on the brain and points out that the body and mind can become overwhelmed and damaged when stress exceeds the recommended max. At the point of "overwhelm" things break down and we may become immune compromised or develop health conditions such as insomnia, depression, anxiety, chronic pain, heart disease, high blood pressure, diabetes, and gastric upset, among others. Being burdened is exhausting, and when we feel stuck and burdened, we may ruminate more about the past and worry about the future. While feeling burdened Veterans also start to feel helpless, as if they have no options for recovery. They think a lot about what they used to be able to do and become angry at the changes in themselves. They feel stuck and burdened by MI. The stages of change model (Prochaska & DiClemente, 1983) reflects that Veterans have choices to make, that change is possible, and that there are risks and benefits to seeking help. Thinking about change is the first step in the change process.

We invite you to read Jack's story below and consider how your burdens affect your quality of life. What is most important in the story is that Jack has a choice and he can decide to lighten his load. He steps out of contemplation into action.

The Burden Bag

Modified Veteran Version from Pernicano (2010)
Used and modified with permission of Jason Aronson.

Once upon a time, a rabbit named Jack moved as slowly as a turtle. He could not hop or run like the other rabbits. He had a huge backpack (rucksack) on his back that weighed him down. It hung nearly to the ground as if it was full of rocks.

A friend who observed Jack's struggle approached him. "Jack, a rabbit is not meant to move as slowly as a turtle. Why are you carrying that heavy backpack? Why don't you take it off?

Jack signed and replied, "It's my burden bag. I never take it off."

The friend asked, "Not to sleep? Not to eat? Not to play?"

Jack replied in a grumpy voice, "I told you, I NEVER take it off."

His friend was curious. "I've never seen a burden bag. What types of burdens do you carry around?"

Jack said, "I don't remember everything in it, because I have been collecting burdens for a very long time. And some of them bother me so much I don't want to look at them too closely."

At his friend's request, he opened the backpack and revealed some of what was within the backpack.

The burdens were stuffed into Ziploc bags and labeled such things as, "Stupid mistakes," "Total failures," "Family problems," "Imperfections," "Betrayals," and "Rejections." The two largest, heaviest burdens were labeled "Unforgivable" and "Unspeakable." They were heavy, like rocks, each bag stuffed full.

His friend remarked that it was no wonder Jack moved as slowly as a turtle. They walked together until they found themselves at the shore of a beautiful lake. A sign by the lake said, "No fishing."

"What is this place?" asked Jack.

His friend replied, "This is a bottomless lake. You can throw burdens in the lake, to lighten your load. You watch them sink and you can't fish them back out." His friend added, "Some people call it Forgiveness Lake. It doesn't matter what you call it. It is open to everyone."

Jack wasn't easily convinced. He did not know what would happen if he emptied his backpack or lightened his load. Jack said, "These memories are important. I can't throw them away like they don't matter."

"Of course, they matter!" said his friend. "And you aren't throwing away the memories—just the weight and pain of them so that you can lighten your load and move forward."

Jack wasn't sure he wanted to handle the unforgivable, unspeakable ones. He didn't know if he deserved to be free of them.

His friend said, "You don't have to deserve it. The lake is here, and it is your choice."

At that moment, Jack realized he had a choice – to remain weighed down by his burdens or to release them. With some fear and trepidation, Jack flung the first burden in a high arc out over the lake. As it hit the lake's clear surface, small circles spread around it, and the burden sank below the surface. Jack felt an unexpected surge of relief. One by one, he threw burdens into the lake. There were a few he was not ready to part with, but the load was much lighter.

When Jack was done, at least for the time being, he was exhausted, because as you know, it is hard work to let go of burdens. He asked, "But what do I do when tempted to collect new burdens?

His friend answered, "That is bound to happen, because, after all, you are 'only rabbit'. You might want to try collecting blessings. Blessings are things like carrots, lettuce, good memories, laughter, and playing with other rabbits. Fill the backpack with blessings, and every day, count your blessings. That will leave less room for burdens. And you can always come back to the lake."

Jack understood he was not meant to move as slowly as a turtle. He was now a work in progress and lightening his load was the first step. Perhaps you, too, will realize who you are meant to be and find a way to lighten your load.

Burdens come in many shapes and sizes. In the case of MI, the heaviest burdens tend to be ones for which the Veteran believes there is no path forward. Guilt is a heavy burden – what you think you "should," "could," or "would" have done to change the circumstances and outcome. Rage, bitterness, or thoughts of revenge poison the Veteran and destroy from the inside out. The Veteran suffers while the object of the suffering may be long gone. The burden of regret over "immoral" military action with heavy casualties or consequences can weary and sicken. The grief of a broken heart brings an endless ache, and failure in anyone's eyes can take them down the pathway of hopelessness.

We all carry burdens from the past, some of which weigh us down and prevent us from living our lives more fully in the present, and it helps release or turn over past burdens. Radical acceptance releases "if-only" thinking and accepts what cannot be changed. It considers the past in context. We encourage you to consider the burdens you carry from MI and to complete the Burden Bag Worksheet (Pernicano & Haynes, 2023). Identify which burdens you want to release to lighten your load (give an example) and pursue a "new normal." Don't worry yet about how you might do that. Naming burdens is a step in the change process.

Burden Bag Worksheet

What Burdens Do You Carry Related to MI?

♦ **"Stupid Mistakes"/Regrets**

_____

♦ **Rejection/Hurts**

_____

♦ **Family Problems**

_____

♦ **Imperfections (Not "Good Enough")**

_____

♦ **Guilt (Healthy or Unhealthy)**

_____

♦ **Loss**

_____

♦ **Grudges/Blame/Hate**

_____

♦ **"Unforgivable"**

_____

♦ **Betrayals**

_____

♦ **Others**

_____

The content in the chapters that follow might help you lighten your load. If you are a loved one or community support, you will want to understand the nature of moral pain and injury. MI is not something you just get over. The healing process is neither helplessness nor hopelessness. Healing from MI is not letting someone off the hook; it is the Veteran finding ways to pull the hook out of himself or herself. The butterfly struggles to emerge whole from the cocoon.

References

Bremner, J. D. (2002). *Does stress damage the brain? Understanding trauma-related disorders from a mind-body perspective.* W. W. Norton & Co.

Carrington Firmin, L. (2022). *Stories from the front: Pain, betrayal, and resilience on the MST battlefield.* Blue Ear Books.

Carrington Firmin, L. (2023). *Latina warrior.* Blue Ear Books.

Frankl, V. (2006). *Man's search for meaning.* Beacon Press.

Merton, T. (1955). *No man is an island.* WordPress.

Pernicano, P. (2010). The burden bag. In *Family-focused trauma intervention: Metaphor and play with victims of abuse and neglect* (pp. 87–9). Jason Aronson.

Pernicano, P. (2012). The cracked glass bowl. In *Outsmarting the riptide of domestic violence: Metaphor and mindfulness for change* (pp. 141–44). Jason Aronson.

Pernicano, P. (2014, 2021). *Using trauma-focused therapy stories: Interventions for therapists, children, and their caregivers.* Routledge/Taylor & Francis.

Pernicano, P. (2019). *Using stories, art, and play in trauma-informed treatment: Case examples and applications across the lifespan.* Routledge/Taylor & Francis.

Pernicano, P. (2020). Floating in quicksand [Unpublished story]. In P. Pernicano & K. Haynes (Eds.), *Introduction to acceptance and forgiveness therapy (Facilitator & Program Handbooks)* (2nd ed.). VA South Central Mental Illness Research, Education and Clinical Center (MIRECC). https://www.mirecc.va.gov/visn16/moral-injury-psychoeducation-group.asp

Pernicano, P., & Haynes, K. (2023). *Acceptance & forgiveness therapy: From brokenness to restoration* [Unpublished handbook] (5th ed.). South Texas Veterans Health Care System.

Pernicano, P., & Haynes, K. (2024). *Introduction to acceptance and forgiveness therapy (Facilitator & Program Handbooks)* (2nd ed.). VA South Central Mental Illness Research, Education and Clinical Center (MIRECC). https://www.mirecc.va.gov/visn16/moral-injury-psychoeducation-group.asp

Pernicano, P., Wortmann, J., & Haynes, K. (2022). Acceptance and forgiveness therapy for veterans with moral injury: Spiritual and psychological collaboration in group treatment. *Journal of Health Care Chaplaincy, 28*(Sup1), S57–S78. https://doi.org/10.1080/08854726.2022.2032982

Prochaska, J. O., & DiClemente, C. C. (1983). Stages and processes of self-change of smoking: Toward an integrative model of change. *Journal of Consulting and Clinical Psychology, 51*(3), 390–395. https://doi.org/10.1037/0022-006X.51.3.390

Tutu, D., & Tutu, M. (2015). *The book of forgiving: The fourfold path for healing ourselves and the world.* D. Abrams (Ed.). HarperCollins.

Worthington, E. L., Jr. (2013). *Moving forward: Six steps to forgiving yourself and breaking free from the past*. WaterBrook Multnomah.

Worthington, E. L., Jr., & Griffin, B. J. (n.d.). *Moving forward: Six steps to forgiving yourself and breaking free from the past* [Online workbook] (2nd ed.). Virginia Commonwealth University. https://forgiveself.com/workbooks/20150903%20 Self-Forgiveness%20Intervention%20Workbook.pdf

Chapter 8

Processing the Impact of Moral Injury

The impact of a potentially morally injurious event (PMIE) begins with triggered moral pain; the way through the pain differs depending on the context, the person's expectations, and hindsight evaluation. Pain may be individual or larger, in situations where we mourn the harm done by our collective hands. Later, using hindsight, what the person tells himself or herself about what happened becomes a story of sorts – a story with meaning, interpretation, and conclusions. The story includes presumed motivations and "what-if" thinking that infers blame and judgment. Moral injury (MI) remains unresolved when the dissonance seems inescapable, which affects the person's thoughts, meaning-making/spirituality, relationships, and day-to-day functioning. Here are some ways Veterans have reported that MI impacts Veterans:

1. Veterans feel damaged, broken, or forever changed by the MI events. Most continue to carry beliefs and conclusions that are inconsistent with what occurred.
2. Veterans maintain silence and secrecy out of fear that others will not accept them.
   Many who spoke up were ridiculed, punished, or isolated from others. Speaking up interfered with promotion, and at times, the truth was disallowed. Some who sought help were discharged or blamed as if they were responsible. Ginger, whose non-commissioned officer (NCO) assaulted her, was disciplined for fraternizing as if she had initiated it.
3. Veterans have strong emotions such as guilt, disgust, apathy, hopelessness, fear, shame, or grief that stem from MI. They judge these emotions as "weak."
4. Veterans judge their vulnerability and imperfection as unacceptable. This was reinforced by a military culture where shows of emotion or human error were considered a liability to the mission.
5. Veterans report an exaggerated sense of responsibility, some of it for things over which they had little-to-no control or for situations for which they were not responsible.
6. Veterans report a loss of faith, purpose, or meaning, and some have religious/ spiritual struggles. They may believe they are unforgivable or abandoned by a

DOI: 10.4324/9781003494263-11

higher power. They may attribute situations to "God's will" instead of the free will of those who hurt them.

7. Veterans with MI often report a disconnect from others. This includes lost sense of worth, loss of closeness with those they care about most, inability to relate to civilians, lost trust from betrayal, lost values, and lost integrity.

The impact of MI is not a one-size-fits-all. Types of MI events (betrayal, participation, witnessing) impact people differently, according to the source of the pain and the individual's response.

Impact of Betrayal

If you believe someone – or the military in general – betrayed you, you may feel bitterness, grief, fear, anger, sadness, and hurt. Being betrayed breeds disillusionment that someone you trusted turned against or hurt you. What happened violated your standards, values, and trust. Betrayal due to race, religion, gender, or sexual orientation may be hushed up or ignored, and justice is not served. To heal from betrayal, Veterans need compassion for themselves and to let go of the past, so they don't carry it or let it define them. Healing from betrayal might involve letting go of "if-only" thinking and realizing you are not responsible.

> Becky was an E4 (specialist) deployed to Iraq. She witnessed shaming and aggressive mistreatment of Islamic prisoners of war (POWs) that went far beyond teasing, even to threats of harm. Becky reported it to her NCO who told her it was "all in fun" and to keep her mouth shut. The cruelty continued, and Becky reported it to the command, resulting in her NCO receiving a reprimand. He told Becky she better watch her back. Shortly after, Becky was pulled from her normal duties and ordered to go on a mission outside the wire with this same NCO. She hadn't been trained for this work, and casualty rates were high. Becky feared retaliation. During the mission there was a "close call" where Becky could have been killed had another battle buddy not intervened in time.

Author Lisa Carrington Firmin depicts the impact of military betrayal through military sexual trauma (MST) in her 2022 publication, *Stories from the Front: Pain, Betrayal, and Resilience on the MST Battlefield*. Stanza 3 from the poem *MST Warrior* reflects the pain of betrayal (reprinted with author permission):

> Overpowered and betrayed by someone I trusted and respected
>   A predator took advantage, exploited my weaknesses
>   With no regard for my humanity. (p. 233, stanza 3)

Impact of Sanctioned Actions

If you participated in sanctioned actions as part of a mission or training, you may feel regret, guilt, sadness, anger, and self-blame when the actions caused harm to others. Your healing might involve learning and accepting that some things are beyond your control despite your best intentions. You might need to forgive yourself for betraying your morals despite the sanction, find compassion for yourself as you would for another in this situation, and consider the context of the event.

> *Jeff's military career was stellar. He was a major in charge of covert operations. "I was very well trained and good at what I did. I directed the operations. The things we did bother me now, and I can't really talk about them except here in therapy. It's like I'm two persons: the me that did horrible things without questioning, feeling, or blinking—I was like a robot on autopilot—and now there's the me that feels ashamed of what I had to do. I feel guilty for doing those things. They don't teach you how to handle that."*

Impact of Deliberate Harm to Others

If you deliberately engaged in unsanctioned harm, you may feel self-blame, guilt, remorse, or hopelessness. Your healing might involve confessing, accepting fallibility, making amends, forgiving, restitution, finding compassion for yourself, and not repeating the same mistakes.

> *Michael's team had a high-performing Muslim enlistee who worked hard and showed leadership potential. They mocked him and made racist comments when he prayed. He was a gentle person who deflected their cruelty. But one day, he joined them in cleaning up after a successful, launched attack on a targeted known terrorist. In "fun," they seated him in the front of a vehicle and made him carry the head of the Muslim enemy in his lap, along with the man's damaged Quran. He said nothing but left the military not long after.*
>
> *Michael was ashamed that he never spoke up on behalf of his Muslim team member, who was kind and hard-working. Michael and the others betrayed their buddy when he deserved their loyalty and support. The cruelty left the other man broken, damaged, and changed. The impact of Michael's MI was shame and guilt. "It's not who I am," he said. "It's not who I was raised to be. He was a good man, and we ruined his career." He*

was disgusted by his previous actions and told no one his story until he came to the VA to process his MI. The silence and moral pain were a heavy burden that tied him up in knots. Confessing his actions to a group of non-judgmental Veterans was a step toward self-forgiveness as his grief, regret, and guilt poured out. The other Veterans helped him release the years of pain, with a plan to make amends and live a life of compassion.

Veterans are not always accepted or understood by their loved ones or communities; what they are willing to share is only the tip of the proverbial iceberg. Some grieve their participation in combat actions and do not want to be thanked for their service. Veterans report they do not find it helpful to hear, "It's not your fault – you were following orders," if they viewed the orders, the war, or their own actions as immoral. It is not realistic to expect someone to "just get over it" when *it* has laid dormant for many years and is causing deep pain. Veterans need an opportunity to absolve themselves of blame, seek retribution, grieve/mourn injustice, and pursue forgiveness for perceived wrongdoing. Many Veterans joined the military at young ages, with the best of intentions, and could not have realized the scope of what they would be asked or ordered to do. Once they joined, their lives, actions, and choices were largely in the hands of leaders they were supposed to trust, some of whom failed them. And for some, they failed themselves and their expectations of being a warrior. What they carry during and after the military becomes a heavy burden, and the path to healing or restoration is often unclear.

The Mental Filter of MI

After going through a PMIE and experiencing strong moral pain, Veterans conclude why something happened and who or what is responsible. The Veteran's behavior may be guilt-worthy, such as acts of undeserved aggression and cruelty. Many Veterans remain silent about deliberate, horrific, insensitive, or illegal actions, and this keeps them stuck in a self-imposed life sentence of emotional pain (Litz, 2023; Pernicano et al., 2022).

These kinds of moral transgressions may result in all-or-nothing mental filters: "I am totally evil," "I am unforgivable," or "I am a monster." Each of us has the potential to take "good" or "bad" actions, as we are all imperfect and fallible. Sometimes, we act in ways inconsistent with our core values. In the climate of war and under extreme stress, we are more likely to engage in behaviors that later bring regret, guilt, or grief. The problem is what to do with moral pain and MI to find a non-punitive path forward. The Veteran requires a safe place to unburden and confess to compassionate, non-judgmental others. It is important to gently hold what Veterans share and not to minimize their pain.

A compassionate response to wrongdoing might be,

Yes, it was heinous, yes it was cruel, yes it was hurtful. We hear you and we accept your imperfection and fallibility. We also see the good in you; you are more than those actions. We encourage you to make amends and to demonstrate the kind of person you want to be. We encourage you to reclaim your moral values and to create purpose and meaning through loving, helpful relationships and kind actions. You are not a monster. The event does not define the whole of who you are, and you have an opportunity now to live your best self.

(Pernicano & Haynes, 2023)

Veterans need an invitation to unburden, confess, and share their truth. This event does not need to be reframed as an acceptable action; rather, the thinking change is about the forgivability of the event and the permanence of the suffering. Compassionate people regret or wish they had not engaged in cruel behavior, and it is crucial to acknowledge guilt or regret and then find a path forward and not let that event continue to define the individual.

On the other hand, some Veterans are not responsible for the named events and deserve no blame. Humans with morals and values point fingers at themselves in ways that lead to unnecessary and unhelpful guilt and self-blame. Cognitive behavioral therapy (CBT; Beck et al, 1979) and cognitive processing therapy (CPT; Resick et al., 1993, 2016) refer to irrational thinking or stuck points about thought patterns that are narrow, filtered, or not fully true. Veterans are encouraged to read more about cognitive behavioral thought patterns in David Burns' *Feeling Good: The New Mood Therapy* (1980). What we tell ourselves after the fact is not always the whole story. When things go wrong, we may try to rewrite history ("what if?") or use hindsight to assign blame. Veterans sometimes use stuck-point thinking to punish, justify guilt, or assign blame for MI. It is important to look closely at one's actual role in the event and consider whether your conclusions are justified. How we are raised and what we are taught affect our beliefs and conclusions when things go wrong.

The just world hypothesis, named by Melvin J. Lerner (1980), might otherwise be called the Walt Disney way of thinking; it sometimes guides our expectations for life. When we are young, we are raised to believe:

1. If we do the right thing, we will get our "happily ever after."
2. That good always triumphs over evil; in Disney stories, the hero defeats the villain, and the good guys win.
3. That those you trust will have your back and come to your rescue under duress.
4. That someone you love will be loyal and faithful.
5. Those who hurt others will get theirs (justice or punishment).
6. That we have control in most situations.

The truth is that sometimes life is more like Grimm's fables:

1. Bad things sometimes happen to "good people," and life is not always fair.
2. Those who hurt others may prevail and may not be held accountable.
3. People we admire and trust can let us down and do hurtful things.
4. We are not always our best selves. Sometimes *we* do hurtful things.
5. Things happen that are outside our control (e.g., natural disasters, accidents, improvised explosive devices, or IEDs).
6. Good intentions sometimes lead to negative outcomes. Negative results do not necessarily mean you did anything wrong.
7. Doing what is right by military standards may no longer feel right in the civilian world.

It is normal to feel moral pain when confronted by a PMIE and to want to figure out why it happened and whose "fault" it is. As a result:

1. We blame ourselves for things that weren't totally our fault.
2. We blame ourselves for things that were not our fault at all.
3. We tell ourselves that we should or could have done something to change the outcome.
4. We judge ourselves as weak or as having failed.
5. We believe we can't find peace until someone pays or justice is done.
6. We punish ourselves for wrongdoing and do not give ourselves the same forgiveness we might offer someone else.

As you look more closely at what you tell yourself about what happened, why you think it happened, and who you believe to be responsible, you will be better able to challenge your conclusions and see beyond the limits of what you have told yourself for so many years. The truth is most events are multi-determined and we limit our understanding when we take a narrow focus.

An example of distorted thinking is, "If I had done something differently, I could have changed the outcome." This may or may not be true, depending on the context and circumstances. If you had done something different, there could still be a tragic outcome. Some distorted thinking is based on military mentality, such as "Failure is unacceptable," "Leadership is fully responsible for negative outcomes," or "Careful planning and execution always bring success." If we live as if our distorted thinking is true, we rewrite history. If we use a new lens to examine distorted thinking, we see things more as they were and not as we wish they had been.

Persons with MI might tell themselves things that compound guilt, blame, or self-punishment. Here are a few examples. It can help ask clarifying questions when analyzing distorted thinking.

I could have changed the outcome if I had made the right decision.

Questions to Ask: When the event occurred, did I act on what I knew at that time? Do I have reason to believe my decision was "wrong"? At that moment, was another decision possible or advised? Did I follow orders and the rules of engagement? Am I sure I could have stopped it or changed the outcome? Could doing something else have made it worse?

Rephrasing:

_____

_____

If I have a good life, I dishonor those who died.

Questions to Ask: How would those who died want me to live? How could I best honor those who died? What would be the point of having a "bad" life? If I could talk with someone who was killed, what would that person want for me? Would those who died want me to keep suffering?

Rephrasing:

_____

_____

What I did is unforgivable.

Questions to Ask: Is there no hope for me if I am imperfect and fallible? What is the benefit of punishing myself for the rest of my life? Would I have done what I did outside the military context or the climate of war? Could I forgive someone else who did what I did? If a fair and compassionate judge told me I was being released, with "time served," what would I do with that freedom? How could I make a difference and pay it forward if I forgive myself?

Rephrasing:

_____

_____

Naming the Pain of MI

Veterans with MI report feeling broken, damaged, or forever changed, and naming the pain is an early step in healing. To name the pain, you remember what happened and the emotions related to the MI. In CPT (Resick et al., 2016), Veterans write an impact statement to examine stuck points. During prolonged exposure (PE; Foa et al., 2019), Veterans record their stories, including details, senses, and emotions. Colorful feeling wheels (Willcox, 1982) can be downloaded from the internet to help identify what the individual felt in the face and aftermath of a PMIE.

Healing from MI includes a grief process, one in which Veterans grieve their losses: loss of innocence, lost values/ideals, loss of others who died or were wounded, loss of integrity, loss of trust, loss of religious faith, and, sometimes, lost faith in military leadership. Moral pain may relate to situations where there is shared responsibility for harm done on our behalf and by our collective hands. When the MI happened, there was no time or permission to process the pain or to grieve. Sometimes leadership called pain "weakness" and ridiculed emotions, which sent the Veteran's emotions to a hidden place where they were buried deep, perhaps deep within the soul. Several writers have described MI as a "soul wound" because of the betrayal of deeply held values (Tick, 2005, 2014; Brock & Lettini, 2012; Wood, 2016). Veterans may avoid thinking about MI because it awakens moral pain; it is important to safely remember, re-experience, and process what they have endured. Whether or not you name it, the individual or community wound is there, like an infected abscess below the surface. It will not heal unless it is properly treated.

Retired Colonel and author Lisa Carrington Firmin poignantly describes the pain of military service and MST in *Stories from the Front: Pain, Betrayal, and Resilience on the MST Battlefield* (2022) and *Latina Warrior* (2023). Her writings are therapeutic for herself and others; her poetry helps others find pathways to healing and resilience.

Stanzas 4–7 from a poem of brokenness, *Fractured*, are reprinted with the author's permission (2023):

Cannot grasp the missing pieces
They slip through so easily,
elusively obscure in my mind

What's left are fractured shards
I try hard to retain every twisted detail But
the blurred bits are never clear enough

I don't remember everything he did to me
It's scary not to know, not to recall each painful part
And, it's even scarier that I might remember it all

To know each excruciating moment would break me
Being fractured keeps me whole. (p. 103)

Figure 8.1 Cracked Bowl Surrounded by Red Brick

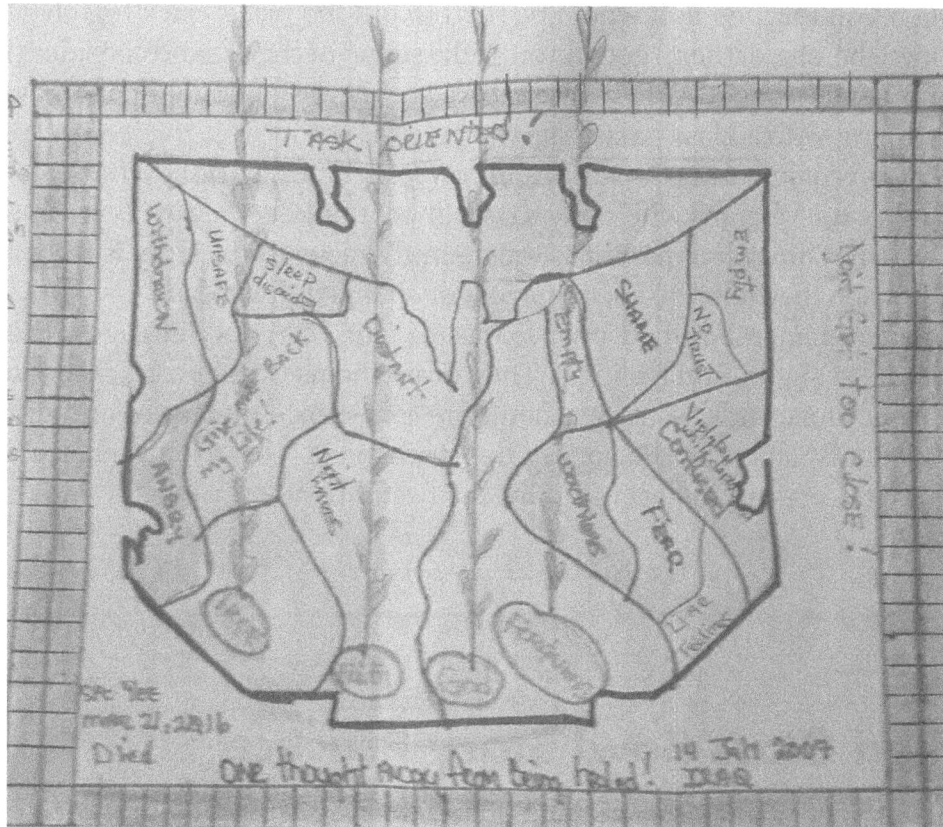

Avenues for naming and processing pain include writing, journaling, meditation, spiritual retreats, art, poetry, music, blogs, or podcasts. In acceptance and forgiveness therapy (AFT), Veterans use drawings (self-depictions of damage and healing) and stories to depict the pain and brokenness of MI. Susan could not find words to describe her MI, and she began her story by drawing herself as a cracked glass bowl, battered and broken after a hurricane. She had been sexually assaulted, and her orders questioned; as a leader, she judged herself to be a failure. The author photographed her drawings, and the Veteran permitted the authors to include her drawings in this book. Her drawing (Figure 8.1) is a clear depiction of the impact of MI. She wrote:

> *My cracks were shame, fear, and confusion, which affected my trust. I keep people out ("don't get too close"). See the red wall? I had guilt and grief. The green shoots are God, hope, and forgiveness, struggling to find their way through the wall. I was cracked - worthless, no trust, distant, withdrawn, angry, and give me back my life! I became task-centered.*

She drew her bowl after hearing the story *The Cracked Glass Bowl* (Pernicano, 2012). Pernicano initially wrote this story, which depicts trauma-related brokenness and grief, for therapy with adult and child trauma survivors. The main character, a glass bowl, survives a hurricane but finds herself damaged and fragile. As a Veteran recently said, "That could be dangerous, you know, a glass bowl broken into shards and ready to cut you if you touched it. It would be hard to put the pieces back together."

The bowl (he, she, or them) goes through the stages of change and considers whether or not to pursue healing. At first, she thinks survival is enough, but she eventually pursues healing with a glassmaker. She struggles as she moves from contemplation to active change, remembering the storm and her vulnerability. The bowl story becomes a core metaphor for Veterans who come to treatment thinking they are *beyond repair*. The listener imagines himself or herself as the main character as the story is read, and they remember when they felt broken, damaged, or changed due to MI.

As listeners remember their own stories of pain, the story engages their senses (sounds, smells, sights, and feelings). They draw themselves as a cracked glass bowl right after the story ends. Veterans silently re-experience memories and moral pain and use symbols, labels, and colors to depict damage. This exercise helps Veterans "share" the trauma and impact of MI for the first time.

Cracked Glass Bowl Story Practice

Doing is more personal and memorable than *reading about* something. Each of us has gone through something unexpected or hurtful that left us feeling broken, damaged, or changed. We invite you to be in a quiet, safe place as you read the following story and picture yourself as the main character. After you read the story, you are invited to draw yourself as a cracked glass bowl. Label the damages and their sources and add colors or symbols as desired. Some injuries might be from childhood, some from military or post-military times. This exercise prepares Veterans to process loss and grief – they revisit the aftermath of the "storm" and the great loss or losses that were experienced. After drawing self as a bowl, there is a Stages of Change worksheet to complete.

The only way to heal the pain of MI is *through it*, not around it or by burying it. For those who wish to do so, you may record the story and listen to it instead of reading it or ask someone to read it aloud. Trauma alert: this story is likely to stir strong emotions and memories.

The Cracked Glass Bowl Part I: The Trauma

(Modified from Pernicano, 2012)

* The reader may refer to the bowl as "she," "he," or "they"
Reprinted and modified with permission of Jason Aronson

The hurricane was finally over, and a small, cracked, green glass bowl bobbed up and down in the ocean. She opened her eyes and looked around at the devastation. It was like a war zone, with uprooted trees and debris scattered as far as the eye could see.

She thought, "It's a wonder I survived the storm!" It was true. The bowl had been lifted off the ground by powerful winds and pummeled by blinding rains, green amidst black. She had been flung into a disorienting darkness, frozen in fear, at the mercy of the storm's destruction. It had been a terrifying experience, and she could not even remember all that had happened.

"How are you feeling?" asked a kind voice. Her friend, the blue bowl, had escaped the worst of the storm and was looking at her with concern.

The glass bowl saw her reflection in the water and cried out with dismay, "Look at me! The storm has changed me. I am so damaged and broken that I will never be the same!"

It was true that the storm had changed her. She had many small cracks on her surface and two long, deep cracks that went all the way through. Straw and dirt were embedded in the cracks; deep gouges and large chips were missing on her edges.

The bowl was exhausted from her ordeal, and she accepted her friend's support and a place to stay. One night became many. Without the support of Blue Bowl, she would have fallen into a hundred little pieces.

The green bowl could not sleep most nights and she could not forget the storm – the smell of the ocean, the overpowering wind, the dark sky, the screams of injured people, fearful children crying for their parents, and flying objects. She had nightmares about the storm, was startled easily, and became nervous at the slightest sign of wind or rain. Others had died in the storm, and she felt guilty sadness that she had survived when they had not. It was as if the storm had penetrated deep within her soul.

Blue Bowl noticed the changes in her friend and wanted to help. She asked, "Have you considered going to the healer?" The healer was a kind, skilled glassmaker who had helped many glass bowls recover after the storm.

"I don't think so," retorted the green glass bowl. "They say the healing is a painful process. I want to put the storm behind me; I don't want to think or talk about it. I want to forget about it and move on. Many did not survive the storm. Maybe survival is enough."

Her friend argued, "Survival alone is never enough. Without the healing, you will be fragile for the rest of your life. The glassmaker helps you talk about the storm. The cracks in your glass melt, and you heal from the inside out."

"Thanks, but no thanks," said the green glass bowl, as she declined her friend's offer.

The cracked glass bowl continued to struggle, until one morning, she woke up and realized that the life she was living was hardly worth living. She told Blue Bowl, "These days, I find it harder and harder to live. My life has no meaning or purpose. Sometimes I feel like giving up. I have decided to go to the glassmaker."

The story parallels the stages in the *Transtheoretical Stages of Change* (Prochaska & DiClemente, 1982), and the glass bowl goes through pre-contemplation and contemplation before deciding to pursue healing. The storm represents a destructive traumatic event personal to the Veteran, and the story often stirs up the senses and emotions. It can be hard to live in the aftermath of a damaging "storm." Perhaps the bowl blamed herself for being *at the wrong place at the wrong time* or regretted going to the beach or not heeding the storm warnings. The storm was not her fault, but how and whether to pursue recovery was her decision to make.

For you, the MI is whatever "storm" left you feeling broken and changed. Like the bowl, you might have been glad to have survived, but later, you felt hopeless or helpless. It is important to process the storm and how you were changed. At one point or another, like the bowl, we decide it is time to get help.

The Cracked Glass Bowl Activity

Instructions

1. The storm represents what you went through that resulted in moral pain and eventual moral injury.
2. Like the cracked glass bowl, you have gone through one or more traumatic experiences. Note: A traumatic experience is something you went through, something you witnessed, something you did or neglected to do, or something you knew about that affected you deeply in a negative way.
3. After a traumatic experience, you may feel broken, damaged, changed, or flawed.
4. Draw yourself in the space below as a cracked glass bowl, your choice of shape and colors. No artistic talent is required. We recommend you draw in silence and let yourself "be" the bowl. You can add elements as things come to you.
5. Draw cracks (deep and surface ones), gouges, scratches, and chips on your bowl. The size of the cracks/gouges can represent the amount of damage.
6. Label the cracks, gouges, scratches, and chips with the traumatic experiences that caused them.

Drawing Space

Veterans answer the following questions based on MI that left them feeling broken, damaged, or changed.

Stages of Change Cracked Glass Bowl Worksheet

(Pernicano & Haynes, 2023)

Contemplation

The bowl sees her reflection and laments, "Look at me! The storm has changed me. I am so damaged and broken that I will never be the same!"

You: "Like the bowl, I felt broken, damaged, or changed."

Describe the damages on your bowl (think about who you were before the MI and who you were after):_____

After your storm, how and when did you first realize you had changed? _____
_____

> *One Veteran wrote, "I had immediate resentment of those involved and distrust of everyone else because I felt like they were spies."*

Consider the greatest damage to your bowl. What was the storm?_____
_____

> *The Veteran continued, "I lost all trust in colleagues, became constantly afraid of being stabbed in the back, and remained tense and guarded."*

The bowl sees that her life is missing something. What was missing in your life after the storm?" _____
_____

The bowl is tired of being broken, vulnerable, and fragile. She is angry and frustrated. She can't do the things she used to do. She contemplates going to the glassmaker. She weighs the risks (revisiting her memories of the storm and the pain of the healing process) with the benefits (healing the pain).

The bowl eventually decides that it is not enough to simply survive.

> *The Veteran wrote, "The bowl can't fix herself; she needs help to come to terms with her trauma & be whole again."*

For you, why is it not *enough* to simply "survive," i.e., to keep living the way you have been living? _____

> *The Veteran replied, "I didn't realize just how bad and toxic it was for me until later, but it's a big part of the reason I haven't gone back to work. I also have to insist on having everything in writing now because of that betrayal of trust."*

Action

At the end of Part I, the bowl decides to go to the glassmaker. She realizes that her current life is not a life worth living.

What are your reasons for going to the glassmaker? _____
_____

> *The Veteran commented, "The bowl doesn't want to let that trauma define who she is or what she does anymore. I'm tired of distrusting and letting these people (who I will never see again) live rent-free in my head. I've done therapy for PTSD [post-traumatic stress disorder] and depression, but it always kept coming back to this issue and events. MI felt like a closer fit to my feelings and reactions."*

Impact of MI: Veteran Bowls of Moral Pain and Injury

There is no right or wrong way to draw yourself as a cracked glass bowl. We are grateful for the Veteran examples below. This first bowl (Figure 8.2) was drawn by a Veteran who broke down in grief and rage after getting news from home that his wife had left him and had aborted their child. He grabbed a weapon and was ready to shoot everyone and himself. A battle buddy stepped in before he could act on his strong emotions. His healed blue bowl (Figure 13.14, Chapter 13) depicts gratitude for the support of other Veterans who lifted him spiritually and emotionally.

> *This bowl represents my mind. The big crack down the middle is me almost losing my mind before I did harmful things to other people. Someone helped me stop before I did something I regretted that would hurt a lot of people. It is hard to live with myself.*

A female Veteran who had joined the military after high school, with idealistic and patriotic hopes of helping and making a difference, drew the next bowl. She blamed herself for being so targeted sexually, then discarded by her opportunistic training instructor. She had not considered the age and rank difference. She judged herself as "stupid" and "naïve." She did not realize he was taking advantage of many women and that he betrayed her trust (Figure 8.3).

> *This is my original bowl. I did it in pencil, things I experienced at the time. Big crack for the sexual/verbal abuse, lying, shame, failure, and fear, looking back, that was a big crack. Holding everything in.*

Figure 8.2 Cracked Bowl of Betrayal, Guilt, and Shame

Figure 8.3 Black and White Cracked Bowl of Naivete

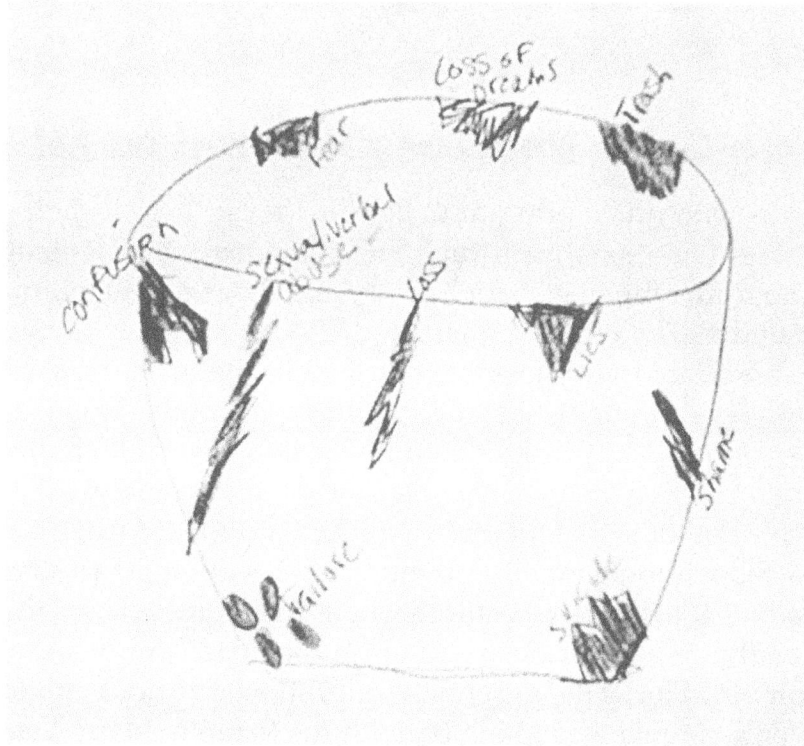

The next bowl (Figure 8.4) was drawn by a male Veteran who reported shame, substance abuse, and spiritual pain. He felt "unworthy," and hid his MI from others. The image in the mirror is how he viewed himself, and outside the mirror is what he presented to others. *Like this Veteran, we hide our pain and brokenness.* His healed bowl may be found in Chapter 12 (Figure 12.5).

If you draw yourself as a cracked glass bowl, we suggest you pick someone you trust to show and describe your bowl when you are done to give them a picture of your moral pain and injury.

Figure 8.4 Cracked Bowl in Mirror

Lamenting Grief and Loss Related to MI

What do we do with our moral pain? Before we can heal, it helps grieve and mourn our losses (emotional, spiritual, and relational), and lament is a way of doing that. The reader might also find poetry and blogs on the internet that speak to your heart and make you feel understood. There was likely no time to process the emotions associated with loss or to grieve in the military. When the event happened, the Veteran might have been told to ignore it, forget it, get over it, minimize it, cover it up, or justify it, and it was not possible to morally do so. By the time a Veteran seeks help, they have had lots of time to analyze the MI but often with little resolution of grief and other painful emotions. Also, over time others may have reacted without empathy to the Veteran's attempts to share with them or even judged what the Veteran went through. PTSD and MI can both be marked by an emotional numbing or desire to erase the "bad" (unpleasant) emotions. Emotional numbing blocks the experience of positive emotions and leaves friends and family wondering what is going on with the Veteran. Many Veterans ignore, bury, or remain silent about their MI, and some even think something is wrong that it still bothers them.

The process of lament helps us express and navigate pain and suffering. Lament, a practice in several world religions, is a petition (to a higher power or benevolent other) for delivery from pain, distress, and suffering. Westermann (1974) notes that the significance of the lament "lies first of all in the fact that it gives voice to suffering. The lament is the language of suffering; in it, suffering is given the dignity of language" (p. 31). Lament is a response to oppression, death, loss, and other tragic or unjust circumstances. The lament of an individual or community is a cleansing, healing ritual that connects people through stories that break the silence.

Lament, then, is:

♦ A passionate expression of grief or sorrow, "crying out" when you feel alone, abandoned, hopeless, frustrated, or mistreated. This grief may be born of suffering, worry, helplessness, injustice, complacency, anger, doubt, and/or hopelessness.
♦ A release of emotion, venting anguish at your lowest points.
♦ A process of asking unanswerable questions (living with ambiguity and the unanswered "why").

As Veterans think about and draw their moral injuries, it activates strong memories and emotions. The military culture sometimes views emotions as "weak," which is not true; certainly, in the heat of the mission, there is little time for emotion. However, what worked in combat doesn't work so well back home. Expressing genuine emotions is healthier than bottling them up or denying their presence.

Lament is a spiritually inclusive – not religious – activity because crying out for meaning is universal during periods of profound suffering. Veterans in AFT have been Christian, Muslim, Buddhist, agnostic, atheist, Jewish, and "no religion." They are surprised to discover that others share similar emotional pain and that no one judges them for their deep emotions. In sharing lament, participants find they are not alone and identify those primal feelings that arise from deep within, such as a growl, moan, rage, or helpless cry.

Retired Colonel Lisa Carrington Firmin laments feeling trapped in "the black hole of life" in her poem, "The Abyss" from *Latina Warrior* 2023 (p. 105, reprinted with permission).

The Abyss

It is not a safe haven
More like an open chest wound that is bleeding out
You feel your very existence draining away

Facing demons of PTSD and MST
Thrust me into The Abyss, the black hole of life
The fragile space between fully living and just existing

I cannot allow myself to stay here
In the dark recesses of my splintered mind
Where pain, fear, guilt, and shame lie

Intense memories of trauma drag me down even deeper
I cannot escape that seductive siren call from the pitch-black void
It whispers just how much easier it would be to succumb

Trying to reconcile the past and the present with my future
Without losing myself permanently in The Abyss
Must fight to break the hold it has on me

The war continues in my head, heart, and soul
Some battles I win, others The Abyss screams it is the victor
Time will tell the final outcome

I will never give up fighting for my sanity
To exist, to live fully in the light, to be whole. For I know I am worthy
The Abyss will not take me down, it cannot win. (p. 105)

The prayer before the prayer (Tutu and Tutu, 2015) is a lament of anguish, yearning, and ambivalence. This teeter-totter ambivalence emerges in lament, for we want help; we are not ready to relinquish what we carry. We want to forgive (after all, everyone says it is a good thing to do), but we are not prepared to ask. Sometimes we would prefer revenge over restitution, and our hearts are locked in bitterness while seeking release. In this prayer, the speaker is not ready for his or her heart to soften. We are reminded of a hardened piece of day-old bread or a tough, old sponge that no longer holds water. As we practice lament, our hearts can soften, to the point that we are ready for the next part of healing.

Elements of Lament

The following are typical elements of a "lament," which we do in the second session of AFT. Veterans with MI contributed the following examples to the program handbook (Pernicano & Haynes, 2023); we invite you to join the process and complete each element yourself.

Element 1: A Metaphor for Pain and Anguish

Metaphors and word pictures are powerful ways to describe situations and emotions. Pick a metaphor that describes what your MI would look like in a picture. Here are some Veteran examples:

I'm walking on a tightrope.
I'm off balance and ready to fall.
I'm sinking without a life vest.
I'm stuck in quicksand.
I'm an iceberg with hidden pain.
I'm trying to outrun lava.
A tornado is swirling around me.
I'm a firefighter with an empty hose.
A dark cloud surrounds me.
I'm trapped in the fog.
I am at the bottom of a dark pit.
I'm a hamster spinning my wheels.
I'm lost driving without GPS.

Write a metaphor (from above, or come up with your own) that describes your pain or anguish.

_____

_____

Element 2: Ask a Question (That Probably Can't and Won't Be Answered)

This is often in the form of a complaint or accusation.

> *How long will this last?*
>> *When will this pain end?*
>>> *Why did this happen?*
>>>> *What is the purpose of this?*
>>>> *How could such a terrible thing happen?*
>>>> *Where were you, God?*
>>>>> *How could they hurt me like that?*
>>>>> *How could I do such a thing?*

Write your question:

_____

_____

Element 3: Express Deep Feelings

What emotions do you experience when you think about your MI story and the cracks in your bowl? You might look at a feeling wheel to help you articulate them. The Feeling Wheel has been credited to Willcox (1982), and many versions are available through a simple online search.

Write one or more strong feelings related to your MI:

_____

_____

Element 4: Beseech

To "beseech" means to reach out, ask, or pray for help, for what you want, for what you need, or for what you are seeking.

> *Help me find…*
>> *I beg for…*
>>> *I cry out for…*
>>>> *I pray/hope for…*
>>>> *I need…*

What do you seek or ask for?

_____

_____

Element 5: Release, Turn Over, Yield

To end the lament, we *surrender* to a power greater than ourselves, like the 12-step concept of "powerlessness." We might turn over control. We might express hope and gratitude that we are not alone. We accept that our own efforts are not "enough" and that help is available.

> *I am thankful for…*
> *I trust that…*
> *I turn over my…*
> *I'm grateful for…*
> *I accept…*
> *I yield…*

Write your yielding statement:

_____

_____

Some write their lament in the form of a poem or song. Following is one Veteran's poem:

Lamentation

Shared with Veteran's permission

I, the daughter of struggle, have been defeated by insensible thieves.
They have plundered my home, pillaged my chambers, and emptied my pockets,
My virtue is lost.
I wander in a desert of my own making, bare, with no shield from the sun,
My skin, blistered and cracked.
The clouds in their anger refuse me shelter,
The springs in their resentment refuse to let me drink.
So shall I die? Shall I lie down? Let my body return to the earth?
*Allow my molecules to heal the earth that **I** plundered, That **I** pillaged?*
My shame runs deep, like groundwater to the well.
Could I not have prevented it?
My sorrow floods the lands and chokes the seas,
Could I not have raised my hands to stop it?
But will tearing my own flesh repay my debt?
Can my fruitless torment provide restitution, or does it simply serve to allow the tyrants

To triumph once again? I have stacked a mountain of stones on the WRONG side of that scale, so much that nothing will ever again,

Bring it to balance. Not my work. Not my surrender. Not my love.

Nothing will ever fill the other side, and the stone of my fruitless agony fill not the scale,

They build a wall that impedes my path,

I must lay down my selfish anguish and suffer instead the pain of dispelling my own ignorance of making mistakes,

Openly admitting my wrongdoing, bearing the righteous anger of those I have wronged,

And changing my behavior,

I will break my back, bloody my fingers, and tear the soles of my feet to drag the heaviest boulders I can find to the RIGHT side of that scale,

And then, if I can make it budge, even the tiniest bit, maybe then,
I will finally deserve peace.

The next lament is a prayer by a Veteran who cries out in moral pain and yearns for healing:

Lament of Guilt, Grief, and Faith

Shared with Veteran's permission

Lord, YOU know I'm still trying to outrun a chaotic and complex past with pains that have affected me for a long time. For decades it has consumed me, hurting those I love, and those around me, leaving its mark on every aspect of my hurting those I love, those around me, and leaving its mark on every aspect of my life. The horrific, negative, and often senseless nature of war has tentacles that reach out far beyond the battlefield. I feel as if I lose ground almost every day. Lord, I find it difficult to believe this is YOUR WILL being done. When is enough enough? I have felt anger, betrayal, guilt, shame, fear, loneliness and depression. On the worst of my days, I felt abandoned, at times, even by YOU. Lord, help me journey to a more loving, peaceful, trusting relationship with family, the world around me, and YOUR children. Help me to understand the events that trouble me and how to deal with them. Lord, YOU know I have experienced painful failure in my attempts at self-care, yet YOU still watch over me. Bless my journey with the caring professionals; you put me in their hands and entrust my care. AMEN

How has MI impacted the reader's life? If you are in a dark place, we encourage you to write a lament, using poetry, song, or narrative, and share it with someone you trust who can be there for your pain. Naming the pain is one of the first steps in healing MI because it breaks the silence and soothes your soul.

References

Beck, A. T., Rush, A., Shaw, B., & Emery, G. (1979). *Cognitive therapy of depression.* Guilford Press.

Brock, R., & Lettini, G. (2012). *Soul repair: Recovering from moral injury after war.* Beacon Press.

Burns, D. (1999). *Feeling good: The new mood therapy.* William Morrow.

Carrington Firmin, L. (2022). *Stories from the Front: Pain, Betrayal, and Resilience on the MST Battlefield.* Blue Ear Books.

Carrington Firmin, L. (2023). *Latina Warrior.* Blue Ear Books.

Foa, E., Hembree, E.A., Rothbaum, B.O., & Rauch, S. (2019). *Prolonged exposure therapy for PTSD: Emotional processing of traumatic experiences - therapist guide* (2nd ed.). Oxford University Press.

Lerner, M. J. (1980). *The belief in a just world: A Fundamental Delusion.* Springer.

Litz, B. T. (2023). The future of moral injury and its treatment. In Perspectives on healing and repairing moral injury. *Journal of Military Veteran and Family Health, 9*(2), 1–5. https://doi.org/10.3138/jmvfh.9.2.ed

Pernicano, P. (2012). The cracked glass bowl. In P. Pernicano (2012). *Outsmarting the riptide of domestic violence: Metaphor and mindfulness for change* (pp. 141–44). Jason Aronson.

Pernicano, P., & Haynes, K. (2023). *Acceptance & forgiveness therapy: From brokenness to restoration* [Unpublished handbook] (5th ed.). South Texas Veterans Health Care System.

Pernicano, P., Wortmann, J., & Haynes, K. (2022). Acceptance and forgiveness therapy for veterans with moral injury: Spiritual and psychological collaboration in group treatment. *Journal of Health Care Chaplaincy, 28*(Sup1), S57–S78. https://doi.org/10.1080/08854726.2022.2032982

Prochaska, J. O., & DiClemente, C. C. (1982). Transtheoretical therapy: Toward a more integrative model of change. *Psychotherapy: Theory, Research & Practice, 19*(3), 276–288. https://doi.org/10.1037/h0088437

Resick, P.A., Monson, C., & Chard, K. (2016). *Cognitive processing therapy for PTSD: A comprehensive manual.* Guilford.

Tick, E. (2005). *War and the soul: Healing our nation's veterans from post-traumatic stress disorder.* Quest Books/The Theosophical Publishing House.

Tick, E. (2014). *Warrior's return: Restoring the soul after war.* Sounds True.

Tutu, D., & Tutu, M. (2015). *The book of forgiving: The fourfold path for healing ourselves and the world.* D. Abrams (Ed.). Harper.

Westermann, C. (1974). The role of the lament in the theology of the Old Testament. *Interpretation, 28*(1), 20–38. https://doi.org/10.1177/002096437402800102

Willcox, G. (1982). The feeling wheel: A tool for expanding awareness of emotions and increasing spontaneity and intimacy. *Transactional Analysis Journal, 12*(4), 274–276. https://doi.org/10.1177/036215378201200411

Wood, D. (2016). *What have we done: The moral injury of our longest wars.* Little, Brown & Company.

Chapter 9

Rethinking Guilt, Blame, and Responsibility

Guilt and Grief

Guilt is appropriate when you do something wrong; it is human nature to experience guilt when we are partly or fully responsible for a terrible outcome. Grief arises when you feel helpless in the face of an unexpected or unavoidable tragic outcome. Pathways for healing from moral injury (MI) depend on the degree of responsibility and avenues for restorative justice, release of guilt, and self-compassion. Key concepts include:

1. Guilt is appropriate when you do something wrong or violate values/beliefs.
2. How you deal with guilt can be healthy or unhealthy.
3. Shame is unhealthy. Shame is a judgment of the *self*. Shame results in someone feeling unacceptable or unlovable. Shame = I am wrong, whereas guilt = I did wrong.
4. Grief and regret are natural responses to overwhelming pain or loss, such as natural disasters, the aftermath of combat, or unintended civilian casualties.

Veterans report guilt for such things as:

1. Deliberate harm or cruelty to others that was unsanctioned or unnecessary.
2. Not reporting a violation of military standards (secrecy, cover-up).
3. Not doing "what's right" per lawful orders or rules of engagement.
4. Blaming someone else for something you did (not taking responsibility).
5. Being complacent and neglecting duty.
6. Imperfect actions that hurt others due to human error or misjudgment, even when they were accidental or unanticipated.

Responses to guilt can be healthy (motivating to restorative action) or unhealthy (moving toward punitive measures and remaining unresolved). To heal MI, Veterans must process and cope with legitimate guilt. It can't be cognitively "argued" or

DOI: 10.4324/9781003494263-12

"debated" away, and the Veteran needs to separate the person (fallible, imperfect, forgivable) from the action that violated core values.

Healthy Response to Guilt

A healthy response to guilt motivates actions that restore trust, repair brokenness, and right a wrong. When you violate deeply held beliefs, values, morals, or standards (military, personal, or religious), guilt, regret, or remorse are understandable. Consider the balance scale that goes up and down on each side as weight is added. Guilt weighs down one side of the scale, and you mindfully and intentionally add things to the other side to restore healthy balance. Healthy ways of addressing guilt include confessing the wrong, taking responsibility for your part, suffering with yourself and others (compassion), and committing to actions that restore balance and repair damage. As mentioned in Chapter 5, different cultures have different traditions to help their members take responsibility when they have wronged another person or the community. A healthy response to guilt includes acceptance of one's imperfection and fallibility and a desire to do differently now.

Punitive Response to Guilt

A punitive, harsh response to guilt does not motivate Veterans toward forgiveness or compassion, and the guilt remains unresolved. Punitive responses to guilt might involve drug or alcohol abuse, suicidal ideation, self-hate, retaliation, or even relationship failures.

A punitive response to guilt keeps you stuck, in that it:

1. Does not accept help from others.
2. Focuses on harsh retribution or revenge.
3. Lacks compassion.
4. Damages relationships.
5. Turns a person into a judge and jury. You miss the opportunity for restitution, amends, or reconciliation.
6. Results in bitterness, anger, blame, and even shame.

A punitive response to guilt has been compared to a substance that consumes and destroys the very substance of an object, such as a poison swallowed, rust on iron, acid on bone, or flesh-eating bacteria on flesh. It eats you alive, from the inside out. The burden of MI need not be punitive, and few decisions and actions deserve a sentence of life in prison. Such a sentence does not honor the past, nor pave the way forward.

Veterans sometimes report *guilt* when they were not responsible and could not have changed the outcome, and in this case, the guilt is misplaced. With misplaced guilt, you *did nothing wrong* but feel responsible because compassionate feelings are mistaken for wrongdoing. Misplaced guilt reflects grief or regret – you feel terrible because of a negative outcome and judge you must have done something wrong. Misplaced guilt may result from unrealistic expectations (aiming for perfection, thinking errors are unacceptable, or desiring total control). You might judge imperfection as unacceptable and vulnerability as "weak." Military training reinforces this. Misplaced guilt ignores the intent and context of the act. It misses "the rest of the story."

The term "survivor's guilt" is often used in a situation where a survivor had no control over who lived and who died; it may be more accurate to call this survivor grief for those who were hurt or died. Some Veterans feel guilt over a freeze/flight/fight reaction, but this neurobiological stress response is an uncontrollable involuntary nervous system response; so is the adrenaline rush and euphoria when you survive a high-risk situation. You don't have to beat yourself up for a normal brain reaction. Guilt sometimes comes during 20-20 hindsight, but it is unfair to judge yourself now for what you did not know then. You can't save everyone: You aren't a superhero. "You can't save the whole world." Medical errors are expected and forgivable. Betrayal does not call for any "guilt" for the survivor.

It is important to clarify reasonable responsibility before pursuing healing for MI. Once you determine what piece of the event's responsibility belongs to you, if any, you can work on forgiveness and pursue actions to restore or repair. Responsibility is complicated, and there are several ways to think about this process. Pernicano (2019) illustrates types of responsibility that vary by factors such as rules of engagement, the chain of command, intentionality, and degree of involvement. Those with MI sometimes engage in black-and-white attribution of responsibility so consider factors (training, chain-of-command, contextual, combat-related, emotional, and cultural) likely to contribute to negative outcomes.

Figuring Out Responsibility for Betrayal, Participation, and Bystander

In the following examples, Veterans blamed themselves for heartbreaking and tragic outcomes. In each case, there are other factors to consider that were overlooked by the Veteran. As you read through, you will likely see that the Veteran confused the outcome with his or her responsibility.

Example of Betrayal

Leslie, a female non-commissioned officer (NCO), was a lesbian in the military before the time of "don't ask, don't tell." She was very private about her personal life and a respected E8. She declined dates and invitations to socialize, instead focusing on her job. She worked out nightly at the gym and ran several miles daily. She traveled alone but felt safe on the base. One evening she left the gym and began her run back to her quarters. She heard feet pounding the pavement behind her and two men pushed her to the ground. "Stuck Up Bitch," one said as they began the sexual assault. She could not see their faces in the dark. She was up for promotion soon and did not want anything to interfere, so she told no one about the assault.

This Veteran blamed herself for the military sexual trauma (MST). She said, "I should have seen them coming, I was not alert. I was weak - I should have fought back. I was stupid to travel alone on base." Her self-blame prevented her from placing full responsibility on the perpetrators. Years later, she finally got help for post-traumatic stress disorder (PTSD) and MI and put the responsibility where it belonged.

Survivors of MST or physical assault may be male or female. They use hindsight to explain why the assault happened and conclude, "It must have been my fault." They sometimes think, "I must have sent the wrong message," "I should have been able to stop it," or "I should have seen it coming." Some offenders blame the victim, which is a form of manipulation. The full responsibility of an assault (at any age) rests with the person who violated the boundaries of trust. The chaplain tells the story of a sexual assault team nurse who had just collected DNA evidence from a rape victim. Afterward, the survivor started to say, "I shouldn't have been there," blaming herself for the events of the night before. The nurse gently but firmly said, "Honey, it doesn't matter if you walked down a dark alley butt-naked! What he did, without your consent, is on him. That was not your fault!" *Nothing* justifies assault, and the victim is not to blame, yet the fact-finding interview after a sexual assault can feel like an interrogation for the victim. Military culture sometimes contributes to or sanctions this type of power, control, and aggression, and the legal system has not uniformly held accountable those who have done wrong. When victims report MST or assault, they sometimes are judged, labeled, or questioned as if they are the perpetrator. When the one who did the assault faces little to no consequences, the individual feels betrayed once again. Victims sometimes decide it is safer not to report, for the sake of career, reputation, and sanity.

Example of Participation

A young man was driving in a convoy on his first deployment. He had not paid close attention during training and tended to be distractible. He did not adhere to safety guidelines for convoy driving and followed too closely behind the vehicle in front of him. No one corrected him. He hit an improvised explosive device (IED) and, because he was following too close, was injured by the explosion, along with several others in a second vehicle. He believed he was responsible and accepted the reprimand that was delivered.

This is an example of legitimate responsibility for unintentional, accidental wrongdoing through inattention and driving too close. However, others shared a portion of the responsibility. Others in the vehicle were accountable for oversight; they should not have let him drive outside the wire under the circumstances. The enemy was also responsible for placing the IED, and sometimes accidents happened even with careful driving. He decided to make amends and to retrain on driving.

Example of Being a Bystander

A military vehicle caught fire and flipped over after an explosion. The Veteran reports he drove as quickly as possible to render aid. Those in the burning vehicle were unable to get out. He froze in shock for a moment, then snapped out of it. A group of five Marines, including the Veteran, struggled for over an hour, but could not "right" the vehicle or save those inside. For years he told himself, "It's my fault they died. If I had not frozen, we could have saved them."

This is an example of a negative outcome despite an appropriate response with good intentions. The Veteran blamed himself for the "freeze" response (part of the flight-fight-freeze) and carried unnecessary guilt. He developed MI because he judged that he "failed" and "could have done more." The evidence did not support his views. He corrected the distortions by realizing, "Freezing was outside my voluntary control. A moment or two would not have made any difference, anyway. It was a tragic death, and I could not have saved them. It is appropriate to grieve the tragic loss and not blame myself."

Example of Participation

Jordan, a former drone operator, blamed himself for a child's death. He had accurately tracked a target. Just as he pushed the button, a child ran into the field and the target moved away. The child was killed. "It is my fault," he said. "This error is unacceptable."

The reality was that the child's death was an accident. The Veteran realized he had acted appropriately and could not have foreseen the child's entry. The Veteran's MI was due to grief over unintended harm. He came to realize that "drones can hit unintended targets. I did not intend to kill a child. I wonder where that child's parents were; they are supposed to protect the child." He had done nothing wrong, and he was competent at his job. He worked to turn his guilt into grief and regret.

Looking at Responsibility

Responsibility for "wrongs" is complex and varies by participation, intention, predictability, and sanction. Contrary to military presumption, a tragic or negative outcome does not mean someone did anything *wrong*.

1. Type of Participation
   - If someone else hurt you, ordered a cover-up, was dishonest, or used poor judgment, you are not responsible. We call this type of MI a betrayal.
   - If you were a bystander, you are not responsible, but you might wish you could have done something to change the outcome.
   - If you were an active participant and something went wrong, responsibility varies by intention, predictability, and sanction.
2. Intention
   - When you had good intentions, but something went wrong, it is appropriate to have grief, remorse, sadness, or regret. This is the case with training accidents or civilian casualties.
   - If you inflict purposeful harm on someone, responsibility varies by sanction.
   - Other factors (emotional overload, lack of sleep, heavy combat, loss of troops, peer pressure) can contribute to decisions and negative outcomes.
3. Predictability
   - You are less responsible when the event is sudden, unexpected, and unpredictable. You might blame yourself, yet you could not see it coming.
   - You bear more responsibility if the event was predictable and intentional unless it was sanctioned and mission-driven.
4. Sanction
   - If an event was ordered or sanctioned, you may still have MI if what happened was at odds with your deeply held beliefs or values.
   - You might carry the burden of secrecy and guilt if there was a cover-up or if you witnessed something wrong and did not speak up.
   - If you engaged in unsanctioned behavior that caused harm, you are more responsible for the outcome.

Responsibility by Type of Involvement (Pernicano, 2019)

Responsibility (and, ultimately, accountability) depends on the type of involvement (Table 9.1). Responsibility also depends on intentions. Each type calls for a different action or response to resolve the MI.

Table 9.1 Responsibility by Type of Involvement

	No Responsibility	Sanctioned/Involved	At Fault/Blameworthy
Type of Involvement	• Victim of the event (betrayal), or • Uninvolved bystander, or • Not responsible for the event	• Participated in assigned military role • Actions were military-sanctioned • Responsibility for the event and/or the outcome may be unclear/debatable/shared	• Stepped outside assigned military role • Took unsanctioned actions or actions outside the bounds of military standards • Deliberately disregarded others
Intentions	You did nothing wrong	Mission-driven activity	• Intentional harm • Not mission-driven
Appropriate Emotional Reaction	• Sadness • Grief • Helplessness • Vulnerability • Anger at betrayal	• Regret (wish for a different outcome) • Vulnerability • Sadness • Grief • Healthy guilt for one's part	• Healthy guilt • Regret • Shame
Resolution (How to Address It)	• Mourn and process • Recognize injustice • Have self-compassion • Release the urge for retaliation or revenge • Pray, reflect, or meditate • Consider restorative justice	• Clarify blame vs. involvement • Consider the context • Grieve and mourn • Have self-compassion • Accept what you cannot change • Confess, seek forgiveness, make amends • Take reasonable responsibility	• Honestly admit • Take full responsibility • Confess, seek forgiveness, make amends, be accountable • Live to make the world a better place
Examples	• Victim of assault or rape • Survivor of an explosion, accident, or natural disaster • Loss of colleague • Not allowed to carry out one's duties (e.g., medic overruled by command and unable to care for an injured civilian)	• Failed rescue • Killed others in the line of duty • Friendly fire or training accident • Medic or command error • Faulty intel resulting in injury/death • Missing an improvised explosive device (IED) that exploded • Ordering a mission without adequate rest that resulted in casualties	• Physical or sexual assault • Covering up a wrongdoing • Desecrating a corpse • Having an extramarital affair • Violating rules of engagement • Unsanctioned torture • Revenge or unnecessary kill

The Responsibility Pie

The Responsibility Pie activity is a practice for evaluating personal responsibility following a negative outcome. It is eye-opening for many Veterans. If you have something to atone for, the burden is less when considering other contributing factors. Most situations, even wrongdoing, are multidetermined in causes or contributions. Pie charts have long been used as a statistical tool to display results, with different percentages given to causative factors.

Early application of the Responsibility Pie dates back to Beck et al. (1979), who helped clients with depression reattribute responsibility more objectively. Similarly, we teach Veterans to appraise personal responsibility before considering guilt, restitution, amends, or forgiveness. The pie exercise helps them identify their piece of reasonable responsibility, as a means of spelling out what they will work on in MI recovery, and to release the rest which is not theirs to carry. It is good to take responsibility for your part of things, and it is good to consider other factors that contributed to the outcome. The exercise offers a new way of looking at those overlooked factors, giving credit where credit was due. It tends to lighten the load of the Veteran's burdens and makes progress more achievable. It is important to examine who and what might be responsible for why something happened, and it is not about blame. Responsibility involves examining a situation, the context, and why things may have turned out the way they did. A person might be responsible to some degree, *and* other factors or persons may also have affected the outcome.

Responsibility Pie Exercise

The pie as a whole represents 100% responsibility. During the exercise, the pie gets divided into portions representing contributing factors to the outcome.

For your scenario, consider an event where you felt mostly or fully responsible. Then, brainstorm possible factors (other than yourself) that may have contributed to the outcome. Make a list of these. The brainstorming can be done as a group activity, but the final call on each factor belongs to the person who owns the story.

Here are some possible factors or sources of responsibility our Veterans have mentioned:

♦ The perpetrator (how often do victims overlook this one?)
♦ Military culture
♦ The enemy

- Other service members who were present
- The commander in chief
- Members of the chain of command
- Need to protect the group
- Conditions of war
- Need for self-defense
- Military values
- Service standards
- Reduced sleep/fatigue
- Physical illness/pain that diminished your own or others' concentration
- Condition of military vehicles or equipment
- Alcohol or drugs that impaired judgment
- The weather
- Lack of support from the command
- Previous combat engagements or close calls that elevated stress
- Place and time you were when it happened
- Other witnesses or non-service members present
- The expectation for obedience/following orders, etc.
- Inadequate justification for the war itself or ulterior motive
- Poor planning and execution
- Other

Once your list is complete, you estimate each factor's percentage of responsibility. Add the pieces to the pie, starting with the largest contributing factor. Add the factors to the pie one at a time, dividing up the pie by percentage, until you get to 100%. Assign your responsibility portion last and edit until you are comfortable with each piece of the pie. You can combine pieces that fall under the same umbrella; for example, you might put the chain of command and communication together if there was a breakdown in leadership communication that resulted in someone getting hurt.

Example Responsibility Pie Exercise

Robert was an Army Special Forces team leader. He led his team as ordered to parachute into a beachhead in Central America. The team took fire and returned fire until the command clarified the threat as friendly forces (a Navy Seal team operating in the same area). Outcome: three friendly casualties. As Robert told the story, we asked him how responsible he felt for this tragic outcome. His response was typical: 100 percent! He had been carrying the burden of those three lives on himself for over 20 years. This incident predated and led to the stand-up of the Special Operations Command, to improve coordination and communication between special operations units from different services.

Besides the Veteran, who or what other factors, persons, or conditions affected the outcome?

Factor	Percentage of Responsibility (%)

Now, put the pieces on a "pie," starting with the largest, and adjust as needed to get to 100%.

Contributing Factors

When we use this case study to introduce and practice the Responsibility Pie as a group, most Veterans identify factors such as chain of command, poor communications, lack of joint operations policies at that time, and inaccurate intelligence. Combined, they get to about 90–95% of the pie. Both groups should have known that the other was in the area of operations. Also, they had excellent training, and when fired on, they fired back without question (1–2%). There is an adrenaline response to taking fire when survival is threatened (1–2%). Central America was in flux, and missions there presented some danger (1–2%). Visibility could have been a factor, depending on the weather conditions.

In the initial sharing of the story, as the group helped Robert complete the exercise, he went from 100% to 15% for himself. Before this group activity, he had never even considered any responsibility for the team leader of the other service, let alone for higher in the chain of command. We celebrate any appropriate reduction in responsibility when supported by the facts. Robert worked on the remaining 15% of personal responsibility with self-forgiveness and amends. While we facilitators and some of the Veterans would have put his responsibility even lower, it was his story and his determination that mattered for his recovery. At the end of the group, he shared that this exercise had been a game changer for him and had helped him get unstuck.

Complete Your Responsibility Pie

1. Complete a Responsibility Pie for yourself, following the steps reviewed earlier. Choose a situation in the past for which you feel a high level of responsibility. We have all done things for which we feel responsible or guilty. In making the list, consider your actions last. Also, focus more on facts than on feelings.

2. Remember a negative outcome does not necessarily reflect blame or responsibility, i.e., a "wrong" decision or behavior. Military assignment of blame in "after-action reviews" may not always reflect accurate responsibility for what happened.

3. You may be partly, fully, or not at all responsible for what happened. Your responsibility pie will point to the next steps for you to resolve what happened. For more help, consider the handout, "Responsibility by Type of Involvement."

After objectively considering all possible factors and assigning each a percentage of responsibility, you can determine your piece of the pie. What do you do with the guilt that remains? There is hope, and we will address this in the next chapter.

References

Beck, A. T., Rush, A., Shaw, B., & Emery, G. (1979). *Cognitive therapy of depression.* Guilford Press.

Pernicano, P. (2019). Responsibility by type of involvement. In P. Pernicano & K. Haynes. *Acceptance & forgiveness therapy: From brokenness to restoration* [Unpublished handbook] (5th ed.). South Texas Veterans Health Care System.

Pernicano, P., & Haynes, K. (2023). *Acceptance & forgiveness therapy: From brokenness to restoration* [Unpublished handbook] (5th ed.). South Texas Veterans Health Care System.

Chapter 10

Practicing Confession and Forgiveness

There is no peace without forgiveness. Whatever you carry – guilt, bitterness, wish for revenge, or self-punishment – hurts you and blocks you from living fully as your whole self; it leaves you in pieces. Once you identify reasonable guilt and responsibility (see Chapter 9), there is a pathway to confession and forgiveness in pursuit of wholeness.

> *Tom was a Lieutenant who did not listen to his platoon sergeant in Iraq. She warned him of a probable ambush on the route they had planned, based on solid intelligence. Yet, in an arrogant desire to look good in the eyes of his commander, he rejected her advice and ended up taking his platoon into a kill zone, unnecessarily losing three of his soldiers and having five others wounded. When we first met Tom, he carried appropriate guilt which needed to be addressed if he ever hoped to live life fully again. Some battlefield events were beyond his control, which we helped him identify, but others were not. He was responsible for a poor choice which resulted in fatal outcomes. His path forward involved self-forgiveness and making amends, all discussed later in this chapter.*

Confession before Self-Forgiveness

Confession brings an offense into the light – out in the open – a step before pursuing self-forgiveness. In the documentary, *Almost Sunrise* (Collins, 2016), Father Thomas Keating suggests to two traveling warriors that sharing brings your actions to light. This is part of the journey toward self-forgiveness. Healing involves honestly admitting, "Yes, I did this." Confessing names something *wrong* that hurt you or someone else. It may also include a willingness to forgive hurt done to you. Confession consists of the desire and willingness to change your attitude, behavior, and emotional response to what happened. This is the "flawed" part of us Worthington and Griffin

DOI: 10.4324/9781003494263-13

speak of (n.d., p. 4, used with permission). It is also important to realize that if you were betrayed, no self-forgiveness is needed; you might acknowledge a desire to release the bitter poison within you while realizing that you could not prevent or stop what happened.

Confession in the presence of others names the pain and lightens the burden of pain. As Malott et al. (2016) state in their group therapy handbook, *Trauma-related Forgiveness* (p. 65, cited with permission):

> *There are few things more terrifying than allowing another person to see our darkest parts. However, the minute that you open up those dark parts to another, light immediately floods in and they begin to look different. Throughout the act of writing your confessional story, you face your own shame, but it is not until another person looks in that you begin to believe that you are not alone. Being accepted only for the outer mask you wear is far less gratifying than being accepted for exactly who you are, including the parts that you loathe.*

In group moral injury (MI) treatment, Veterans become a safe community in which to confess to each other; receive compassion rather than judgment; learn to have compassion for themselves, as they would a friend; become accountable, with restitution/amends; and commit to living in the present, one day at a time.

Models of Confession

Confession releases pain and prepares someone to offer or receive forgiveness; it is not limited to a religious process. In acceptance and forgiveness therapy (AFT), the authors discuss several models of confession. For instance, in the *12-step model*, you work the 12 steps with the help of a sponsor (benevolent other). You agree to be subjected to a higher power, engage in self-examination, develop a moral inventory (responsibility for harm to self/others), and commit to change. You become part of a forgiving community, examine yourself daily, and live one day at a time.

In the *religious model*, you subject yourself to a higher authority such as a priest or minister. Many religions teach the concept of "go and sin no more" through prayer, forgiveness, grace, penance, and moving on with the rest of your life. If someone hurt or betrayed you, you might turn them over to the "court of a higher power" and stop being their spiritual judge.

In the *legal model*, you go to court and subject yourself to a higher authority, admit your wrongs, accept responsibility, and receive the consequences, such as restitution, probation, life restrictions, paying a fine, serving time, or being *released with time served* (something that resonates with many Veterans). Upon release, you commit to following the rules or conditions of parole/probation.

In the *relational model of confession*, you share something about the MI event with a compassionate counselor or loved one, even if you fear rejection, disgust, withdrawal of love, or loss of respect. This opens the door for additional support in your recovery. The writers encourage Veterans to share a small part of their story in testing the waters, to learn if they can trust another with more of their story. Sometimes, for instance, a spouse or partner cannot hear the extent of their Veteran's full story, yet Veterans could practice with a small piece of it. Also, if what you want to confess will hurt the other person, confession might better be made to a neutral third party.

Lastly, there is a *private/internal personal acknowledgment model*. Here, you simply write it down (some Veterans find meaning in journaling), commit to change, give back to society/others, make a sacrifice, or serve others. You have confessed only to yourself, yet you have chosen to take deliberate steps toward healing.

The following is an example of an AFT worksheet designed to help Veterans engage in private confession.

Call to Confession: Name the Pain

(Pernicano & Haynes, 2023)

None of us are perfect, and we carry burdensome memories of times we were not our best selves. We invite you to complete your private confession. When you are finished, consider if there is any call for action, such as an apology, restitution, or amends. After each statement, you might write or say, "I am imperfect *and* worthy. I seek forgiveness."

"I hurt someone else. I violated human rights, values, morals, or sacred beliefs."

_____

"I hurt someone through inaction, silence, ignoring, or looking the other way."

_____

"I continue to block forgiveness of myself or someone else."

_____

"I blamed myself for something that was not my fault."

_____

"I blamed someone else for something I did."

_____

"The burden I carry has hurt me and those around me."

_____

"Someone hurt me badly. The bitterness I carry is hurting me more than it is hurting them."

_____

"I let the past or someone else define me."

_____

"I have been unwilling or unable to release my bitterness about what happened."

_____

Other: _____

Metaphors of Forgiveness

Forgiveness is hard to define. For many Veterans, a metaphor helps clarify what forgiveness might feel like to the individual (Pernicano & Haynes, 2023). Each metaphor reflects a different aspect of forgiveness. The creative metaphors offer flexible options for pursuing forgiveness.

Which of these metaphors represents forgiveness for you? (Or write your own metaphor.)

1. Picture yourself handcuffed to the past, surrounded by self-blame, guilt, or bitterness. Forgiveness is finding the key and then using that key to unlock the cuffs. Once you are uncuffed, what will you do to pursue peace?
2. Picture yourself wearing a heavy rucksack full of rocks. Some belong to you, and some are not yours to carry. Forgiveness is dumping some rocks out of the rucksack to lighten your load. What is left will be easier to carry and deal with.
3. Picture yourself discarded in a landfill, broken, and battered. Someone finds you and offers help. They see beauty and value in you that you do not see in yourself. They offer help. Forgiveness is accepting help and knowing that you are worth the effort.
4. Picture yourself dumping your burdens in the lake and then filling the almost empty burden bag with blessings. Forgiveness is letting yourself experience gratitude and counting your blessings.
5. Picture yourself being eaten alive on the inside by corrosive memories that create intense and unresolved guilt, anger, grief, regret, bitterness, etc. Forgiveness is taking an antidote to the poison to dissolve the negative emotions and healing from the inside out.
6. Picture yourself as a sponge, full of dirty water and no longer able to clean. Forgiveness is rinsing out that sponge and then compassionately filling it with clean water. Imagine what you would pour into the sponge for renewed purpose and function.
7. You decide to use the clean sponge to wipe up a mess that is partly of your own making. Thousands of others join you, with thousands of clean sponges, to restore beauty to what was lost.
8. Picture yourself floating in quicksand. Forgiveness is turning around and using the rope ladder to climb out. Now, where will you head as you continue down the path?
9. You have been on a long journey down the river with a locked box of your worst memories. You let them out of the box and listen while they shriek and moan. Together, you grieve the past and paddle together in a new direction.

10. You turn the person who hurt you over to your higher power (benevolent other). Be creative. You might beam them up or use a spiritual dumbwaiter. Hand them over. Now, they are out of your sight, mind, and heart. You no longer have to serve as judge and jury.

11. Picture yourself in a court of acceptance and forgiveness as the judge releases you with time served. The judge suggests you now live your life with purpose and meaning, accepting failure and worth.

12. Your anger has kept you on the far side of a large canyon. You find the bridge you were searching for and cross to the other side. As you cross, your anger and bitterness lessen, and when you reach the other side, you resume your journey.

13. You are planning a rafting trip down a long river. When you get to the location, some "ghosts from the past" join you there. They have lived rent-free in your head for many years and intend to go with you on this journey. Picture yourself asking their forgiveness, saying goodbye, and starting your journey without them.

14. Other (write your own): _____

_____

Which metaphor(s) "feels like" a path to forgiveness for you? _____

_____

Forgiveness involves a choice to let go, a purposeful action, and a symbolic release of pain. This in turn allows each of us a path forward. One or more of these metaphors might identify where/how you are stuck and the next steps on your journey of forgiveness and healing. Each represents a way to release MI and move toward healing. None of them are punitive, but each suggests letting go, releasing pain, or moving in a new direction. Willingness is the first step in the process of forgiveness.

A creative next step might involve building a short story around your chosen metaphor and seeing where it leads you. Why? Metaphor is a different form of language and communication. It helps us step outside the box when considering forgiveness. Consider this example:

I am in the court of acceptance and forgiveness when the benevolent judge calls for me to rise. I don't want to be here. I can never forgive myself for what happened. The judge is releasing me with time served.

What do I say to the judge? _____

_____

As I think about why I am in prison, I explain it to the judge. What do I say? _____

_____

The judge tells me I am released for time served, because no one gets life in prison for what I experienced.

What is my response to the judge? _____

_____

The judge says I can lead a more meaningful life outside of prison.

I argue with the judge, even though I wonder how this might be possible. What do I say?

_____

In the end… _____

_____

Most of the metaphors above can be turned into stories of acceptance and forgiveness. Acceptance might be a way of saying, "This happened and I am no longer going to deny that it happened or consider other ways it might have turned out. I try to rewrite the story or change the ending when I dwell on the past. I can't change what happened, but I *can* change how I react now."

Letter Writing from a Benevolent Other

Self-forgiveness is a tough journey out of pain, and it helps when Veterans consider how they are viewed by a benevolent other of their choosing. Since AFT respects different forms of spirituality and religion, Veterans choose a benevolent other consistent with their worldviews. The writers use the term "benevolent other" similar to that of a "higher power" in a 12-step program. A benevolent other is the Veteran's identified source of unconditional positive "grace" or acceptance. A benevolent other considers context and intentions and will encourage the other person toward purpose and meaning in life, regardless of prior actions or inactions. We encourage the Veterans to see themselves through the eyes of this benevolent other. Veterans see themselves compassionately through the eyes of their dog, sibling, military leader, battle buddy, family member, friend, the Pope, or the Divine.

A letter writing project invites Veterans to use the lens of someone else's caring eyes when struggling with forgiveness (see more on this project in Chapter 11). Epston (2009) describes the legacy of letter writing as a clinical practice. Veterans write a letter from someone who cares for them unconditionally, sees good in them, and has compassion for them. This gestalt-like technique allows them to "hear the voice" of someone who loves them and wants them to find peace. This letter often stirs compassion for themselves and encourages them to make peace with the past. Consider this Veteran's story and subsequent letter:

Michael blamed himself for sleeping during a jeep accident in which the front passenger was killed. Granted, he was only a rear passenger, off duty, and not wearing night vision goggles (NVGs). The dark was pitch black and he had been awake for 48 hours. It was supposed to be a routine transport. Who was to know that the driver would not be wearing his NVGs and that another piece of equipment would shatter their window and impale the front passenger? The driver may have fallen asleep and was later court-martialed. Michael was abruptly awakened by the cries of the man in the front.

The driver had become emotionally unhinged, and it was Michael who stepped up, telling him to keep the man as still as possible until medics arrived. Michael held the man's hand, prayed with him, talked comfortingly to him, and promised to notify his family. Despite efforts, the man died shortly after. Michael contacted the man's family and told them about the efforts he had made. He grieved with them as they mourned their loss.

Michael was stuck in his "what-if?" grief and self-doubts. He chose for his benevolent other the man who died. We suggested he see himself through that man's eyes. Here is his letter:

Dear Michael,

The night I died was the darkest night. Even with NVGs, it was hard to see, and that other vehicle came up out of nowhere. We didn't have time to get out of the way or get their attention. I was so glad you were with me that night. It happened so suddenly. I couldn't move; my heart was pounding, I cried out, and then I felt your hand in mine. You called my name and told me it would be OK. I'm glad you said it, even though I didn't believe you. Having you there was good. I didn't want to die alone, and our driver was a mess. Hearing your voice calmed me. I was pretty sure I was dying, but you were there. My family remembers you as a kind and compassionate man. No one should have to die alone. They were grateful that I made it home to them and that you told them about me and what happened. They know it wasn't your fault. You need to let me go, Michael. Please don't carry me with you any longer. My time came, and your time will come, and what matters is that, because of you, I did not have to die alone.

Love you, man.

The process of self-forgiveness starts with willingness more than readiness. Punitive guilt does not leave room for grace. Most Veterans have more than "served their time" (emotionally, spiritually, and relationally) as if giving themselves a life sentence in prison. Sometimes we ask Veterans in a group to add how many combined years they suffered and carried the burden; the total may be in the hundreds! Most begin to realize that enough is enough, and we suggest they consider "time served" to envision a path forward.

Time Served

Pernicano (2023) in Pernicano & Haynes (2023)

A man once appeared before a benevolent judge in the Court of Acceptance and Forgiveness. He had struggled to accept and forgive things from his past, and he carried a heavy burden of guilt and pain. He was serving a self-imposed sentence of life in prison, without parole.

The judge asked him to stand up, and said, "You have been in this prison a long time. I would like to hear your story." The man stood up. He was reluctant to tell his story because he knew it would stir up his painful memories. But not talking about it had not helped, so he hesitantly did what the judge asked.

After he finished, the judge said, "You are free to go—with time served. It is time for you to be released. No one deserves life in prison for what you have told me. You have served many years in this dark and painful place. Go collect your things and reclaim your life."

The man went back to his cell and locked himself in.

Later that day, the guard came by the cell. He asked the man, "Why are you still here? It's time for you to go. The judge released you with time served." The guard laid the key by the cell door.

Two days later, the man was still in his cell. He had not used the key. The guard came and said, "I gave you the key to the cell door and it is still there on the floor." The guard picked up the key, unlocked the cell, opened the door, and said, "You are free to go. What are you waiting for?"

The man had many reasons for why he had remained in the cell. He was still in pain, and he was not sure what to do next. He told the guard, "It's not that easy. Being free to go is about two things: one part is your mind, knowing it is time, and the other part is spiritual, wondering if you deserve it or if you are willing to stop carrying it. I'm working on freeing myself. Until I accept what you offer me and free myself, I'm not really free to go."

The guard was baffled and said, "Well, in the court's eyes, you are free to go. So go, and continue your journey of mind and spirit somewhere else."

For some, it is not enough to be freed by a benevolent judge, with time served. Someone else may free you, but you remain bound by your inner pain and struggles. Freeing yourself and releasing your pain is not as easy as it seems. And yet, it is your decision to make. Remaining in emotional prison is not a path forward.

The man finally collected his things and left the jail cell. He would find the key to free himself in mind and spirit. He would reclaim his life. But for now, he would continue his journey as he searched for acceptance and forgiveness.

Questions About Release from Punitive Guilt:

1. What is your life sentence for (i.e., self-imposed emotional punishment)?
2. What gets in the way of you forgiving yourself?
3. What is the benefit of staying in jail? What is lost?
4. Comment on "time served" (how many years have you served for your moral pain and lived with the MI?).
5. Releasing yourself from an emotional prison involves self-forgiveness or letting go of the bitterness of betrayal. What types of restitution, amends, or positive practices might help you leave your emotional jail and move forward on your journey?

Jim, a skilled medic, struggled with guilt over a woman's sudden death in Iraq. She had come to sick call for what looked like a boil on her breast. He suspected a clogged duct, gave her some antibiotic ointment, and said, "Go put hot compresses on it, then report for duty tomorrow." What turned out to be a flesh-eating bacteria spread rapidly and went septic by morning. The blood infection shut down her organs and she died several hours later, delirious with a fever of 105 degrees. "I missed it," he said. "I was in too much of a hurry. I should have cultured it. She died because of my error." He did not believe in a higher power and punitive guilt had kept him in chains for 20 years. "I don't deserve a good life," he said, "because she lost hers." When he heard about time-served, the wheels started to turn, and his eyes lit up. "I'm wasting what life I have. I can accept time served. I can forgive myself and ask her [in a letter] to forgive me. I can visit her grave. I can accept my imperfection and restore some value and integrity."

Worthington's Forgiveness Model (Included with Author Permission)

See Chapter 5 for the story behind the REACH model (Worthington, 2001); the model is detailed in an online workbook (Worthington & Griffin, n.d.). This model of forgiveness teaches Veterans to balance guilt/fallibility/imperfection with grace/compassion/worth and extend compassion to themselves and others. Suffering "with" and "for" yourself is a new idea to many, but when we step back and examine the context of MI, we see the potential for acceptance and forgiveness. Here is the model, with descriptions added beneath each step from Pernicano & Haynes (2023):

Step 1: Decide to Pursue Forgiveness
> This decision is at the head level. It is the stage of willingness.

Step 2: Put the Responsibility Where It Belongs
> Responsibility pie can help with this. What is your piece of responsibility? What other circumstances or persons share that responsibility?

Step 3: Challenge Unrealistic Expectations
> Give up perfectionism. You are fallible. Others are fallible. What about your situation being unrealistic?

Step 4: Reduce Rumination (Worrying)
> When you can't stop thinking about something, focus on something else that is more positive rather than trying to suppress the negative. For example, when you say, "Don't think of someone in red underwear," it usually has the opposite effect.

Step 5: REACH Steps for Emotional Forgiveness
> (Compassion = suffer with, in a way that you feel pain and want to step in and help)
>> R = *Recall* the hurt that was done (this may include a process of confession). Name it and feel the moral pain of what happened.
>> E = *Empathize with the person (self or another who hurt you).* Consider your own or someone else's humanity. Accept permission to fail. Feel compassion for the hurt person. Consider the context in which the MI happened.

A = *Altruistic forgiveness.* "Altruistic" means giving forgiveness with no strings attached. Be kind to yourself or speak kindly of the other, as you would someone you care about in a similar situation. If you are not ready to forgive, think of your metaphor (let go of the poison) and seek willingness.

C = *Commit to forgiveness.* Mark your forgiveness journey with a symbolic ceremony or ritual. Consider time served or a metaphor of forgiveness that commits you.

H = *Hold onto forgiveness.* Recognize this as a process or journey, one day at a time. On low days, return to your commitment to keep going.

Step 6: Realize Human Beings Are Flawed but Precious

Accept failure. If you "failed" or hurt others, accept your mistakes and human limitations. Stop carrying punitive guilt.

Accept value. If you were betrayed, you did not deserve it, and the betrayal does not define who you are. If you hurt someone else, that does not define the whole of who you are, and you still have value. Others see good in you even when you can't see it in yourself. Accept support from others (family, friends, church, pastors, pets, and therapists).

Step 7: Live Your Best Version of Yourself with Room to Fail

Forgiveness frees you to pursue peace and live compassionately. Make amends, pay it forward, engage in restitution, or restore relationships when possible and advisable. Don't put yourself back into situations where you will be hurt or betrayed.

Forgiveness is complicated; it does not excuse, deny, or minimize what happened. Offering or receiving forgiveness is sometimes life-changing. A clip from the movie *The Mission* (Joffé, 1986) depicts a waterfall climbing scene. It powerfully illustrates the turning point in self-forgiveness for slave trader Rodrigo Mendoza, in the context of the community of the slaves' ancestors extending forgiveness to him. The chief and villagers have received forgiveness training from the Jesuits living in their community. Thus, a young villager, directed by his chief, shifts a knife from Mendoza's throat to the rope securing the burden of a bag of armor Mendoza has dragged up the cliff. The villager cuts the rope and pushes the load over the cliff, where it splashes into the river far below. Mendoza's self-judgment turns to tears of relief as he visibly releases his load among the community of those whose relatives he has enslaved. Forever changed by the experience, he lives with and defends the village for the rest of his life.

The clip prompts a discussion of self- and other-forgiveness in a community context. MI often occurs in the context of a community, and it is largely resolved in a community of fellow Veterans with MI. Veterans contribute to each other's healing in a powerful therapeutic way. The movie clip illustrates that: 1) the tribe experienced terrible betrayal, 2) the slave trader sought to make amends to the tribe and himself, and 3) the slave trader took a new perspective as he moved forward, ultimately becoming the bodyguard for the tribe.

Coping with Betrayal

In the case of *The Mission*, the tribe was ready to forgive the slave trader's betrayal. However, forgiveness is a process that takes time. As we move in that direction, we can adopt a stance of willingness to:

- Commit to practicing self-compassion.
- Practice letting go: "I don't like or trust you, but I don't have to hate you. I can stop being judge and jury. What you did was wrong. I do not have to let it define or control me. I deserve better."
- Recognize that accountability belongs to the one who hurt you. Don't let what happened continue to control or define you.
- Speak up for yourself or educate others. You may blog, volunteer, speak to elected officials, or share what happened. You may pursue restorative justice by using your voice and speaking the truth.
- Live by your values. Release bitterness. Living with compassion rather than retaliation makes a powerful statement.

In their poem *The Prayer Before the Prayer*, Tutu and Tutu (2015) speak of the difficulty of forgiving others and the willingness to release anger as an early step.

Describe your willingness to move toward forgiveness of yourself or others:

_____

_____

_____

Making Amends

When you have wronged others, even unintentionally, you may decide to make amends. This action rights a wrong, heals brokenness, and restores wholeness. You might:

1. Engage in restitution or make amends.
2. Make the world a better place by paying it forward, living out your values, and becoming your best self.
3. Practice compassion.
4. Take responsibility and hold yourself accountable for choices and behaviors.

A Vietnam Veteran returned to the village that haunted him, many years after the war had ended. There he met an old man, like himself, who had fought the same fight, likely against one another. They talked of the war, wept, and shared a peace ceremony. They acknowledged a new friendship; together, they started a foundation for relocated Vietnamese needing help to settle in the US. Making amends quieted his grief and the cries of those he had hurt.

Guilt responds to confession, forgiveness, and restorative justice. Guilt expressed in unhealthy ways is punitive and eats you alive from the inside out. It remains unresolved and may turn to shame ("I am bad"). While you cannot *undo* what you did, you *can* accept responsibility for your actions and put them in context. Some Veterans tie amends to what they did. It doesn't have to be a direct tie; for instance, you may not be able to return to the battlefield, as the Vietnam Veteran did. But indirect amends work, too. For example, if children were harmed, you might invest time or money in a charity such as Compassion International that serves children (https://www.compassion.com). If you acted non-compassionately, you might show compassion through volunteer service. By giving back with compassion, you heal your soul and find peace.

How have you been making amends or planning to make amends?

_____

_____

Other Considerations

You can change how you think about your MI by putting it in context, writing a letter, completing a responsibility pie, or considering a new point of view. If you lost someone close to you or think that you should have died instead of them, consider what advice that person would give you if they were here today. Ask, "What would that person want for me?" or "What would I want for the other person if the roles were reversed?"

_____

_____

You might practice seeing yourself through the eyes of a benevolent other, i.e., take the perspective of someone who loves you unconditionally. What would you say to the benevolent other about your struggle to accept and forgive the past? Consider the benevolent other's response to you, i.e., what would the benevolent other suggest you do to find peace?

_____

_____

Responding to the Compassion of Others

Forgiveness is not a feeling. It is a set of intentions, actions, and practices that start with the head and move to the heart (Worthington & Griffin, n.d.). REACH, time served, and *The Mission* reflect that:

♦ Offering and accepting forgiveness are choices.
♦ Our higher power is bigger than our circumstances or failure.
♦ Rituals and ceremonies are important.
♦ There is power in the community.
♦ Our efforts can prepare us to receive emotional healing and forgiveness.
♦ Compassion is powerful.
♦ When we *offer forgiveness*, we free the other person to move on. We free ourselves of a heavy burden of anger, bitterness, etc. The man with the knife *did not yet know* the slave trader's decision to turn his life around, yet he gave him that opportunity.
♦ When we *experience forgiveness*, we are released to find a new purpose and move on. When others forgive us (even when we don't *deserve it*), we become capable of self-forgiveness and self-acceptance. The movie's main character spends the rest of his life serving the tribe, i.e., making amends.

A Veteran's Story of Guilt, Self-Forgiveness, and Reconnection

Wes was a retired senior non-commissioned officer (NCO) in the Army Reserves. As a leader, he was directly responsible for the welfare of his soldiers during the unit's monthly two-day battle training assemblies (or "drills") along with the two-week annual training. He and other like-minded leaders (both officers and NCOs) cared for their soldiers even between battle assemblies.

Wes was an extrovert with a pleasant, positive demeanor, yet highly critical of himself. As the group sessions progressed, Wes began to show a more fragile side, some cracks in his facade. He was hurting and carrying a heavy responsibility. Finally, as we came towards the end of the group sessions, Wes shared his MI story. One of his junior enlisted soldiers, "Private Jones," had been reaching out regularly in the weeks leading up to their battle assembly. Jones's girlfriend had left him, and Jones wasn't handling it very well. He called a number of times under the influence of alcohol, barely coherent, and didn't respond well to his NCO. Finally, Wes had had enough. He didn't answer the last call that came just a day before their battle assembly. He planned to let the young man sober up and deal with this matter face-to-face, during their training weekend.

Unfortunately, Private Jones didn't show up for the training, and Wes learned that Jones had killed himself. By the time Wes made it to our group, several years had passed and he, like many Veterans, claimed 100 percent responsibility for this heart-breaking incident. Suicide triggers a unique form of guilt and shame for the survivors. As a pebble thrown into a pond creates a ripple effect on the water, suicide creates its own ripple effect of guilt among all those left behind, wondering what they could have said or done or not said or not done differently.

The Veterans in the group mourned with Wes (a testament to the power of group treatment!) and noted that his grief was evidence that he, a senior leader, truly cared for his soldier. He was not a leader who was only in it for him or herself. As Wes shared his Responsibility Pie exercise, he noted more objectively that he was not alone in the chain of command for this soldier; many other officers and NCOs carried some responsibility for the young man's well-being. And unique to the Reserves and Guard, managing soldiers between monthly battle training assemblies is difficult, as soldiers are scattered geographically. Wes realized that Private Jones's personal life was just that: personal, and that the military had nothing to say about his relationships outside of military duty time, as long as he was able to accomplish his duty mission. Finally, Wes concluded that suicide is ultimately the responsibility of the one who takes their own life. Answering that one phone call would not necessarily have changed the eventual outcome. As hard as we try (and the military puts a ton of time and effort into it), ultimately it is virtually impossible to stop someone from dying by suicide if they do not cooperate with others in seeking help.

This sad story illustrates the unresolved grief work often behind MI. Rather than finding healthy ways to grieve, Veterans turn to self-blame and impose a life sentence without parole until they realize that it is time to grieve their losses. Guilt may blind Veterans from seeing the big picture. In this story, the non-commissioned officer (NCO) could have answered the phone call, but taking the call would not guarantee the prevention of a later suicide. His guilt could have been confessed in appropriate ways and dealt with. In all fairness, he *had* answered previous calls, which proved unproductive due to the soldier's drunken state. He wisely reasoned that he would see the soldier soon anyway. No one can predict the future although Veterans quickly blame themselves when they cannot.

Through grief work, this leader found a path forward to self-forgiveness and was also able, as a result, to be there more fully for his fellow Veterans. After a female Veteran shared about sexual trauma, he said he would like to "meet that guy in a dark alley." He became a safe *big brother type* for the other Veteran, helped her rebuild trust in others, and, through that, found a little healing himself.

Healing occurs through interactions, compassion, and acceptance alongside others. Wes befriended a young soldier in the group, and their relationship steadily grew. Wes was compassionate and encouraging to this young man, and they sat together, sometimes cutting up and other times relating more like a father and son.

One week the young Veteran spoke of spending a lot of time with a friend named "Jack," who turned out to be Jack Daniels. He had been emotionally broken by several combat-related events that involved civilian deaths and a child being used as a human shield. He felt hopeless about his actions as a soldier and now struggled as the father of a young child.

As the young man spoke of suicidal ideation, Wes jumped in with care and concern. Looking back, Wes was paying it forward and making amends for his past. He genuinely cared for the other group member. Wes offered the first validation after the young man shared his story in the group, pointing out his courage during very tough circumstances. The young man tearfully confessed he felt forgiven and supported in ways that were new for him. He had real friends and was relying less on "Jack." Wes embraced him and referred to his strengths and hope for his future.

*The young man came to the group a few weeks later and proudly announced that his young son had spent the weekend with him on school break (after a long absence). He had promised to use a kit to make a gingerbread house with his son. They discovered many broken pieces as they opened it, which moved his son to tears. The soldier shared, "In the past, I probably would have said, 'What the F***' and thrown it away. But he was crying so hard. I hated to see him cry, so I hugged him and said, 'We'll fix this.' I said, 'It's like that story of the cracked bowl in the group. We'll put the pieces back together!' We used lots of icing and, piece by piece, we built that gingerbread house. He was so happy!" He got a little tearful and, as Wes patted him on the shoulder, the young man said, "See, I'm putting the pieces back together in myself, and in my life!"*

Wes had come full circle in his role with a younger soldier. Together, they were healing their moral injuries. The young man was finding new meaning in being a father, and an older NCO was healing his guilt through their relationship.

References

Collins, M. (Director). (2016). *Almost Sunrise* [Film]. Veterans Trek Production.

Epston, D. (2009). The legacy of letter writing as a clinical practice: Introduction to the special issue on therapeutic letters. *Journal of Family Nursing, 15*(1), 3–5. https://doi.org/10.1177/10748407083311

Joffé, R. (1986). *The Mission* [Film]. Warner Bros.

Malott, J. D., Smigelsky, M. A., Whiteford, R., & Smith, M. (2016). *Trauma-Related Forgiveness Group Therapy* [Unpublished manual]. Memphis VA Medical Center.

Pernicano, P., & Haynes, K. (2023). *Acceptance & forgiveness therapy: From brokenness to restoration* [Unpublished handbook] (5th ed.). South Texas Veterans Health Care System.

Tutu, D., & Tutu, M. (2015). *The book of forgiving: the fourfold path for healing ourselves and the world.* D. Abrams (Ed.). Harper.

Worthington, E. L., Jr. (2001). *Five steps to forgiveness: The art and science of forgiving.* Crown.

Worthington, E. L., Jr., & Griffin, B. J. (n.d.). *Moving Forward: Six Steps to Forgiving Yourself and Breaking Free from the Past* (2nd ed.). [Online workbook]. Virginia Commonwealth University. https://forgiveself.com/workbooks/20150903%20Self-Forgiveness%20Intervention%20Workbook.pdf

Chapter 11

The Healing of Sharing Your Story

Not sharing your moral injury (MI) story is like pretending that a wound will heal without treatment while flesh-eating bacteria destroy from within. A soul wound (Tick, 2005, 2014; Brock & Lettini, 2012; Wood, 2016) is unlikely to heal without help because of the meaning ascribed and the unresolved moral pain. Until the wound heals and leaves a clean scar, the damage will continue to cause pain. Telling your story, with acceptance and forgiveness, is like healing from the inside out (Pernicano, 2012).

As you prepare to talk about your MI, keep the focus on your healing and not on stirring-up anger, resentment, bitterness, guilt, or hopelessness. When you first describe what happened, it may stir deep emotions. The purpose of sharing is to make meaning of what happened so that you see it in context, accept what you cannot change, feel compassion for yourself, and tolerate imperfection. You begin to understand that what happened does not need to define you; it is part of you but not the whole.

Trauma-Informed Storytelling

Cavanaugh et al. (2019) provide a helpful guide for telling and processing a trauma-focused story safely and healthily. Sharing your story with others, in the context of respect and compassion, provokes empathy, contributes to understanding, and expands your perspective. Others can provide feedback to challenge assumptions/ generalizations, humanize unintended outcomes, create bridges, and build a community based on shared humanity. Cavanaugh et al. indicate there are benefits to sharing stories in a group because the storytelling is beneficial for the teller and the listener: individuals better "understand their own experience, find the strength to share their voice and gain confidence in the power of that voice" (slide 13). Participants become an instrument for change.

DOI: 10.4324/9781003494263-14

It helps to keep it simple, so "don't get stuck in the weeds" or become side-tracked by explanations, dates, names, or other unnecessary details, as they can become confusing or take you off-topic. As you edit out irrelevant portions, you get to the main points on your timeline: what happened, which values were violated, your emotional response to what happened, what blocked your healing, and what you told yourself. Then, point out what is helping you change through acceptance, compassion, forgiveness, or release. Tell the listeners your hopes for healing and the ways your listeners have encouraged you. Be concise and credible in what you share, keeping to facts more than impressions or conclusions that may be unwarranted (such as irrational, punitive, or hurtful comments).

As you think about your story, consider the context, so you see the social forces or other factors that contributed to your MI. Cavanaugh et al. (2019) suggest you anticipate and prepare for possible triggers and the unexpected. You may not have fully healed from some parts of your story, and you don't have to expose all the details to make your point. Remember that you are in control of the language and the emotions. Focus on where you are now and how your story got you there. You can find strength in your story, as it will impact others as you tell it, perhaps giving them courage and willingness. Your story might be just what someone else needs to hear.

Compassion for Yourself

Telling your story of MI is a way of healing from the inside out, sealing your cracks (Pernicano, 2012), "cutting your rope" (see "The Mission," Joffé, 1986), and building connection. Having compassion for yourself (suffering with and for yourself) is a way of seeing yourself through a new lens, in which you can be both flawed and valuable (Worthington & Griffin, n.d.). It is part of the process of acceptance and forgiveness. MI often comes from interpersonal trauma where trust is violated by others who hurt you or by your actions. Sometimes Veterans feel *abandoned* by a higher power, or they develop suicidal ideation when they judge themselves to be beyond hope. One Veteran said, "I'm like the Hulk. I try to stay in control, but one thing triggers me and I'm that huge, angry, scary monster. I have lost who I used to be, and now I hurt the people I love."

Telling your story is a form of confession. Sharing your story in the presence of compassionate others is restorative, letting you acknowledge and accept your fallibility and worth (Worthington & Griffin, n.d.). Telling your story can be a pivotal change point as you confess pain, identify the impact, take reasonable responsibility, help others who struggle, and share a pathway to hope and healing. Being in a community with trusted others lightens the load of heavy, long-carried burdens.

Those who listen to your story *hold* the pain and, like a kind mirror, reflect compassion and concern. This is not acceptance of actions that caused moral pain; it is acceptance of the past which cannot be changed, along with the Veteran's imperfection, fallibility, and connection to humanity.

We recommend that when ready, you share your story with a trusted other, such as a therapist or chaplain, who cares about you. Choose someone who will show compassion and provide affirmation. Sharing your story is a way of owning your imperfections and seeing your value through the eyes of others. Litz (2023) points to the importance of spending time with compassionate others and practicing compassion day-to-day. Confession can be soul-cleansing and free you to live a life consistent with your values from this point forward. You cannot change the past, but you can choose how you respond to it now through your decisions and actions. The following exercise will help prepare you to tell your story of MI.

Letter from a Benevolent Other

In Chapter 10, the concept of letter writing was introduced. We encourage you to write a letter from a benevolent other before sharing your story of MI. It can help to see yourself through the eyes of a compassionate and benevolent other. Letter writing lets you view yourself through someone else's eyes. When the primary author was in therapy training in the late 1970s, we learned techniques to connect with our clients. For example, we used role play, practicing something you want to say or do with someone else, to find the right words and confidence. We also used a mirror technique where you spoke to yourself in a mirror. The person in the mirror could be a helpful coach or a nay-saying bully, but you learned how to respond on your behalf. We also used psychodrama, which was like setting up and carrying out a little play, and everyone in the group played a role you assigned them. The therapist was quietly behind you and whispered encouraging things you might want to say, to give you courage to express yourself. This was a helpful technique to prompt someone to speak up about something painful or difficult to reveal.

Another therapeutic technique that dates back many years is therapeutic letter writing. This practice has been used widely in narrative and family therapies (Epston, 2009; White & Epston, 1990). Pennebaker and Evans (2014) describe the benefits of expressive writing. Letter writing puts the writer in someone else's shoes, perhaps someone unable to communicate, maybe deceased, potentially unsafe, or otherwise out of reach. The goal is to resolve an otherwise unresolvable situation or to allow a new lens or frame of reference. It permits the writer to write as himself or herself or as someone else, which moves the writer into imaginary realms of possibility.

The letter might communicate any of the following: something wished for, honest communication of hurt or loss, anger over betrayal, or desire for forgiveness. Generally, these letters are not sent, to allow for vulnerability and genuine emotions. Litz et al. (2015) use letter writing in adaptive disclosure therapy, a treatment for MI, to communicate with a higher power, someone you harmed, or someone who harmed you.

In acceptance and forgiveness therapy (AFT), the Veteran writes an imaginary letter to himself or herself from the vantage point of a "benevolent other." The other person is defined as someone who cares for the Veteran unconditionally. The letter is about what that person wishes for the Veteran to be able to heal and find peace. We had to spell out, *"No criticism!"* when one Veteran wrote a letter from his son and, as an aside, became very critical of the Veteran's parenting. Veterans have crafted letters to themselves from battle buddies, military leaders, clergy, the Pope, professors, family members, and God. One Veteran could not think of anyone and then chose to write from his dog who loved him no matter what and was always happy to see him.

Veterans might also write other kinds of letters when they struggle with bitterness or self-forgiveness. Here are some examples of possible letters, and remember, they won't be sent.

1. If you were abused when you were younger, you can write a letter to your abuser to share your thoughts and feelings and tell the person directly how their actions affected you. It holds them accountable and brings release even though you don't send it. You might burn it or dissolve it in water.
2. You can write a letter requesting forgiveness from someone you hurt. Describe what happened and the context. Tell them what you remember about them and your awareness of the hurt you caused.
3. If you harmed or hurt someone else, you might write a letter of forgiveness from them to you. This letter does not excuse what you did, but it encourages you to live a life of compassion and reminds you of the context in which the hurt happened if that is pertinent.
4. If someone betrayed you, you might write a letter to them. This letter calls them to be accountable and points out the wrongness of their actions. You can tell them of your anger and hurt. You might remind them they can no longer define you or travel with you in your mind and heart. Tell them how you will leave them behind.
5. Write a letter to someone you lost. Express caring for them and your wishes for them. This is a letter of compassion. Tell them what you remember about them.
6. Write a compassionate letter *from* someone you lost. This letter includes what they would wish for you going forward. They might suggest how you could best honor and remember them. They might encourage you to find peace.

Here are two Veteran examples (Pernicano & Haynes, 2023):

Sample letter #1: A letter from someone who loves you unconditionally, without judgment

I am sorry to see you struggling with so much anger, sadness, guilt, and pain. You continue to carry such a burden from the past, and I hope you find peace and forgiveness. No one can walk in your shoes, and at the same time, you might find a new pair that can carry you where you need to go. I am here for you in your struggle. I would gladly take some of your load to help you heal. Even though you wish it had been different, it is what it is. I hope you find a way to accept what happened and move forward. You served our country and did it well. You can't save the whole world. Remember that YOU are more than what happened during your service time. I love you, unconditionally, and nothing you could do, say, or think can change that.

Sample letter #2: A letter to someone who has experienced betrayal

You have carried this burden for so long, and I wish I could help you release your pain. You joined the military with good intentions to serve our country; you were betrayed. You lost faith in others and maybe even in yourself. I love you, NO CONDITIONS, and because of that, I see what happened to you through a different lens. I am here for you. I have heard you question what you might have done or not done that could have changed what happened to you. You weren't responsible for what happened, and it isn't fair for anyone, including you, to question or doubt your response to what happened. Your reactions make sense, given the circumstances. I hope you find peace and realize the injustice of what happened. It is OK to release the burden and live as you were meant to.

Your Letter

Who loves you unconditionally and writes you a letter of encouragement?

_____

What is the main message?

_____

Your Letter from a Benevolent Other

_____

_____

_____

_____

_____

_____

_____

_____

If you choose to try this expressive letter writing, we recommend generally that you write but not send it. You can do what you want with it later: burn it or write it on dissolving paper, swirl it around in warm water, and watch it dissolve. You might read it to someone before letting it go.

After you write your letter, you may experience renewed self-compassion and be more aware of what Worthington & Griffin (n.d.) refer to as the you that is valuable, worthy, and loved. These authors remind us to balance out our awareness of imperfections with the truth that we are precious and loved. It is time to consider telling your story. If you have been on the fence about telling your story, the letter may help move you from contemplation into action.

You might picture a scale that balances with weights. On one side sits the moral pain and MI. What can you balance it with on the other side? We suggest that compassion, acceptance, and forgiveness sit on the other side and that they can balance out the pain, guilt, bitterness, and blame. If you don't add something to the other side of the scale, you will continue to be stuck and burdened. You are not likely to find peace with an unbalanced emotional scale.

You might be held back by wondering how others will react to your story and whether they will judge you. Ask, "What is the worst thing that can happen?" If you were a gambler, what are the odds that you can tell your story *and* receive compassion from those who listen? And once you tell your story, what are the odds that you might feel relief or inner release, perhaps even peace? Is it possible that their reactions will not be those that you expect? Is it possible that they might see you more through the lens of your benevolent other? This is especially true if you tell your story to others who care about you and share your desire for release and peace.

If you decide not to tell your story to someone else, we suggest you write it out and read it to yourself. Give yourself affirmation and compassion to balance out the other side of the scale. Then choose a life that continues to restore the balance, one in which you live out your values, relate to others in kind ways, and choose acceptance and forgiveness, one day at a time. It is your story to tell (or not), and it is up to you to identify and meet your needs for well-being.

Telling Your Story

Prepare well to share your story of MI. Sharing one's story with peers and taking responsibility for one's part in what happened is restorative, and it frees you to move forward to live out your values with good intentions. The affirming response of others is priceless and sometimes unexpected, and you will feel touched by the compassion offered. As you tell the narrative story of your MI, be sure it is about only one MI; otherwise, the experience can become overwhelming for you or your listeners. You might pick the deepest crack or chip on your bowl or consider which injury has been most troubling or problematic post-military. A young Veteran once came prepared to tell 25 stories! He had a note card for each MI event – good intentions but overload. We honored his intentions, but it was emotionally exhausting for him and perhaps others. Please start with just one story and follow up later with others now that you have a format to use. This is getting your feet wet, not plunging into a raging river that will drown you.

We suggest you write out the story, stay focused, and then share it face-to-face with someone who will listen and respond compassionately. Your story is shared in person, not by text or email. It is a face-to-face, "I look you in the eye, and I feel your pain." The word "compassionate" means "suffering with" (together) through unconditional caring, so choose a listener or listeners who will refrain from judging your humanity, intentions, or actions, nor will they minimize your concerns. Before you tell your story, we suggest you "suffer with" *yourself* and perhaps even remember how much younger and vulnerable you were and what you encountered that you could not have anticipated. You might picture that younger "you," who had good intentions as you began your military service.

The person to whom you choose to tell your story could be a clergy person (priest or pastor) if you think their spiritual views have room for grace and atonement. After confessing, you might engage in a ritual of release. Then you can think about ways to make amends, pursue justice, or engage in restitution.

Before you share, we suggest writing out your story, organized into three parts.

Part I describes MI that left you feeling broken, damaged, or changed because it violated your core values. It can be something you did, something you witnessed, or something that betrayed you. Part I can be 10–15 minutes. It is the part about moral pain and violation of values.

♦ What happened, and how did it violate your values or moral beliefs? Share the important details of the event as well as your feelings (moral pain).
♦ What level of responsibility do you think you carry? Try to stick to the facts about what happened and not what you wish had happened.

Part II describes the *impact* of what happened, such as how you changed after the military or after the MI event. This part might take 10 minutes.

♦ How did it affect you, i.e., what was the impact on your life? (Refer to your worksheets from "Floating in Quicksand" or "The Burden Bag." Who were you before the event, and who have you been after the event? Feel free to include metaphors.)
♦ How long have you been carrying this burden?
♦ How did you try to deal with it, and what happened (justice, injustice, retaliation, punishment, kindness, etc.)?

Part III, the most important part, describes how you will move toward hope and healing, with compassion for yourself and others. As you describe hope and healing, you might have some ideas about how you will live, or continue to live, by your values, as your best self. Part III is about how you plan to re-establish purpose and meaning, connect with others meaningfully, and live out acceptance and forgiveness. This part might take about 10 minutes. Remember, you are a work in progress.

- Has anything in this book helped you in your journey of healing?
- Has anything in your daily life helped in the journey of healing?
- Do you have ideas about what you want to do toward hope and healing?
- You are a work in progress. What do you want to work on for hope and healing?
  - Forgive yourself.
  - Forgive someone else.
  - Give yourself compassion.
  - Practice gratitude.
  - Practice compassion.
  - Not let the MI define you.
  - Lighten the load – empty the rucksack or cut the rope.
  - Release the poison.
  - Find peace within.
  - Make amends.
  - Accept time served.
  - Carry out restitution.
  - Remind yourself of your worth and accept your failures.
  - Connect with others.
  - Live your best self (by your values).
  - Other.

In AFT, after the Veteran tells/reads the outlined story of MI, the group members offer empathy, encouragement, and support *without advice*. A ritual of offered forgiveness and compassion includes the group reading a response to the Veteran and the Veteran "accepting" the offered response. If you tell your story one-on-one, you can follow this same process.

The (group) responses to the Veteran are below. The first is for MI of guilt and grief related to participation, witnessing, or aftermath (usually some form of dehumanization), and the second is for betrayal (racial, gender, sexual, military). There are slight differences in what is offered (forgiveness, compassion, release, justice). We refer to cutting their rope and sharing their pain. The betrayal response may be adapted for non-military betrayals, such as a spouse's infidelity.

After being affirmed and receiving a ritual of compassion and forgiveness, the Veteran writes a few words about what will be released on a small piece of dissolvable rice paper and stirs it into a bowl of warm water. This ritual is reminiscent of "The Burden Bag" (Pernicano, 2010) and *The Mission* (1986), where pain is released into water. As a metaphor, water is cleansing and refreshing. Veterans cry, smile, and exclaim as the "magic paper" dissolves (or, as one older Veteran said, "drowns"). They seem surprised at the release they feel, even when they know what is coming.

Veterans must offer one another affirmation, not advice or solutions, and there is no comparison to others' stories. It is a judgment-free zone of empathic listening, and the group's members surround one another with compassion. The Veterans, whether on a virtual screen or face-to-face, help the other person move from unforgivable to forgivable, noting courage, strength, and other attributes they have witnessed in the Veteran during group sessions.

You might ask a benevolent other to read one of these responses after you tell your story:

Response to Guilt, Witnessing, or Participation

Thank you for sharing.

You entered the military with good intentions. We sent you into harm's way and put you into situations where atrocities or tragic outcomes were possible.

We share responsibility with you for all that you saw, for all that you did, and for all that you failed to do.

We recognize your story includes actions, thoughts, and feelings you believe were wrong and hurtful.

We receive you as part of this community of flawed human beings and as part of the flawed human race. With compassion, we offer you release from your emotional prison with time served.

We extend to you the gift of forgiveness for whatever actions you took or did not take. Let us help you cut your rope and forgive yourself.

Response to Betrayal

Thank you for sharing.

You entered the military with good intentions. We are outraged that your ideals and trust were shattered by the harmful actions of others or by military culture.

They took your best, did not protect you, and discarded you in the landfill of betrayal. Your voice was not heard, and justice was not served.

We understand and accept whatever actions you took or did not take during or after what happened.

We share your grief, loss, and pain, and extend to you the gift of compassion.

We encourage you to release whatever burdens you carry, especially undeserved shame, self-blame, anger, or bitterness. Let us help you cut your rope.

It is time to pursue peace and restore your trust and faith in others.

No matter what you are carrying, we encourage you to lighten your load by sharing your story when you are ready. This is not what one Veteran called "cheap forgiveness." We are not telling you it is "okay" or to merely "get over it." Like Frankl (2005), we suggest that you can react to your suffering meaningfully and that punishment is not a healing pathway.

Veteran Examples

A retired Marine, Jerry blamed himself for losing emotional control during a difficult deployment. He described his "cocky" frame of mind, and said, "I hurt a kid. I was an a-hole. We traveled outside the wire every day. We took and returned fire. One day, near the FOB [forward operating base], this little kid came looking for treats. I smiled at him, but it was a mean smile. He never knew what was coming. I beat up that little Afghan kid. I tore into him for no reason. They pulled me off him and he ran home crying. For a long time, I dreamed about him. I remained callous for a long time; I wonder how he felt about Americans after that. A little heartless. I was pretty angry and skeptical when I came to this group. I told you my story, and now I can let it go. You listened, heard it all, and you came back. You didn't run away. Now I've let myself out of jail." As his paper dissolved in a bowl of warm water, he laughed and said, "It's gone. I'm leaving it there. I give myself time served. I am doing so much better, I can hardly believe it."

Ryan, a retired non-commissioned officer (NCO), referred to his "two best friends." As he told his story, he revealed that he was living with the "ghosts" of two villagers he interrogated in Vietnam. After he got the info he needed, he pushed them out of a helicopter to their deaths. "They went with me to prison and still talk to me in my nightmares. I thought what I did was unforgivable." His MI roots were legitimate guilt, self-blame, and shame. The other Veterans spoke to him about the climate of war and how they could feel his guilt, regret, and pain. They extended compassion and encouraged him to forgive himself. They reminded him of his caring heart and how he had helped others in the group. He began to cry as he dissolved his paper in the water. "This is my story and the key that unlocked it," he said. "I was falling apart, ready to hit bottom and end my life. This group gave me one last chance at recovery. I healed in the group. My story and the key that unlocked it went into the water. I will leave it there, never to be retrieved. I have released myself with time served. I am a new creation. I did not believe it was possible. Never forget, never return, CLOSED."

Amy shared, "I have never told anyone about what happened in the military. I almost didn't join this group because I knew I would be expected to tell my story. I didn't want to tell it in a group with men. I punished myself for so many years. After all, I thought what happened was consensual, because I went to his house and didn't fight him off or scream. I froze when he started to grab me and take off my clothes. He never asked if it was OK. He outranked me. I pulled away, and he pulled me back. He said no one would believe me; it was his word against mine. I didn't date in high school, and my family attended church. I thought sex before marriage was wrong. During this group, I realized what he did was rape. I did not consent. He was my superior and he took me to his house. His wife was not home. He said he had to pick up some papers and needed my help to do some work. There was no work. I was new to the Air Force and wanted to please my superiors. I blamed myself for not speaking up. I carried those memories in silence and shame. No more!" she cried as she put her paper in the water and stirred it to dissolve. "There! He is not going to define my life anymore. I am doing things I stopped doing, I am taking back my life. And you all have given me the courage to do it. Not all men are bad like him, I learned that with you in this group."

This is your healing process, and you are the one who will define your pathway of healing from MI. We suggest you have compassion for yourself as a fallible yet worthy human being. You are more than your MI, which will always be part of you, and you don't have to let the past continue to define you. After all, most young men and women joining the military have no idea what they will face and enter with good intentions. We believe that no matter what happened then, you can now choose to live compassionately and make the world a better place. We hope you will take time to grieve your losses, mourn the past, and choose to live daily as your *best self.* Acceptance means giving yourself forgiveness and grace going forward.

References

Brock, R., & Lettini, G. (2012). *Soul Repair: Recovering from Moral Injury after War.* Beacon Press.

Cavanaugh, K., Belton, K., Dowel, V., Finley, S., Grassette, A., Peery, D., Rios, A., & Ryais, C. (2019, August 11). *Trauma-informed storytelling.* Presented by the National Consumer Advisory Board. https://nhchc.org/wp-content/uploads/2019/08/ti-storytelling-1.pdf

Epston, D. (2009). The legacy of letter writing as a clinical practice: Introduction to the special issue on therapeutic letters. *Journal of Family Nursing, 15*(1), 3–5. https://doi.org/10.1177/10748407083311

Frankl, V. E. (2005). *Man's search for meaning.* Beacon Press.

Joffé, R. (1986). *The Mission* [Film]. Warner Bros.

Litz, B. T. (2023). The future of moral injury and its treatment. In Perspectives on healing and repairing moral injury. *Journal of Military Veteran and Family Health, 9*(2), 1–5. https://doi.org/10.3138/jmvfh.9.2.ed

Litz, B. T., Lebowitz, L., Gray, M. J., and Nash, W. P. (2015). *Adaptive disclosure: A new treatment for military trauma, loss, and moral injury.* Guilford.

Pennebaker, J. W., & Evans, J. (2014). *Expressive writing: Words that heal.* Idyll Arbor.

Pernicano, P. (2010). *The burden bag. In Family-focused trauma intervention: Metaphor and play with victims of abuse and neglect* (pp. 87–89). Jason Aronson.

Pernicano, P. (2012). *Outsmarting the riptide of domestic violence: Metaphor and mindfulness for change.* Jason Aronson.

Pernicano, P., & Haynes, K. (2023). *Acceptance & forgiveness therapy: From brokenness to restoration* [Unpublished handbook] (5th ed.). South Texas Veterans Health Care System.

Tick, E. (2005). *War and the soul: Healing our nation's veterans from post-traumatic stress disorder.* Quest Books/The Theosophical Publishing House.

Tick, E. (2014). *Warrior's return: Restoring the soul after war.* Sounds True.

White, M., & Epston, D. (1990). *Narrative means to therapeutic ends.* W. W. Norton.

Wood, D. (2016). *What have we done: The moral injury of our longest wars.* Little, Brown & Company.

Worthington, E. L., Jr., & Griffin, B. J. (n.d.). *Moving Forward: Six Steps to Forgiving Yourself and Breaking Free from the Past* (2nd ed.). [Online workbook]. Virginia Commonwealth University. https://forgiveself.com/workbooks/20150903%20Self-Forgiveness%20Intervention%20Workbook.pdf

Chapter 12

Stories and Metaphors for Restoring Wholeness

Moral injury (MI) approaches and practices have similar core ingredients but are packaged differently. Many refer to forgiveness, compassion, relational connections, and meaning-making. Viktor Frankl (2005) wrote about making meaning from suffering, with ingredients including compassion for self and others through meaningful works and loving relationships. Desmond Tutu and his daughter Mpho Tutu (2015) wrote about forgiving as a pathway to healing. They depict forgiveness as a journey to heal our broken parts and become whole again. Worthington and Griffin (n.d.) point out that the path to forgiveness includes self/other empathy and awareness that we are all flawed and valuable and imperfect and worthy. Litz (2023) points to confession and compassion for self and others, suggesting it may be too much for those betrayed to ask them to consider forgiving the offender. Pernicano and Haynes (2023) encourage Veterans to confess wrongdoings, accept responsibility without punishing blame, show compassion for self and others, and restore wholeness. A contemplative monk, Thomas Merton (1955), in *No Man Is an Island*, wrote that our existence is intertwined with that of others. Loving ourselves and others involves the desire to live, recognizing that life is a gift and that the greatest good is what we can give others. Giving to others brings out the goodness in us.

Metaphors and stories facilitate healing in trauma-informed care (Pernicano, 2014, 2019). Metaphors paint word pictures that are easily understood. When traveling the river of life, you need a helmet and a paddle because you may encounter rocks, white water, or dry places. You ensure you have what you need to survive and know that the river goes somewhere, even if you don't know where it ends. If you are on a ship that capsizes in the ocean, you join others in a life raft, wear a life vest, and paddle to get through the worst. Dumping burdens from a rucksack lightens the load. Taking an antidote to the bitter poison you swallowed is life-sustaining. Treated wounds heal, and your scars become reminders of your resilience and restoration. You can wear your MI battle scars without shame or guilt. Broken bones are stronger after they heal, mushrooms thrive in excrement, and wine grapes grow best in rocky soil. Perhaps the reader already realizes that there are many ways to depict and pursue the healing of an MI.

This chapter brings core metaphors of healing, wholeness, and post-traumatic growth found in acceptance and forgiveness therapy (AFT). Many metaphors depict

DOI: 10.4324/9781003494263-15

trauma and recovery; the stories and metaphors in this chapter are about creating beauty out of brokenness. One or more of them may ring true for you as you consider your journey of hope and healing.

The Self-Weaving Tapestry (Previously Titled *The Unraveled Tapestry*, Pernicano, 2010)

Veterans with MI return in their minds and hearts, time and time again, to the worst moments and memories of their lives. For them, it is as if their lives have contained no good, and we know that is not true. What *is* true is that betrayal, grief, guilt, and pain are captivating, and they steal our hearts and our awareness of the good in ourselves and others. Even in the *Harry Potter* series, good usually balances out evil; however, during the threatening moments, it is hard to see the good that will come. If we keep re-reading Chapter 3, we will never figure out what happens in Chapter 8. Life is like that: we get stuck in prior chapters and fail to move forward to new chapters of our life story.

This story reveals a *Harry Potter*–like fantasy kingdom where people are born with a self-weaving tapestry. The tapestry adds threads by itself, both dark and light, as the person goes through life's pain and joy. The story is about weaving together the dark with the light of our lives to see beauty in the whole. Pernicano wrote the original story to help families put their lives back together after abuse, sexual assault, substance use, incarceration, involvement with child protective services, and other life struggles. Veterans listen to the story, identify bright threads throughout their lives, and then name the darker threads of pain. Each draws and shares a personal tapestry. Individually or communally, this story opens the door to meaningful discussion of what has been hidden in the closet and what can be restored to the whole.

The Self-Weaving Tapestry Story: The Dark with the Light (Pernicano, 2010)

(Previously *The Unraveled Tapestry*, Reprinted
and Modified with Permission of Jason Aronson)

There once was a Harry Potter-ish type kingdom where each person was given a self-weaving tapestry at birth. It held memories of life events. Whenever a good thing happened, a bright-colored thread would weave itself in. When something bad happened, a dark thread would be woven in. For most people, there were more bright than dark threads, and the tapestry became a beautiful reflection of the person's life.

One person who lived in the kingdom hated the dark threads because they were a reminder of the sad, tragic, or awful things that had happened. For that person, it was as if a spotlight was on the dark threads. The person said, "I hate the dark threads. I don't want to look at them or think about them. I don't want to remember those things. I'll just get rid of them." The person removed all the dark threads and locked them in a box in the closet.

A friend came by to visit not long after that, stared at what was left of the tapestry on the wall, and asked, "What have you done to your beautiful tapestry?"

The person said, "What do you mean? I fixed it. I took out the dark, ugly threads. Now I won't have to look at them or think about them. It's better this way."

The friend replied, "The tapestry was the beautiful whole of you. Hiding the dark threads can't destroy or make them disappear, and the pain you experienced was real. But life includes the dark with the light and the good with the bad. Your tapestry is not whole without the dark threads. Look at it—there is so much missing."

It was true. The tapestry was no longer whole. There were huge holes among sagging bright threads. Many important parts were missing; it was a sorry remnant of what had been there before.

The friend added, "The dark threads are part of you, but they don't have to define you. You might want to retrieve the dark threads from the closet and weave them back into the tapestry. This time, put them where you want them. You can't change what happened to you, but you can change how you look at the threads and find meaning in the whole."

The person considered what the friend had said. It did not help to hide the dark threads. The person took the dark threads out of the box in the closet and wove them back into the tapestry, placing them where they seemed to fit. The person started to accept the dark with the light and to see and accept the beauty of the whole. After all, we all need to find meaning in the darkness and light of our lives.

I hope you, too, will discover ways to accept the beauty of your "whole," to be restored, the dark with the light. Like the tapestry, you are a work in progress.

Consider some bright and dark threads of your life. We suggest you begin with bright threads (people, events, circumstances), as they may be less at the forefront when you struggle with MI.

Story Application:

1. Search online for coloring page or weaving template and download your choice.
2. Make a list of bright threads in your life (from birth until now) that have given you joy, love, pride, accomplishment, growth, happiness, and/or satisfaction. These might be people, experiences, or events.

3. Label some of these positive things on the tapestry threads and color them in bright colors.
4. Make a list of darker threads in your life (from birth until now) that have given you grief, anger, sadness, shame, or emotional pain. These might be people, events, trauma, or MI.
5. Label some of these negative things on the tapestry threads and color them in dark colors.

Veteran Example

Figure 12.1 is an example of one Veteran's tapestry and his description. For this Veteran, the story and drawing task helped him describe emotionally vulnerable and memorable places of his life. You will see that this individualized activity becomes a form of meaning-making.

The white is like purification or the healing process we are going through. You can see it goes black to gray, bottom to top. There are yellow areas where the light shines through. The pink is my daughter, overlapping with my brown; she meets the brown and it is together. Purple is hope. It sounds cheesy but a simple drawing, like the paper in the water, feels like healing. You can see the dark with the light. I wasn't sure I wanted to do this group. Now we told our stories, and we are on the same page. As you go up, more yellow, the hope and healing. You can see I'm improving, there is more yellow on top. I put more yellow than dark at the top. I won't forget the dark memories, but they are less painful.

Figure 12.1 The Self-Weaving Tapestry

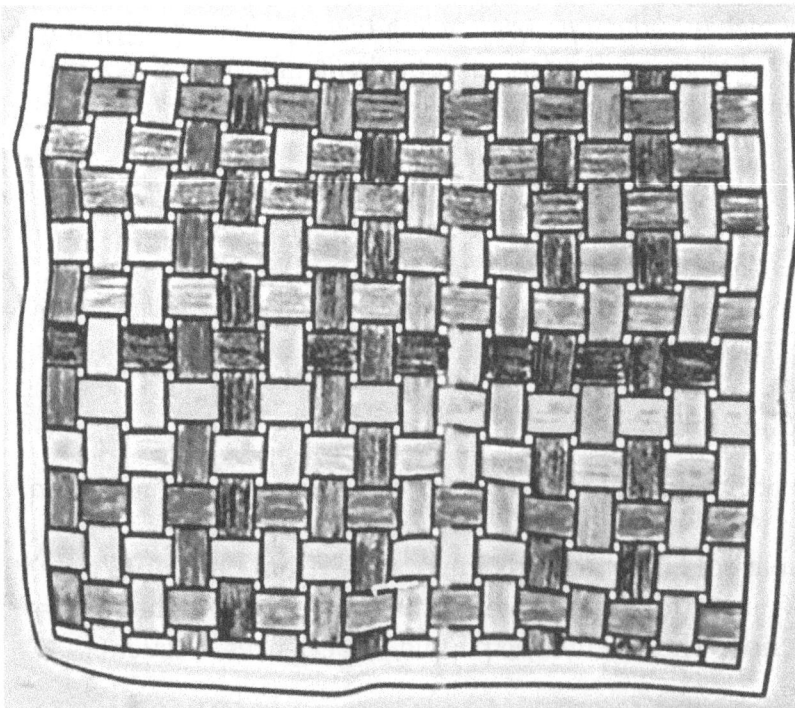

Japanese Kintsugi Pottery: Embracing your Battle Scars

A second model of healing MI comes out of the Japanese tradition of *kintsugi*, which represents post-traumatic growth. This Japanese art tradition is called the "golden mend," but it might also be called fancy superglue healing. A similar Japanese philosophy of *wabi-sabi* means finding beauty in broken or old things. Kintsugi artists restore broken pottery with precious metals like gold or silver; the repaired item is considered more beautiful and stronger than before the break. We sometimes see cracks as ugly imperfections, and we hide them from the world or throw the broken objects away. Many internet blogs describe and depict kintsugi, revealing beauty out of brokenness. We all crack, chip, and break in the face of overwhelming stress, yet we do not have to stay broken and fragile. And we don't have to throw our brokenness in the trash.

An online blog from The Mend Project (2019), "The Art of Kintsugi: How Scars Beautify and Unite Us," notes that each scar tells a story. Some scars are visible, while others are invisible, and they remind us of the dark times in our lives, times we felt broken or defeated. Many people settle for *survival* because they view MI as a permanent, unacceptable part of them. The Japanese teach that scars can signify healing and survival. Those who survive abuse or other types of MI are living examples of kintsugi. It takes tender, loving care to restore the beauty of a broken object. Hannah Braime (2014) writes, "Through Kintsugi, the cracks and seams are merely a symbol of an event in the life of the object, rather than the cause of its destruction."

The following short story, beginning with part of a church sermon by Holly Wilson (2018), led me to think about how those with MI hide their cracks.

Hidden Cracks (Pernicano)

A church sermon by Pastor Holly began: "A woman had collected and displayed glass and ceramic items in a cabinet for many years. After she died, her daughter went through her mother's belongings and discovered that each item had a crack. The woman had positioned the items away from view, to hide the cracks. In doing so, she could not fully enjoy them. We do that. We hide our cracks from the world when we are ashamed, embarrassed, or guilt-ridden, afraid that our cracks or imperfections will be judged as ugly or unacceptable."

We endure the brokenness and pain of moral injuries that are cracks and divots in our souls. MI changes the very substance of who we are and what we believe in. We are shattered by the betrayal of those we trusted. We hurt others and can't fathom who we have become. In the fog of war or mind-blowing combat, we lose sight of ourselves and barely recognize the ghosts who return home. Lies become truths until we no longer know which is which. As we hurt ourselves and others, new chips and cracks emerge over the years. We avoid thinking about what happened and turn our cracks to the wall. Soon, the mirror reveals only brokenness to our troubled eyes.

Let's leave the land of would, could, and should, and journey together to the land of acceptance and healing. We can hide our flaws or embrace them as our golden seams. We can come out of hiding with other broken vessels and put our pieces back together with resin and gold. Let's celebrate our golden seams. Let's move from brokenness to beauty, from useless to purpose, from cracked to restored.

We can support one another in healing by sharing our brokenness. Omid Safi (2017), a professor at Duke University, poignantly writes about the Japanese traditions of kintsugi and wabi-sabi (https://onbeing.org/blog/omid-safi-illuminating-the-beauty-in-our-broken-places/). "Wabi-sabi means finding beauty in old or broken things. First, you lovingly repair them, and then you find beauty in them." He points out that we are all broken and alludes to the vulnerability in loving someone who has been broken and healed and made whole again, where the cracks are golden. His poem reminds us that we heal one another through kintsugi and wabi-sabi. We offer one another the gold of compassion. Veterans experience this as they share and gently hold one another's vulnerability and pain. They begin to understand that they are not alone in their pain or healing.

Illuminating the Beauty in Our Broken Places

(Safi, 2017, shared with his permission)

Give me someone who knows their own vulnerability and sees mine,
Give me someone whose cracked spaces are golden,
Give me someone who has helped do Kintsugi to my cracked spaces,
Give me someone who is open to me doing Kintsugi to their cracked heart.
So friends, Wabi-sabi-me.
Let me Wabi-sabi you.
Let's repair each other,
Let's seek what's cracked in each other,
Let's heal our broken spaces,
Let's fill what's broken with gold.
May we emerge more beautiful, more whole, and luminous.
Come and see the beauty in my cracked spaces,
I see the beauty in yours,
You are not a heart that I will discard,
Do not discard me.
We can emerge from this healing golden, more beautiful.
May all that is cracked and broken be healed, be illuminated.

The Cracked Glass Bowl Story, Part II (The Healing)

Weaving a tapestry and mending with gold resin are ways to restore the whole. You can also heal from the inside out, starting with the brokenness of a glass bowl after a storm. When a glass bowl is damaged, it has several choices. The bowl could stay in contemplation, stay fragile, and rely on her friend to care for her. She could use superglue to put the pieces back together or even patch herself with golden resin like the Japanese art form of *kintsugi*. However, in this story, the glass bowl contemplates and decides to go to the glassmaker. Even though it will be painful to tell her story and endure the heat, it will result in healing and joy. Metaphorically speaking, when we choose to go to the glassmaker, we become a new creation, a little at a time. We become more than before, adding color, revising our form, and creating new meaning and purpose. Healing is a work in progress, and subsequent *damages* can be healed through the same process.

In the story, "The Cracked Glass Bowl," the bowl first thinks it might be *enough* to survive. Her friend suggests that survival alone is not enough because it leaves us fragile and unable to thrive. The main character decides to pursue healing, which may involve some pain but result in a new creation. A new creation can be repurposed to function and live fully.

The bowl is *each of us*, after a storm, feeling pain and unsure what to do next. After Veterans complete their confession and story, they are ready to envision hope and healing. We do not leave the bowl in a state of brokenness. She enters the action stage of change and participates in her healing. The bowl and her friend visit a glassmaker *healer*. The bowl tells her story and collaborates with the glassmaker to design a restored self. The heat is painful but allows her to seal her cracks from the inside out.

The Veterans choose colors, shape, and purpose for their envisioned transformation. They reveal their new creation alongside their first damaged bowl, a visual reminder that healing is possible. Veterans describe the growth they are experiencing and point out themes, colors, and symbols that represent that growth. Their drawings and descriptions are rich depictions of transformation. We invite you to read Part II of the Cracked Glass Bowl (Pernicano, 2012) and, once again, imagine yourself as the main character. Draw yourself as a new creation, with hope and healing. Finish by completing the Stages of Change worksheet.

The Cracked Glass Bowl, Part II: Becoming a New Creation

(Pernicano, 2012, Reprinted with the permission of Jason Aronson publishers)

The cracked glass bowl and her friend, the blue bowl, went together to the glassmaker's studio. Everyone knows that you should not try to pursue healing alone. The glassmaker explained the healing process: "You will tell me what you want to look like at the end of our work together. Tall and thin, off-centered, perfectly balanced, short, and broad, whatever. I can add colors to the green if you would like a change in your hue, or I can mix in swirls of gold. While you are in the oven, you will feel your glass soften and melt, and the cracks will blend or disappear. We will talk about what you went through in the storm because talking about your experience is part of healing. Afterward, you will be new and different. Some say it is like becoming a new creation."

"A new creation," said green bowl. "I can hardly imagine myself as anything but a cracked, damaged bowl." Then she asked, "How will I know when you are done?"

The glassmaker replied, "You guide the process and tell me when we are finished. When you are satisfied with the results, I will take you out of the fire for the last time to let you cool. After cooling, your glass will be smooth – no chips or gouges. You might find yourself better able to cope with your memories of the storm."

They worked together, and the glass bowl went in and out of the oven. The glass bowl told the glassmaker what she remembered about the storm. At first, the red-hot fire and painful memories brought tears to her eyes, and she cried out in anguish. She felt vulnerable and exposed as she relinquished control, endured the searing heat, and surrendered to the healing process.

It was a lengthy process, because, as you know, healing takes time. It is hard to say how or when she knew she was "done" but she did know, and she said, "I'm ready to go home now and live my life." The glassmaker reassured her, "You are a work in progress. You can come back if and when new cracks arise. And don't worry if you seem a bit off-color at first. Your true colors will come out as the glass cools."

It was true. After only a few minutes, there was a dramatic transformation. The now cooled lavender-bluish-green bowl was a work of art, a re-creation. She had chosen a simple form, with smooth flowing lines, swirls, and blends of color. She was a bold statement and well-balanced. One small bubble of her original green color remained unblended. The now sealed cracks reflected her courage and strength.

"Thank you," she said. "I would not have believed that such change was possible."

"Change is always possible," the glassmaker replied.

The glass bowl met her friend in the waiting area and Blue Bowl said, "I was going to ask you what took so long, but it is obvious. I might not have recognized you without that one small green bubble. Your essence is the same, but you are very different."

She replied, "I am more different than I believed possible. The oven's heat was painful, but the glassmaker's fire and telling my story have freed me. I am a work in progress. The remaining cracks are reminders of what I have endured, and I don't have to hide them."

This story might remind you that healing, although painful, is worth the effort. It is not enough to simply survive a storm, cracked and battered. When you are ready, I hope you will take a leap of faith to move beyond your storm and become a new creation, a beautiful work in progress.

The bowl becomes a work in progress instead of a cracked display of brokenness. She reaches a point of acceptance and willingness. She believes that healing is possible and knows she will be different after she goes through the healing process. Healing, like working a 12-step program, involves accepting what you cannot change, changing what you can, and knowing the difference. Wishing you could change the past is part of the grief process, and trying to change it is a futile waste of energy. You can't possibly know how it would have turned out if you had changed history. You imagine it would have been better, but it could have been the same or worse. It was what it was, and it is what it is. You will never finish the book if you keep re-reading an earlier chapter.

New Glass Creation

(Pernicano & Haynes, 2023)

Instructions:

1. Draw yourself as a "new creation" bowl or other glass creation (your choice of shape and colors). As a new glass creation, you are "the same and different," and you are "becoming restored," as the cracks of trauma start to heal "from the inside out." Consider what might be helping you seal the cracks.
2. Add something to your bowl that personally represents hope, self-compassion, peace, forgiveness, healing, or restoration.

Drawing Space

After you draw yourself as a new creation, please consider the following questions. The bowl is now at the action phase of change. She has weighed the risks and benefits of getting help and has visited the glassmaker. It can take some time to reach that decision, and we encourage you to think about ways you may still be stuck in MI or whether to move in a new direction.

The Cracked Glass Bowl Stages of Change Worksheet

(Pernicano & Haynes, 2023)

This is the stage where the bowl commits to change by seeking help to heal her brokenness and pursue "a life worth living."

The bowl has a supportive friend to help her through the change process. Who will support you through the change process?

_____

_____

Who or what is your glassmaker?

_____

_____

What is the heat that will seal your cracks?

_____

_____

What does it mean to the bowl that she will be "a new creation … the same and different?"

_____

_____

What does it mean to you that you can become a "new creation … the same and different?"

_____

_____

What will help you continue to heal from the inside out?

_____

_____

How will your life be different as you seal your cracks?

_____

_____

Bowls of Hope and Healing

Drawing the self as a new creation helps Veterans envision hope and healing. After confessing and sharing their pain, Veterans begin to report changes in their lives: that things are different at home, they are less angry, or they have returned to church. Some notice positive changes in their relationships, such as the young Veteran who did not want to disappoint his young son and fixed the gingerbread house. We ask them to share their drawings with the group to celebrate growth and change.

Following is the story of the Veteran who killed two young Vietnamese after interrogating them, pushing them from a helicopter on a whim. His first bowl started whole, in the air, like the villagers who fell to their deaths (upper left). The series of bowls in Figure 12.2 is him falling over the years, and he loses parts of himself as he falls, ready to shatter at the bottom; he explained he had often thought about ending his life. He saw himself as worthless, falling apart, originally with no process for recovery. He said the group gave him "one chance at recovery" although he was skeptical about being "forgivable." As he showed us his bowl (Figure 12.2) he said:

> My two 'best friends' from Vietnam haunt me, they are with me each day. I can't forgive myself for what I did. I started whole. My bowl fell from me that day and it has kept falling for over 50 years. There was no process of recovery, no hope of forgiveness. The bowl fell and as it fell it got more and more cracks in it. It is about to shatter. I was left with one chance to save the bowl. If I couldn't save it, it would shatter and sink into the ocean (me).

Figure 12.2 Falling to Self-Destruction

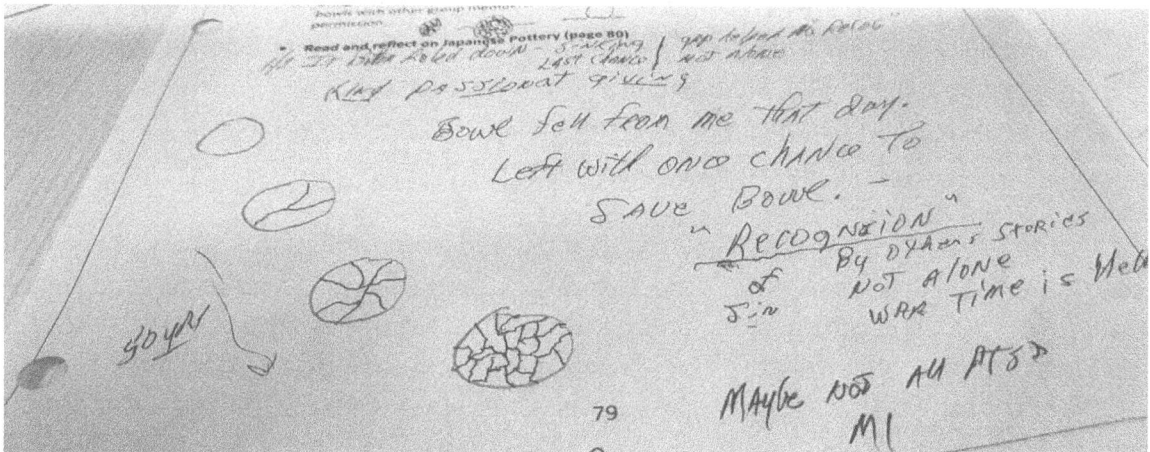

Figure 12.3 Healed by Compassion and Forgiveness

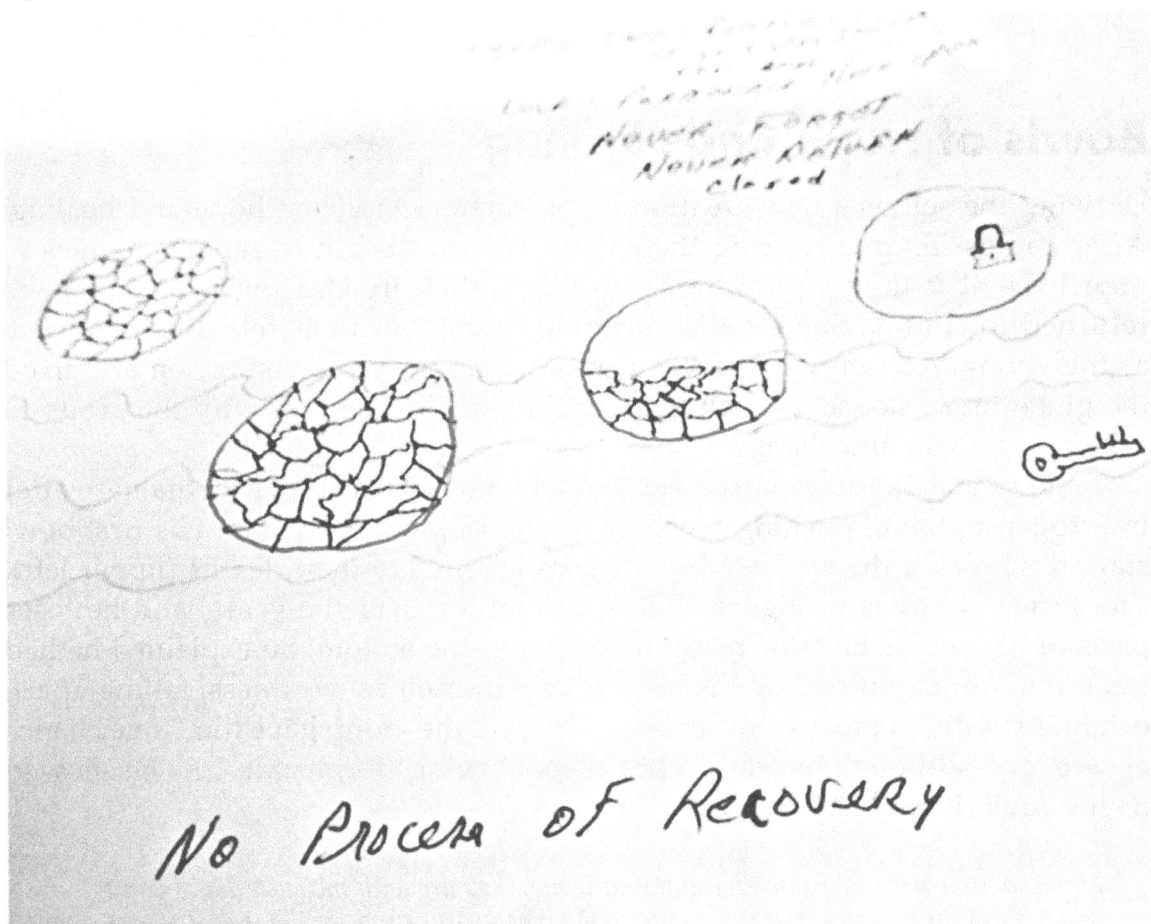

Eight weeks later, this Veteran smiled as he shared his new creation (Figure 12.3):

I'm leaving them there. The moral injury program brought unexpected healing, and the relationships have been life-changing. This group, with dynamic stories and recognition of sin, showed me that I am not alone, and wartime is hell. The bowl healed before it shattered and sank into the ocean. It healed in the group. The story and the key that unlocked it went into the water. Now there is yellow tape on the bowl, like the gold, and the cracks are gone. I have accepted time served, I am a new creation. I did not believe it was possible. Never Forget, Never Return, CLOSED.

Confession – telling the MI story to a trusted someone else – is an important component of healing, and for this Veteran, it provided an avenue to acceptance and forgiveness. Compassion heals unhealthy responses to guilt and enables Veterans to restore connections with self, others, and higher power and realign with their core values. Participatory forgiveness lays down a path to atonement and amends.

Figure 12.4 Removing the Wall

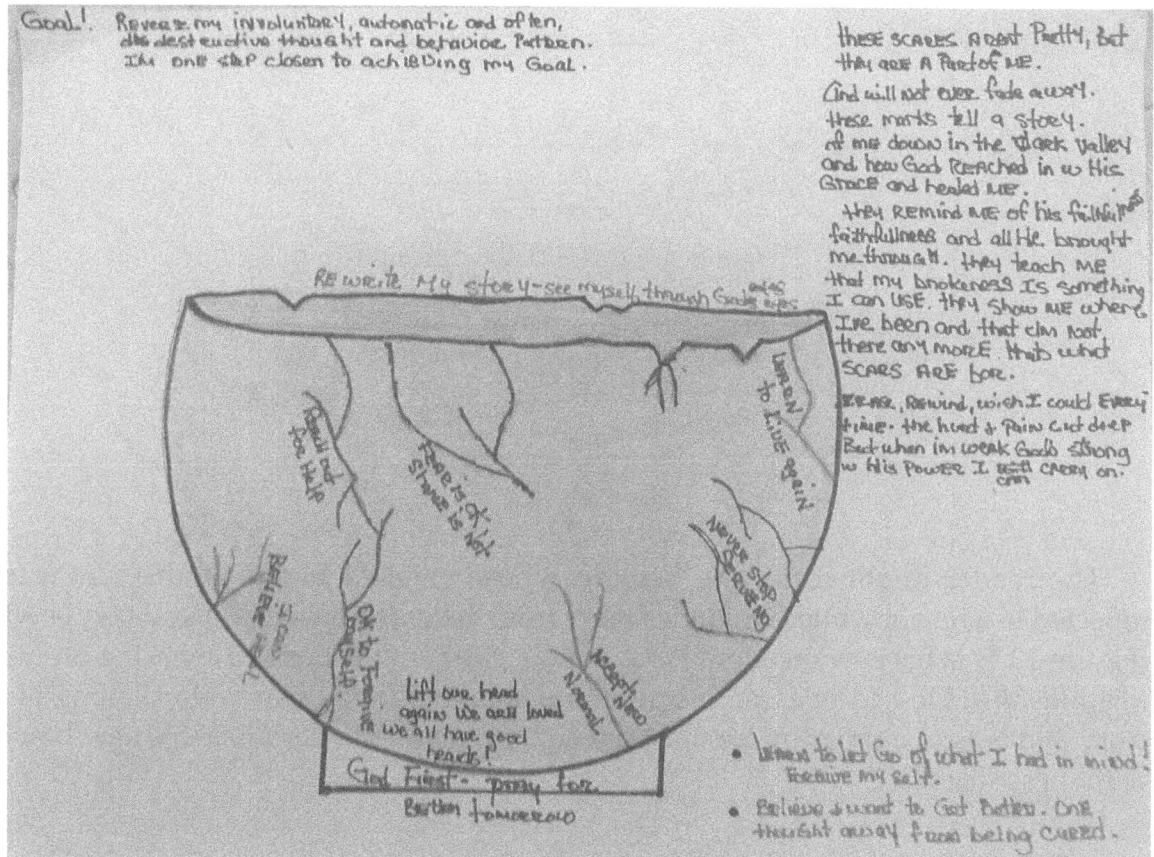

The reader might remember Susan's walled-off bowl from Chapter 8 (Figure 8.1). She survived severe betrayal and did not believe she could tell her story of military sexual trauma with male Veterans in the room. She was in the group with two other women, and each discovered "some men can be trusted," as the male Veterans expressed protective outrage for what had been done to these female group members. The following Figure 12.4 is her new creation, the red wall gone and the bowl with gold. Her words are as follows:

When I told my story, I saw caring, and you were with me [the others in the group]. I got through it, and now I can leave it behind. My mission is not done. I carry my soldiers who were behind me, and I carry each of you. They mentally judge you in the military, and I did it too. Now I have a new set of eyes. The yellow color is hope, at my core. I get to rewrite my story and see myself through God's eyes. The green is some cracks that have melted. I know I can heal because I believe I can heal. I get to live my new normal. I'm learning how to live again. I'm going to frame these and keep them as reminders. No more walls.

Figure 12.5 Reshaping and Fusing into a New Whole

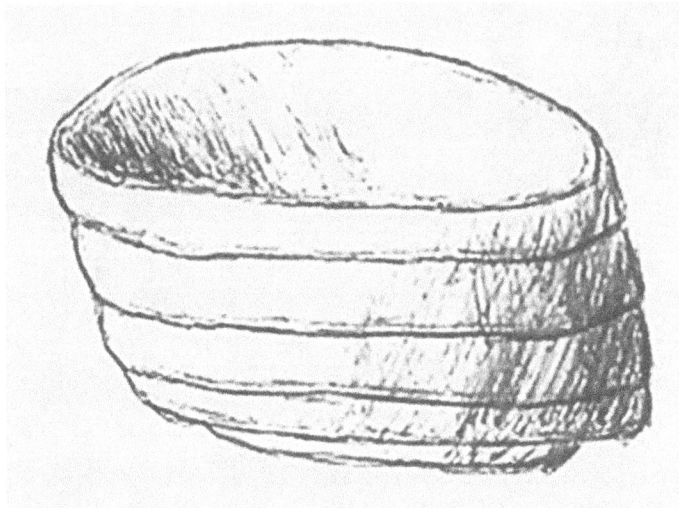

The reader might recall the Veteran whose cracked bowl (Figure 8.1) was reflected in a mirror while he hid the cracks from the outside world. The above bowl (Figure 12.5) is his new creation. He was now clean and sober and working on his relationships. He had released his guilt and shame into the water after telling his story and was in a program for spiritual enhancement. He describes his new bowl with these words:

Like in the story, it has been melted down and reshaped into a whole new bowl. Some shards of glass have been fused into it from the previous bowl. It has function and purpose, and it will hold whatever you put in it.

This Veteran's first bowl 8.3 was black and white with prominent holes, reflecting lost innocence and betrayal by a training instructor. She drew her new creation (Figure 12.6) as a pink flower pot with a small plant growing. The transformation is striking.

I never imagined that group therapy is what this is like. I didn't expect to feel safe. It brought a lot to me. You're going to see a huge transformation. Now, pink and green. I got more out of this group than I got out of other mental health. I couldn't have done it by myself. Now I'm a flower pot. Melted down completely, there are sealed cracks that will always be there. Some cracks are good, they're not all bad. It is where I was. This is a seed, the future, I'm going to grow from my flower pot now, instead of being in that bowl. I have a vessel to grow and keep getting better. I don't know how I'm going to handle not being here. This is Grandmother's favorite color – my favorite color. She had a kind of green paint color on her walls. Green is growth, we can't live without plants.

The stories and metaphors in this chapter reflect that we all have cracks and can pursue healing in one way or another because efforts to hide our cracks leave us

Figure 12.6 New Growth in a Flower Pot

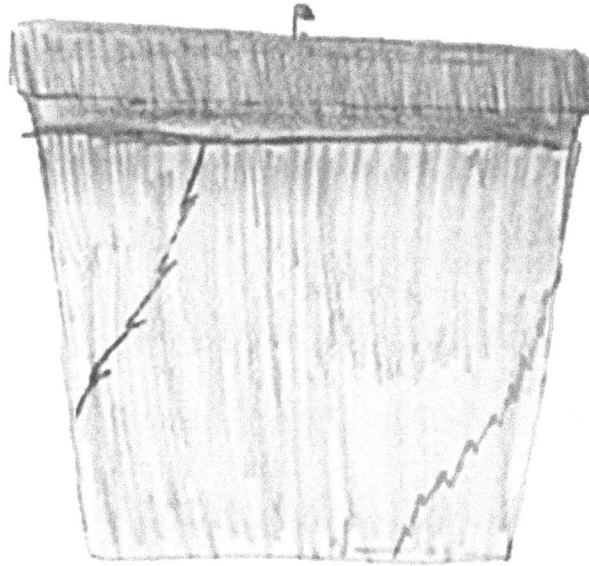

fragile. How would you look if you pursued wholeness? Do you need to get some dark threads out of the closet? Will you painstakingly put yourself back together with gold resin? Or will you go to the glassmaker and seal the cracks? Use whichever metaphor appeals to you and stop hiding your battle scars, as they are evidence of what you endured. The cracks did not cause your destruction; they reveal the beauty in your healing and restoration.

References

Braime, H. (2014, April 29). What Japanese pottery can teach us about feeling flawed. *Authenticity/Self Care and Self-Kindness.* https://www.becomingwhoyouare.net/japanese-pottery-can-teach-us-feeling-flawed/

Frankl, V. E. (2005). *Man's search for meaning.* Beacon Press.

Litz, B. T. (2023). The future of moral injury and its treatment. In Perspectives on healing and repairing moral injury. *Journal of Military Veteran and Family Health, 9*(2), 1–5. https://doi.org/10.3138/jmvfh.9.2.ed

Merton, T. (1955). *No man is an island.* WordPress.

Pernicano, P. (2010). The unraveled tapestry. In *Using metaphor and play in child therapy: Of magic and miracles* (pp. 18–20). Jason Aronson.

Pernicano, P. (2012). The cracked glass bowl. In *Outsmarting the riptide of domestic violence: Metaphor and mindfulness for change* (pp. 141–44). Jason Aronson.

Pernicano, P. (2014). *Using trauma focused therapy stories: Interventions for therapists, children, and their caregivers.* Routledge/Taylor & Francis.

Pernicano, P. (2019). *Using stories, art & play in trauma-informed treatment: Case examples and applications across the lifespan.* Routledge/Taylor & Francis.

Pernicano, P., & Haynes, K. (2023). *Acceptance & forgiveness therapy: From brokenness to restoration* [Unpublished handbook] (5th ed.). South Texas Veterans Health Care System.

Safi, O. (2017). Illuminating the beauty in our broken places. *The On Being Project*, Duke University. https://onbeing.org/blog/omid-safi-illuminating-the-beauty-in-our-broken-places/

The Mend Project. (2019, October 24). "The Art of Kintsugi: How Scars Beautify and Unite Us." https://themendproject.com/the-art-of-kintsugi-how-scars-beautify-and-unite-us/

Tutu, D., & Tutu, M. (2015). *The book of forgiving: The fourfold path for healing ourselves and the world*. Harper.

Wilson, H. (2019). *Church sermon on brokenness and healing*. University United Methodist Church. San Antonio, TX.

Worthington, E. L., Jr., & Griffin, B. J. (n.d.). *Moving Forward: Six Steps to Forgiving Yourself and Breaking Free from the Past* (2nd ed.). [Online workbook]. Virginia Commonwealth University. https://forgiveself.com/workbooks/20150903%20Self-Forgiveness%20Intervention%20Workbook.pdf

Chapter 13

Post-Traumatic Growth and Continuing the Journey

Veterans in acceptance and forgiveness therapy (AFT) have been Hispanic, Black, Jamaican, Puerto Rican, Native American, White, Pacific Islander, and more; ages late 20s to early 80s; male and female; enlisted and officers (both non-commissioned and commissioned); Buddhist, Muslim, agnostic, atheist, humanist, and Christian; and from every combat era since Vietnam. MI develops across all socio-economic strata. Some with MI have endured adverse childhood experiences and cumulative risks throughout their lives that are known to impact academic achievement and adjustment. Core values, relationships, experiences, and systems of meaning-making/spirituality influence the development of MI and the healing process before, during, and after the military.

MI is not a diagnosis with symptoms; healing from MI is more than symptom reduction. Like the bowl in *The Cracked Glass Bowl* (Pernicano, 2012), it is not enough to survive; Veterans need an opportunity to heal and thrive. Veterans completing AFT often describe what might be termed post-traumatic growth (PTG) in their self-depictions of hope and healing. They report closeness with those in the group, improved trust, self-acceptance, restored appreciation for life, hope going forward, and new meaning/purpose. The blue glass heart (Figure 13.1) was Paul's expression of gratitude for connection and emotional healing.

> *During week three, Paul described the impact of MI as he bitterly declared, "I have no feelings. My feelings died after the war. The military took my humanity. It turned me into a machine–a monster–and I was good at doing what they wanted. I did terrible things. I am no longer capable of love."*
>
> *Paul wrestled with his grief, guilt, and self-blame, and in week 9, Paul told his story of MI. He became tearful as the other Veterans affirmed him. They spoke of his loving heart, how he listened without judgment to their stories, and showed compassion for them. He was not heartless, and they expressed care for him.*
>
> *Paul reached into a bag the following week and pulled out six beautiful blue glass hearts. "These are for you," he said. "You opened my heart and I feel love for each of you. My feelings didn't die. Now they are restored by your acceptance and forgiveness. I am a new creation and my cracks are sealed." That session ended with hugs, and the blue glass heart sits on my desk.*

DOI: 10.4324/9781003494263-16

Figure 13.1 Opening Up a Closed Heart

PTG is evidenced by "positive psychological changes as a result of struggle from trauma or life-changing events" (Tedeschi et al., 2018, p. 345). PTG changes are reflected in a greater appreciation of life, increased personal strength, improved closeness in relationships, positive religious/spiritual change, realignment of life priorities, and increased positive values (Tedeschi et al., 1998). PTG is a "transformational outcome" (Evans et al., 2018, p. 267) following a trauma-related struggle. The five domains of PTG closely parallel Frankl's (2006) ingredients for meaning-making: relating to others, appreciation of life, spiritual change, personal strengths, and seeing new possibilities.

Veterans in AFT often report PTG dimensions of change following the healing ritual, tapestry presentation, and sharing of their pre-post glass bowls. The instructions on the cracked glass bowl drawing task are to depict "damage" related to MI, and later "hope and healing"; how they do so is unique and revealing.

Pernicano et al. (2022) rated 22 matched pairs of bowls for dimensions of MI/recovery present in drawings/descriptions, pre-post therapy. Veterans described ways they were broken, damaged, or changed due to MI. Their cracked glass bowls reflected lost purpose and meaning, self-blame, and broken connections with others or higher power. They voiced hopelessness, futility, and resignation. The second set of drawings (hope and healing) were brighter and more colorful, reflecting healing, growing acceptance, and self-forgiveness. These new creations were described as partially or fully repaired with sealed cracks, bases reinforced, and some with gold inlay. Their new glass creations reflected renewed purpose and functionality. Veterans added symbolic elements that depicted hope, purpose, faith, trust, openness, self-care, and increased connectivity (to other group members, higher power, family, etc.).

Dimensions of Brokenness and Damage

Damage to the Self

"I was on a treadmill, everything leaking out."
"The top rim is worn away and eroded."
"A lot of collateral damage. It's broken my heart."
"The black spots are like cancer on my heart or soul."
"Parts of me are missing."

Interpersonal Damage

"My supports have cracks too; my cracks have spread to them."
"I am hidden from others."
"This crack that looks like a bullet hole is the wound that never heals. I have caused collateral damage."
"I have caused hurt to others."
"Here is hurt from others."
"No one touches me."

Failed/Defeated

"I could never do enough. Perpetrating violence, taking part in oppression."
"I am a bad person."
"It is hard to live with myself."
"My bowl = guilt."

Here are some examples of dimensions of healing.

Restored or in the Process of Healing

"I'm learning how to repair and take care of myself."
"I put the pieces back together."
"I can learn from my scars through acceptance of the scars."
"I am overcoming shame and fear."
"It is a total transformation."
"It is a whole new bowl."

Reconnected or Re-Engaged (Spiritually, Interpersonally, and Intrapersonally)

"The new bowl includes Christ, the cracks are not as pronounced; some are starting to disappear."

"I am held up by all of you (group members). You are my base, you are holding me up."

"These colors represent my religious faith and my hope in God, a stained-glass window, a symbol of hope."

Surmounting or Overcoming

"The cracks that are left aren't as deep. They will be with me forever, and that is OK. Now I can help others, with compassion."

"I am blooming, growing out of my brokenness. Now I am giving back, creating a worthwhile life."

Self-Accepting or Positive Self-Appraisal

"I have a new set of eyes, to see myself through God's eyes."

"The yellow is hope."

"I put a lid on it, to keep the BS from coming up."

A Veteran struggling with moral pain and injury is like a butterfly struggling to leave the cocoon. If you rescue or release it, the wings will not grow strong because the struggle prepares it to fly. Each butterfly must go through its struggle, and each struggle is different. We are not suggesting that it is good to suffer, but we affirm Frankl's (2006) perspective that suffering is part of the human condition, and there is no inherent meaning in suffering other than how we respond to it. We make meaning out of suffering through our actions and interactions. Some have said that pain is inevitable, but suffering is not. The butterfly somehow knows it will fly once it pushes through the last barrier to freedom.

Veteran Stories of Healing and Growth

We end this book with several Veteran examples that instill hope. We honor their struggles; we trust you also will celebrate their successes. Each Veteran is on a journey from pain to restoration. MI sometimes develops out of intentional wrongdoing, but it sometimes results from poor timing, unexpected circumstances, or others' decisions, some of which are beyond our control. There is often no answer to the question, "Why?" A better question is, "What is my chosen path forward?"

Strength comes from shared vulnerability and compassion; suffering with others becomes less lonely and instills empathy and hope. Somewhere along the way, Veterans build new connections with others and begin to thrive. *The Cracked Glass Bowl* story (Pernicano, 2012) suggests we should not pursue healing alone. In a group context, Veterans become benevolent others, to hear and gently hold pain, and the group members carry one another through the pain.

Figure 13.2 Cracked Bowl #1: Loss of Meaning and Purpose

The drawings and descriptions above and below are those of Veterans who completed AFT, 90 minutes per week over 12 weeks, along with hard work in between. We gathered some participants together recently, and they reported (5–6 years later) that the program was a catalyst and that their progress continued after the group. Healing has continued through purposeful living, ongoing acceptance and forgiveness, spiritual grace, and meaningful relationships. This section of the book celebrates their healing and shows that healing is possible. Case details have been generalized or changed to protect Veterans' anonymity.

Figure 13.2 reflects the Veteran's loss of meaning and purpose.

Example 1: Cracked

My original bowl was black and white, dark and light, with deep cracks, pieces missing, speech without words, in darkness. The bowl is no longer useful, you can't use it. My old nature, this is what I was. I was shattered by military experience. I lost something. We were something before, we meant something before. I didn't even have a name for it. Now, I know it is moral injury.

Figure 13.3 reflects broad healing across many dimensions.

Figure 13.3 New Creation #1: Flowers in a Vase

Example 1: New Creation

I did that reimagining piece – before, during, and after. First, I transitioned through a self-weaving tapestry story. Then the new story of the bowl going to the glassmaker. The bowl reshapes into a vase, can be used for flowers, and is black and white based. It's useful: you can drink from it and cook in it. This is my proposed new creation. The lines – each stands for something: love of God, faith and prayer, wife and children, family, friends and brothers, resilience, empathy, forgiveness, healing, restoration, hope, and peace. 12 aspects of positive things I'm trying to lay hold of. My shading on the vase is a J for Jesus. New, outside myself, meaningful interactions, benefits I can provide to mankind, positive things, instead of dwelling on the old nature, the first bowl. I'm moving to something more life-giving and life-fulfilling. Get past it and move forward. I feel lighter, having everyone listening – they were empathic, loving, and gracious. This group is life-changing. I've been sharing with family members. For me this has moved way too fast, I wish it wasn't ending. The most significant group interaction I've had with the VA [Veterans Affairs] since I got out 11 years ago.

Table 13.1 is this veteran's description of emotional transformation he attributed to the 12-week group.

Table 13.1 Transformation of Veteran #1 Emotions

From	To
Anger	Hope
Confusion	Awe
Bitterness	Amazement
Helplessness	Thankfulness
Depression	Wonder
Anxiety	Fullness
Sorrow	Excitement
Regret	Meaning
Rejection	Purpose
Illusion	Spiritual
Constrained	Valued
Limited	Confident
Frustrated	Free
Disillusioned	Successful
Withdrawn	Inspired

Table 13.1 Transformation of Veteran #1 Emotions (*continued*)

Numb	Loving
Embarrassed	Respected
Remorseful	Creative
Weak	Curious
Shame	
Guilt	

When contacted about including his material in the book, this veteran replied, "Thank you for contacting me - it means a lot to me and my wife - and is God's reminder to me of the good work you are doing with our Veterans. Your next publication will inform and help many people. I want you to know that the Moral Injury group was a great catalyst to move me forward in self-understanding, perspective, deep historical contemplation, healing, positivity, gratefulness, and hope. It is God who gives us peace."

Figure 13.4 reflects grief and loss over inescapable death of war.

Example 2: Cracked

This first one is a dark chapter in my life. There is remorse, guilt, shame. There is grief. The blood – red – is the death of others. There is no vision yet and I am sinking. This blue is water. There is no solid base.

Figure 13.4 Cracked Bowl #2. A Dark Chapter in Life

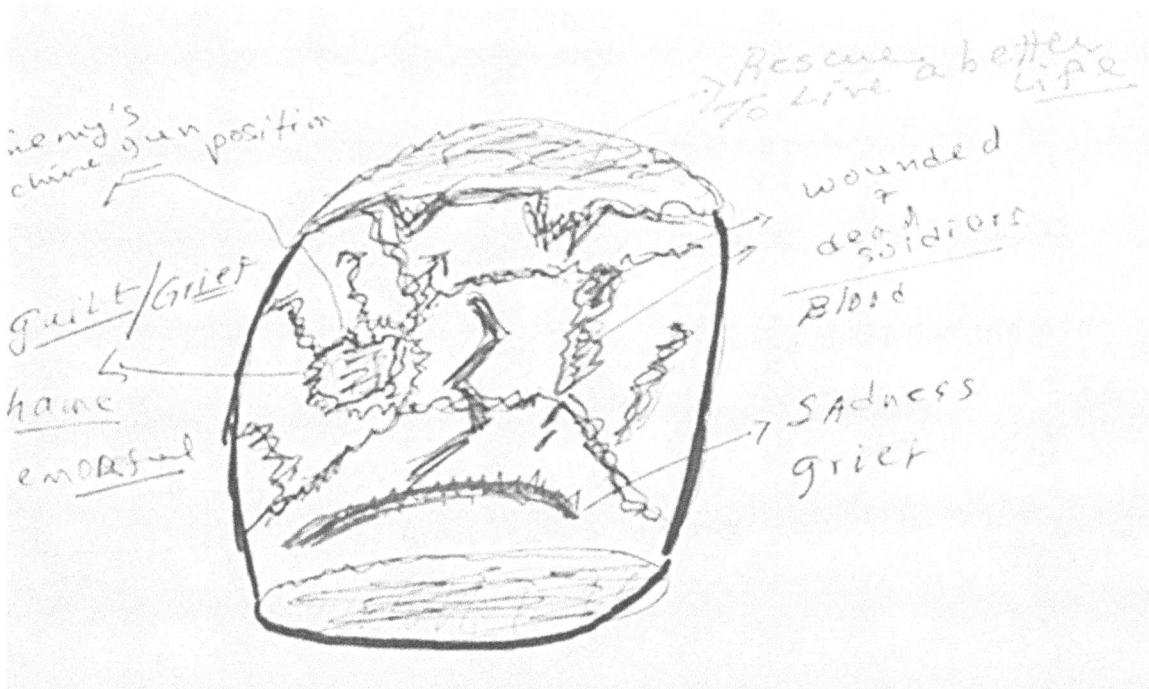

Figure 13.5 New Creation #2: A Dove Flying Free

Figure 13.5 is a beautiful depiction of spiritual and emotional "transformation," with a strong base and recognition that the memories are his forever and that he has come out of the darkness into the light of hope.

Example 2: New Creation

The new one is very different, it is the difference in me right now. Transformation. That's gold – a cross. This gold represents freedom and it goes all the way to the top. It is over those killed and means 'rest in peace.' I was a teacher, and the base is a strong brown base – see the right angles? This is what we need – a strong base. The cracks that are left are not as dark – they are the memories I will have forever. I put a sun up here – we need some lightness in our lives. The grey is the past.

Figure 13.6 reflects deep anger and hatred at who the Veteran had become following betrayal.

Figure 13.6 Cracked Bowl #3: Betrayal of Trust

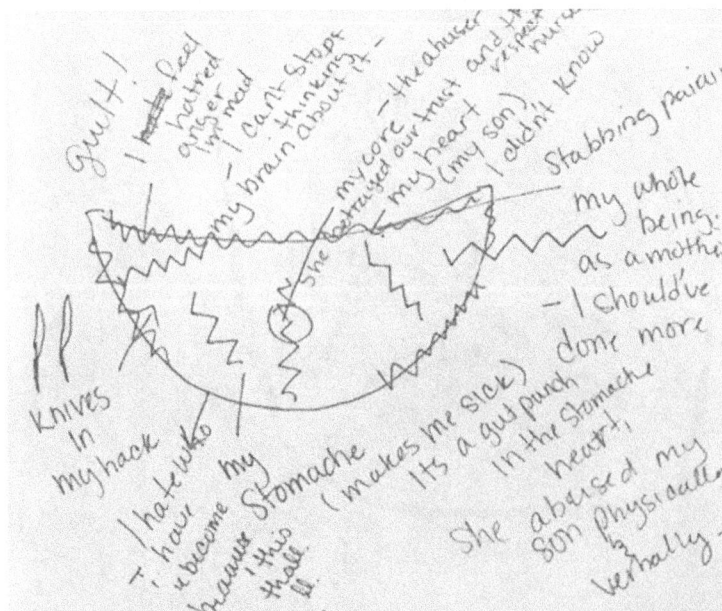

Example 3: Cracked

I felt a lot of hatred and anger. It was just like I had hated who I had become. And when I drew the glass bowl, I couldn't find anything positive, not one piece of me that was positive… There was a lot of negative stuff on her. Like I had knives in my back. That was my core and my whole being was pretty much cracked.

Figure 13.7, a healthy tree being nurtured by Veteran's tears, reflects new growth and pursuit of wholeness.

Example 3: New Creation

I knew I needed help because I couldn't do it myself. It's not my fault. I can't control who she was/is as a person, but I can control how I feel and act towards others. I had to forgive myself for thinking I was less of a parent or that I did something wrong when I didn't. I did a different type of bowl for my new bowl, surrounded by my tears. They are watering the tree and my tears overflow. The bowl is whole, and I am growing from it. I still have the tears, but instead of keeping them in and drowning myself in them, I let them come out. I will continue to grow and heal with new branches and leaves. That's my symbolism for growth. You guys were the ones who supported me through this change. I don't want to be the same. Instead of waking up mad, I wake up to a new day, and perspective. I continue to grow by embracing my roots. And getting closure, they'll never close completely but they will mend. And it's okay to have battle scars.

Figure 13.7 New Creation #3: The Tree of Life

Figure 13.8 Cracked Bowl #4: The Wound That Never Heals

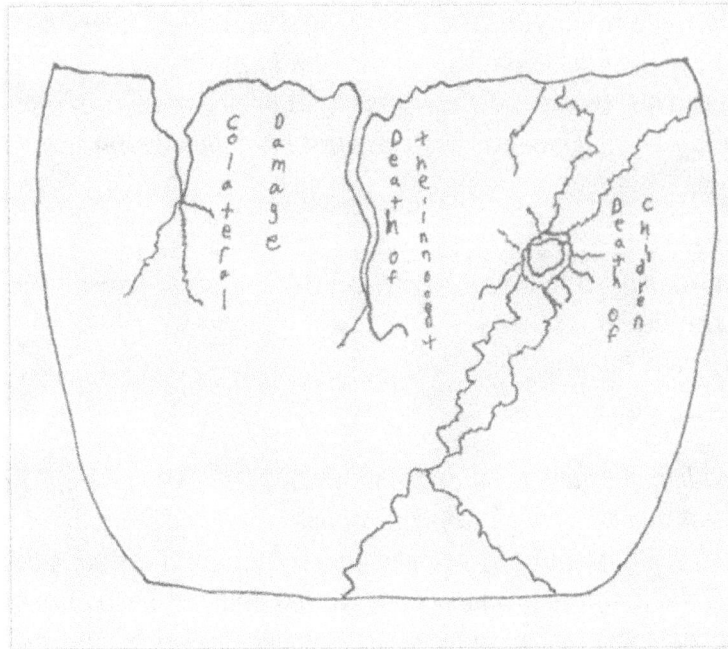

Figure 13.8 depicts the places the Veteran served and grief and loss at the death of innocents.

Example 4: Cracked

You can see the top rim is worn away and eroded. The most damage was here – Baghdad, Tigres, and more. Serious pressure cracks are running into the bowl. A lot of collateral damage. It's broken my heart. Death of innocents. The crack that looks like a bullet hole is the wound that never heals.

This Veteran's new creation (Figure 13.9) reflects durability and a new foundation, a "stained glass window, a symbol of hope."

Figure 13.9 New Creation #4: Stained Glass New Creation

Example 4: New Creation

The new bowl is a rebuilding, a work in progress, I am mixing gold and patching with different materials. It is a new base – my foundation. The new rim represents durability. The colors - mahogany is the cross, the rope is purple, and the green is water. These represent my religious faith and my hope in God. It is a stained glass window, a symbol of hope.

This Veteran attended the first AFT group in 2018. Recently, he wanted the authors to know how he had changed after AFT. "PTSD sometimes masks moral injury (MI), and I think MI needs to heal first. I healed in spirit through forgiveness, then mind and body later. It is life-changing; mixing science with spirituality, and it works! You have created a legacy to give Veterans their life back." He recounted his growth after the program: changing his diet, exercising, hiking with his son at Lost Maples, and traveling to participate in his Naval Officer Commissioning. He now walks without a cane.

Figure 13.10 suggests hopelessness and guilt.

Example 5: Cracked

The following bowls are those of a Vietnam-era Marine Corps Veteran in his 70s who completed the program. He became dear to our hearts, as he struggled and eventually transformed his MI. Online groups are hard for older Veterans who are not tech-savvy, and this Veteran admitted in Session 1 to being visually impaired, unable to read the workbook we mailed him, as well as hearing impaired, unable

Figure 13.10 Cracked Bowl #5: Vietnam Vet Guilt

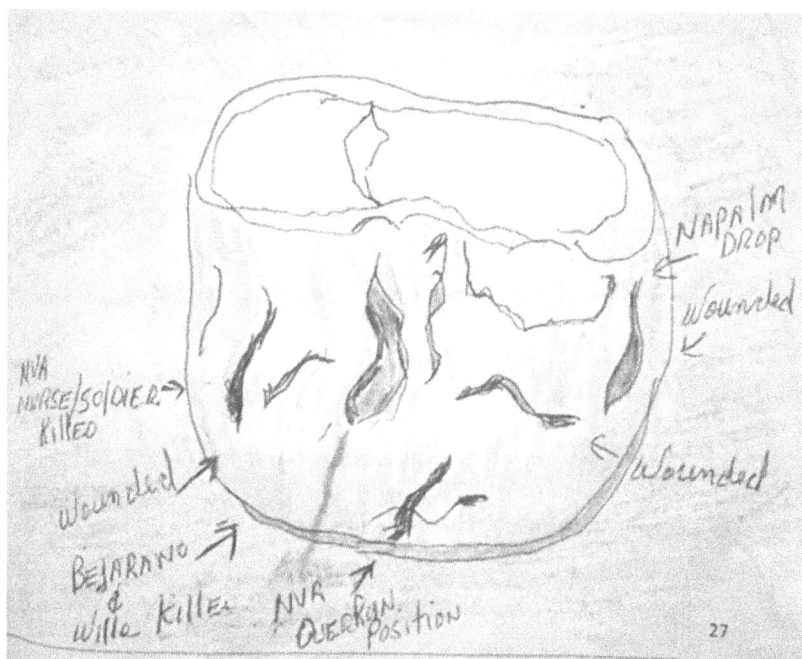

Figure 13.11 New Creation #5: Hope, Faith, and Love Teacup

to hear well online. He was unsure how to mute his mic when not speaking. With the help of his grandchild and some headphones, he prevailed and overcame these obstacles one by one.

He initially felt responsible for the deaths of his buddies who, despite his warnings, rushed out of their protective hooch into the chaos of a firefight only to be carved down by the enemy. He had carried the whole weight of their deaths on his shoulders all of his life. In Session Two he drew the cracked glass bowl that represented his life to that point. He shared about both bowls towards the end of AFT.

This is my old cup when I came in, all kinds of scars all over my body, scars inside of me in my heart that hurt; full of scars, water coming out of it. I was going to take my life and got referred to this group. I didn't want to be here.

Figure 13.11 reflects this Veterans hope and healing.

Example 5: New Creation

The group's been really helpful. I have a new outlook on life. This is my new cup, a whole new transformation. I play the guitar, and I was praying in Spanish while I sang to God: 'You're the clay-maker, I'm the clay, transform me into a new being.' And God said, 'I will make you right through fire. I want you to praise me, learn how to forgive, I want your smiles.' Hope, faith, love. I learned that from you guys. I have hope now. I came so close to pulling the trigger. In the Marine Corps, they

Figure 13.12 Cracked Bowl #6: Shadowed Pain

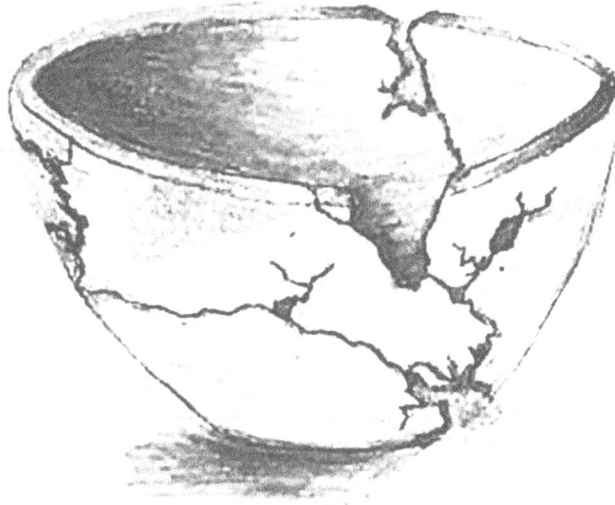

said we never leave nobody behind. That ain't true. We are human: we bleed and cry, not as tough as they say we have to be. I don't want to take my life now; for once I'm spending more time with my family, going to my grandchildren's baseball games. I want to be with them. My faith is back, I'm back with God. I'm a work in progress.

Figure 13.12 reflects Veteran's perceived guilt and brokenness from deployment events that involved children.

Example 6: Cracked

This Veteran was very quiet, sharing sparingly. Throughout the group sessions, she listened carefully, and when it came time to talk about her MI, she spoke briefly and stuck tightly to the outline. Her progress was most visible in the following drawings. When we asked her permission to use them in our writing she said, "You can do anything you want with them, but if I had known you were going to use them, I would have worked harder on them." She is modest about her artistic abilities. Her words:

This is me, my moral injury. Cracks, chips, down to the bottom. Ready to fall apart. The damage is from deployment events [children] that I can't talk about. I am a bad person. I feel numb. I put my battles before everyone and everything.

Figure 13.13 reflects hope going forward.

Example 6: New Creation

I underestimated the power of sharing in the moral injury repair group. I found that, as I shared, some of the pain diminished; not all of it, but some of it. It really surprised me. This bowl is my vision of hope – strong, solid, and balanced. I am not there yet, but some of my cracks are sealing, and in this group, I felt accepted.

Figure 13.13 New Creation #6: Vision of Hope

MI carries an increased risk of alcohol use and suicide for Veterans, and we encourage the Veterans Affairs (VA) and other caring professionals to ask about MI or to administer the Moral Injury Outcome Scale (MIOS; Litz et al., 2022) routinely for the sake of early intervention. The Veteran who almost engaged in a mass shooting and suicide after his wife left him for his best friend became quite attached to his fellow Veterans. His new creation bowl (Figure 13.14) represents the connections Veterans make with other Veterans as they forgive themselves and their trust is restored.

There is a new color, from green (a rubber band of courage that was ready to snap) to blue (without cracks). I am held up by all of you (the group members). You are my base, you are holding me up. I am stronger and releasing my anger in better ways.

Figure 13.14 New Creation #7: Lifted by Other Veterans

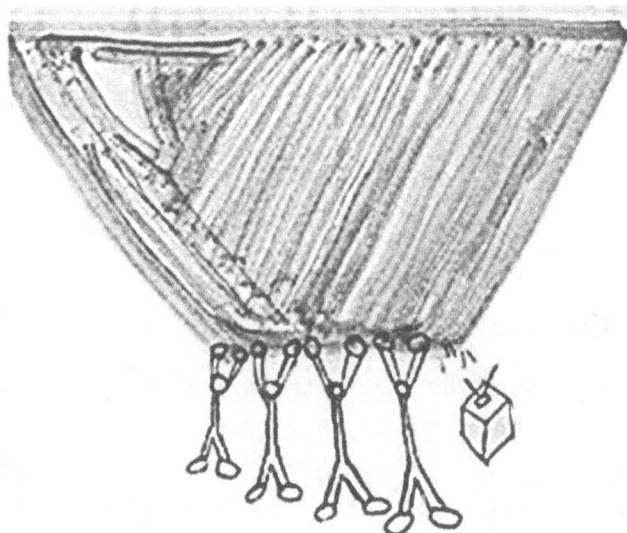

Continuing the Journey

The journey of healing MI is lifelong. Metaphorically speaking, you may encounter white water, rocky places, smooth floating, and dry spells when paddling down the river of life. Be sure you have a paddle, life jacket, helmet, and provisions as you continue your journey. We encourage Veterans to get help for MI through the VA, Vet Centers, or the community. Going forward:

1. Know your triggers and have a few available phone numbers for support day or night (including the Veterans Crisis Line: dial 988, then press 1 for Veteran-centered care).
2. Each night when you go to bed, count your blessings (gratitude) and forgive your human imperfections.
3. Each morning when you wake, let yourself experience curiosity about what might come your way and how you can pay it forward, show a small act of kindness, or make one person's day a little better.
4. Show compassion for yourself and others, whether or not you think it seems *deserved*.
5. Hang out with fun, value-based, compassionate others. This will help you make the world a better place within your circle of influence.
6. Engage in self-care, including things that bring you joy.
7. Consider the Whole Health program at a local VA. Providers offer holistic programs such as mindfulness, acupuncture, tai chi, yoga, aquatics, nutrition, chiropractor, etc.
8. Do something with others: a chorus, instrumental group, hikers, bikers, kayakers, Wounded Warrior programs, volunteers, etc.
9. Meditate or practice your version of spirituality for purpose and meaning.
10. Get professional help if you are still stuck in the weeds.

You have a word for it now: "MI." As one Veteran said:

The peace has become a thankfulness that I have a label. I'm able to call it what it is – moral injury. I've made it concrete – it's not flying in the air. I've been carrying it for over 50 years. I couldn't control what happened, but now I have something to do, to deal with it. It's progress. I want to give other people a better perception. I used to blame God for everything, I hated God. During the 12 sessions, I realized I could change my view of God's behavior. God wasn't hateful, he was always there. When I was feeling pain, screaming, and crying, he listened to me. I went to thinking I had a loving God. God changed and my life changed. God had always been there. I handed it over. I know that I'm loved. I listened as people were sharing, I paid close attention to their stories, and now we are doing all this closure stuff. Other Veteran stories helped me measure myself – I'm really thankful for that. Like talking about the potholder and weaving it all together. We are all woven together.

Veterans who serve our country are a treasure, not meant to be in the news as a tragic statistic. In the final story, "The Quest," Pernicano (2023) brings you to the end of one journey you traveled in these chapters and encourages you wherever you are headed.

Collectively, we (family, caregivers, spiritual leaders, counselors, and the community) share a journey with Veterans, and it is up to us to welcome them home; they will heal as we create meaningful places for them. Veterans signed up to serve when they were "young and dumb" (a frequent Veteran quote), not knowing or anticipating what would be asked of them nor fully equipped to do it. Some sought gainful employment or G.I. Bill education, and the military became a means of survival with affordable housing and rations. No one signs up for or anticipates betrayal, bullying, racism, or abuse. No one seeks moral quandaries or moral pain. Whether enlisted or drafted, Veterans don't get to choose where they are sent to serve. Ideals and patriotism were shattered for many by what they encountered. Regardless, there is a journey forward for each.

The Quest

Pernicano (2023) in Pernicano and Haynes (2023)

There once was a person on a journey, a quest to restore his soul and seek a treasure. A wise person had suggested he take this path and keep moving forward. He had been promised a treasure at the end of his journey. When he reached the end, it would be revealed.

It had been a very challenging journey. First, he had been caught in a terrible storm that nearly drowned him. He survived, torn and battered, then continued down the path. Next, he fell into quicksand, and it was a long while before he discovered a ladder behind him and climbed out. As he climbed out, a heavy rucksack labeled "burdens" was there, with his name. He put it on and continued along the path. It weighed him down and slowed his progress.

"Where is this treasure?" he asked; he wondered if he had traveled in the wrong direction or lost his way on the path. He was exhausted, and he needed a rest. As he came to a beautiful lake, he sighed in relief. Then he saw others coming into view, emerging from other paths around the lake.

They moved toward one another and sat on the cool grass.

The man said, to the others, "I was told to take that path and keep moving forward. I was promised a treasure at the end of my journey."

The others said, "We were told the same thing." As they talked among themselves, they realized that each path had the quicksand with the rucksack beside it and that each path led to the lake.

One traveler added, "The wise person also told me to carry the rucksack on my back until I reached the lake, then to take it off and see what lies within. Maybe the treasure is inside the rucksacks."

Each opened their rucksack and examined the burdens within, personal things they had been carrying for a long time. Inside were instructions to "Lighten Your Load." "I don't know if I want to do this," each one said, "but I will trust the wise person and follow the instructions. I want to find that treasure."

Each released burdens into the clear waters and, as they disappeared below the surface, each experienced profound relief and shared joy. The bright sun shimmered on the lake.

A feast appeared before them; they would have a shared celebration at the lakeside. They gathered in a circle and began to enjoy the feast, telling one another of their life experiences.

The wise person appeared, as if out of nowhere. "I can see that you have come together to celebrate a shared journey. Your path continues now, and I wish you well as you travel forward."

"But where are we going?" they asked.

"Forward," said the wise person. "Ever forward. I am not sure where the path goes, but it will take you forward."

"We came for the treasure," they said. "Where is the treasure you promised?"

"It is here," said the wise person. "You are the treasure. Each of you is a treasure. Share it as you go. You carry compassion, forgiveness, and acceptance with you, and that is all you need."

The treasure within is often revealed in a shared journey with others. For that, we are grateful.

We hope you find your path to the lake, where you can rest and share a meal with others before you continue your journey. You can connect, share your pain, and discover the treasure that is you.

References

Evans, W. R., Szabo, Y. Z., Stanley, M. A., Barrera, T. L., Exline, J. J., Pargament, K. I., & Teng, E. J. (2018). Life satisfaction among veterans: Unique associations with morally injurious events and posttraumatic growth. *Traumatology, 24*(4), 263–270. https://doi.org/10.1037/trm0000157

Frankl, V. (2006). *Man's search for meaning.* Beacon Press.

Litz, B. T., Plouffe, R. A., Nazarov, A., Murphy, D., Phelps, A., Coady, A., Houle, S. A., Dell, L., Frankfurt, S., Zerach, G., & Levi-Belz, Y. (2022). Defining and assessing the syndrome of moral injury: Initial findings of the moral injury outcome scale consortium. *Frontiers in Psychiatry, 13*, 923928. https://doi.org/10.3389/fpsyt.2022.923928

Pernicano, P. (2012). The cracked glass bowl. In *Outsmarting the riptide of domestic violence: Metaphor and mindfulness for change* (pp. 141–144). Jason Aronson.

Pernicano, P. (2023). The quest. In P. Pernicano, & K. Haynes. *Acceptance & forgiveness therapy: From brokenness to restoration* [Unpublished handbook] (5th ed.). South Texas Veterans Health Care System.

Pernicano, P., & Haynes, K. (2023). *Acceptance & forgiveness therapy: From brokenness to restoration* [Unpublished handbook] (5th ed.). South Texas Veterans Health Care System.

Pernicano, P., Wortmann, J., & Haynes, K. (2022). Acceptance and forgiveness therapy for veterans with moral injury: Spiritual and psychological collaboration in group treatment. *Journal of Health Care Chaplaincy*, 28(Sup1), S57–S78. https://doi.org/10.1080/08854726.2022.2032982

Tedeschi, R. G., Park, C. L., & Calhoun, L. G. (Eds.). (1998). *Posttraumatic growth: Positive changes in the aftermath of crisis*. Lawrence Erlbaum Associates Publishers.

Tedeschi, R. G., Shakespeare-Finch, J., Taku, K., & Calhoun, L. G. (2018). *Posttraumatic growth: Theory, research, and applications*. Routledge. https://doi.org/10.4324/9781315527451

Chapter 14

Conclusion with AFT Program Data

A variety of situations trigger moral pain. The world has witnessed moral pain associated with COVID-19, including people dying alone, relatives separated from their loved ones, and healthcare workers forced to triage services with a lack of medical resources. We have experienced moral pain in the face of worldwide inhumanity (consider Africa, Russia, ISIS, Taliban, Hamas, Ukraine, Cuba, and other areas in the Middle East). Regardless of politics, we experience moral pain at children separated from parents at borders, deaths of innocents during combat, mass shootings in schools and houses of faith, religious and racial threats, wrongful incarcerations, child abuse, human trafficking, loss of youth to fentanyl and other drugs, limited availability of health care, alcohol-related road deaths, and other grief-worthy situations. There are many ways in which moral pain results in moral injury (MI), and – for the authors – raising awareness about MI may save lives and improve the quality of life for those who bear pain.

Risk Reduction

One way to save lives is to screen for and treat MI. Those who do not seek help face increased risks, especially in the case of guilt for perpetrating harm or violating the rights of others. Early evaluation and triage are beneficial to identify Veterans with MI and to determine best-fit intervention(s). Providers might use the Moral Injury Outcome Scale (MIOS; Litz et al., 2022) as a screening tool in inpatient and primary care settings, substance use programming, and post-traumatic stress disorder (PTSD) specialized treatment settings.

DOI: 10.4324/9781003494263-17

Benefits of Healing MI

Self-disclosure and compassion from other Veterans build trust and reinforce integrity. The sharing rituals shift Veterans from moral pain to hope and do much to reaffirm values and integrity. Veterans develop compassion for themselves and others and become ambassadors for those still struggling. Veterans report other benefits as well, such as reduced alcohol use, renewed spirituality, improved relationships, tighter bonds with one another, relief at release, and changed perception of the MI event and their response. Silence and avoidance are non-restorative, so whatever your role in the life of a Veteran, encourage them to pursue professional help or spiritual guidance for meaning-making, acceptance, and forgiveness.

Quantitative Measures of Change

Veterans ask if healing is possible, and we provide data that supports MI intervention. We have used the following measures in our work:

+ The MIOS (Litz et al., 2022), administered during the 4-week education program, before and after the 12-week therapeutic program, measures the baseline and type of reported MI.
+ Psychological distress is measured using the Brief Symptom Inventory 18 (BSI-18; Derogatis & Melisaratos, 1983); it contains three 6-item scales assessing somatization, depression, and anxiety, rated on a five-point scale from 1 (not at all) to 5 (very much), and an 18-item Global Severity Index (GSI), which are transformed into standard T scores (see Franke et al., 2017). The BSI-18 has good internal consistency, reliability, and validity. Scores above 70 are considered high clinical distress, 65–70 moderate clinical distress, and below 65 subclinical distress. A T-score change of five is considered clinically meaningful.
+ Psychological flexibility is measured with the Acceptance and Action Questionnaire (AAQ-II; Bond et al., 2011). The Veterans Affairs's (VA's) computerized patient record system (CPRS) uses the original ten-item version of the measure, with higher scores representing greater flexibility. Scores on this measure reflect improved acceptance.
+ We measure PTSD symptoms using the PTSD Checklist (PCL-5; Weathers et al., 2013), a valid and reliable measure of PTSD. There are different suggested cutoffs, but generally, scores above 34 point to possible PTSD (with or without MI).

♦ The Religious and Spiritual Struggles Scale (Exline et al., 2014) screens for spiritually-related struggles. Types of religious and spiritual struggles include supernatural, interpersonal, and intrapersonal. Six factors include divine, demonic, interpersonal, moral, ultimate meaning, and doubt.

Table 14.1 summarizes 2020–2023 outcomes (16 completed cohorts of 3–8 Veterans each) for acceptance and forgiveness therapy (AFT; Pernicano & Haynes, 2023), using paired, two-tailed t-tests:

Table 14.1 AFT outcomes 2020–2023

Measure	Mean/SD, Before Group	Mean/SD, After Group	Significance p value	Effect Size Cohen's d
Brief Symptom Inventory-18 (BSI-18) Global Distress $N = 41\ t(40) = 4.97$	M 71 SD 5.79	M 64 SD 7.19	$p < 0.01$	1.10
BSI-18 Depression $N = 41\ t(40) = 4.46$	M 70.24 SD 7.25	M 61.8 SD 9.72	$p < 0.01$	0.98
BSI-18 Anxiety $N = 41\ t(40) = 4.67$	M 70 SD 6.56	M 63 SD 8.7	$p < 0.01$	0.98
BSI-18 Somatic $N = 41\ t(40) = 3.60$	M 67.17 SD 8.25	M 60.44 SD 8.69	$p < 0.01$	0.79
Acceptance and Action Questionnaire-2 (AAQ-2) $N = 46\ t(45) = -3.71$	M 29.3 SD 10.60	M 37.46 SD 10.47	$p < 0.01$	0.77
PCL-5 (PTSD Checklist) $N = 49\ t(48) = 4.08$	M 52.33 SD 14.79	M 40 SD 15.13	$p < 0.01$	0.82
Meeting PTSD Criteria on PCL-5 (> or = 35)	$N = 42/49$ 85.7%	$N = 31/49$ 63%		
Religious and Spiritual Struggles Scale (RSS) $N = 19\ t(18) = 2.50$	M 64.79 SD 23.06	M 47.32 SD 19.89	$p < 0.05$	0.81
Moral Injury Outcome Scale Total $N = 30\ t(29) = 3.94$	M 32.4 SD 8.37	M 23.83 SD 8.89	$p < 0.01$	0.99
Moral Injury Outcome Shame $N = 27\ t(26) = 2.50$	M 15.7 SD 6.65	M 11.3 SD 6.39	$p < 0.05$	0.67
Moral Injury Outcome Trust $N = 27\ t(26) = 3.85$	M 16.93 SD 4.17	M 12.43 SD 4.10	$p < 0.01$	1.09

Mental Health Benefits of MI Intervention

Although MI is not a mental health (MH) diagnosis, those with MI often report MH symptoms of depression (mental rumination, dysphoria, social withdrawal, negative self-evaluation, anhedonia, irritability, guilt, and blame), anxiety (*what-if* thinking), sleep interruption, and lost motivation/hope. These impact relationships, work, and daily functioning. Veterans who pursue help for MI, through AFT and other MI programs, report beneficial changes.

AFT results in reduced depression/anxiety, improved acceptance, reduced spiritual stressors, and reconnection to self and others. Acceptance and forgiveness help Veterans reappraise the past and accept what they cannot change. The PCL-5 reflects significantly lower PTSD symptoms, perhaps due to resolved guilt and shame, cognitive flexibility, reduced avoidance, improved acceptance, and processed grief. Veterans shift to a more flexible mindset to address rigid MI stuck points and redefine responsibility. Most report fewer symptoms of religious and spiritual struggles which likely maps onto their acceptance and forgiveness through compassion and confession. Veterans improve trust on the MIOS, as expected in a process group with self-disclosure. Reduced shame likely relates to forgiveness and lessened guilt.

Qualitative Measures

Qualitative results parallel the quantitative ones, as Veterans release pain by sharing their stories with other Veterans and depict their growth through metaphors, drawings, and self-descriptions of hope and healing. Qualitative data (drawings and descriptions of bowls and tapestries) point to changes in self-perception, increased acceptance, pursuit of forgiveness, hope, and meaningful connections with spirituality, purpose, meaning, and others. Veterans reconnect "up" (spirituality and meaning-making), "within" (intrapersonally), and "between" (interpersonally), depending on the MI. Veterans describe burden release and renewed intentions for value-based living. Many opt to continue with a support group to stay connected to other Veterans, and chaplaincy has begun an aftercare program to continue growth and reduce relapse in the stages of change. Pernicano et al. (2022) are studying Veteran-reported pain and brokenness and meaning-making which results in post-traumatic growth, hope, and healing. Veteran descriptions of cracked glass bowls and tapestries consistently reflect renewed purpose, restored worth, and positive meaning-making.

Many Veterans in AFT have previously attended evidence-based practices (EBPs) for PTSD and still carry guilt, moral pain, and confusion, suggesting more is needed. The stories and metaphors in this book – combined with group activities, interactions, and practice assignments – facilitate Veteran processing of MI. Many Veterans who commit suicide have not accessed VA services; we need to reach those in the community, through Vet Centers, places of worship, and universities. Haynes offered the first 4-week university-based group in 2023. A Veteran recently suggested peer-to-peer support for those with MI, i.e., connecting program graduates to other Veterans.

Propelling Change in Military Culture

Military culture and "rules" or "truisms" contribute to the development of MI. We might better prepare service members for potentially morally injurious events (PMIEs) and connect them to resources when indicated. We typically do not expect those we trust to betray us, but the possibility needs to be addressed. Colonel Carrington Firmin (2022) has stepped up awareness of military sexual trauma (MST), and she clarifies that no one is fully safe from unexpected harm. The military culture remains top-down, and survivors of sexual trauma only recently have had avenues for reporting outside their chain of command. Hopefully, as awareness rises, there will be a reduction of wrongdoing within a previously misogynistic, male-dominated, hierarchical culture. Veterans speak of racism, fraternization across ranks, abuses of power, and threats to integrity. We encourage survivors to break the silence and pursue justice so that professionalism and respect become the expected standard for all who serve.

The military is only as strong as its leadership, and many exemplary leaders provide value-based leadership, yet one *rotten apple can cause much damage*. Poison from within spreads when not addressed, and fear instills silence. Leaders must model and instill moral integrity and emotional resiliency. Veterans of all ranks and service eras speak of the need for a paradigm shift in leadership and military culture, especially as scandals continue. We need to redefine what it means to be a strong, compassionate person who endures difficult circumstances and to destigmatize and normalize MI and MH-related symptoms, during or after deployment. Those who serve could not have anticipated the consequences of war or legitimate wrongdoing; to some degree, we are all complicit in moral pain, including the ones back home who sent Veterans to war. Moral injuries will one day be recognized as wounds that can be healed and transformed into *battle scars* that need not be hidden.

Community Awareness

Honest engagement with Veterans fosters empathy, transparency, and understanding.

Many excellent MI services are being developed and provided, and with increased awareness, there could be increased grassroots support and outreach. Resources are scarce for providers to conduct clinical trials, but we can collaborate and disseminate promising practices. Primary care providers can screen for MI routinely, as they already do for other mental/physical health-related issues, and we can reduce the silence and stigma that bring alienation and isolation. We hope this book raises awareness of MI and inspires compassion for those suffering moral pain. One day, MI services will be available where Veterans live, work, serve, and worship; they may wear their *battle scars* proudly, and we may welcome them home.

References

Bond, F. W., Hayes, S. C., Baer, R. A., Carpenter, K. M., Guenole, N., Orcutt, H. K., Waltz, T., & Zettle, R. (2011). Preliminary psychometric properties of the acceptance and action questionnaire – II: A revised measure of psychological inflexibility and experiential avoidance. *Behavior Therapy, 42*(4), 676–88. https://doi.org/10.1016/j.beth.2011.03.007

Carrington Firmin, L. (2022). *Stories from the front: Pain, betrayal, and resilience on the MST battlefield*. Blue Ear Books.

Derogatis, L. R., & Melisaratos, N. (1983). The brief symptom inventory: An introductory report. *Psychological Medicine, 13*(3), 595–605. https://doi.org/10.1017/S0033291700048017

Exline, J. J., Pargament, K. I., Grubbs, J. B., & Yali, A. M. (2014). Religious and spiritual struggles scale [database record]. *APA PsycTests*. https://doi.org/10.1037/t36191-000

Franke, G. H., Jaeger, S., Glaesmer, H., Barkmann, C., Petrowski, K., & Braehler, E. (2017). Psychometric analysis of the brief symptom inventory 18 (BSI-18) in a representative German sample. *BMC Medical Research Methodology, 17*(14). https://doi.org/10.1186/s12874-016-0283-3

Litz, B. T., Plouffe, R. A., Nazarov, A., Murphy, D., Phelps, A., Coady, A., Houle, S. A., Dell, L., Frankfurt, S., Zerach, G., & Levi-Belz, Y. (2022). Defining and assessing the syndrome of moral injury: Initial findings of the moral injury outcome scale consortium. *Frontiers in Psychiatry, 13*, 923928. https://doi.org/10.3389/fpsyt.2022.923928

Pernicano, P., & Haynes, K. (2023). *Acceptance & forgiveness therapy: From brokenness to restoration* [Unpublished handbook] (5th ed.). South Texas Veterans Health Care System.

Pernicano, P., Wortmann, J., & Haynes, K. (2022). Acceptance and forgiveness therapy for veterans with moral injury: Spiritual and psychological collaboration in group treatment. *Journal of Health Care Chaplaincy, 28*(Sup1), S57–S78. https://doi.org/10.1080/08854726.2022.2032982

Weathers, F. W., Litz, B. T., Keane, T. M., Palmieri, P. A., Marx, B. P., & Schnurr, P. P. (2013). *The PTSD Checklist for DSM-5 (PCL-5)*. Scale available from the National Center for PTSD at www.ptsd.va.gov

Index

Note: Page numbers in **bold** refer to tables.

www.ingramcontent.com/pod-product-compliance
Lightning Source LLC
Chambersburg PA
CBHW081739270326
41932CB00020B/3325